CLINICAL CHILD PSYCHOLOGY

CLINICAL CHILD PSYCHOLOGY

Editors

Radhey Shyam,
Azizuddin Khan

KALPAZ

Clinical Child Psychology

Rs. 750

ISBN: 978-81-7835-761-4

Published in 2009 in India by
Kalpaz Publications
C-30, Satyawati Nagar,
Delhi-110052
E-mail: kalpaz@hotmail.com
Phone : 9212729499

Lasser Type Setting by: Quick Media, Delhi
Printed at : Singhal Print Media, Delhi

Contents

Preface

With the advancement of knowledge and technical know how, the field of psychology has undergone major changes and has expended enormously. In a span of about one hundred thirty years it has progressed well in term of the theoretical advancement of its knowledge base and psychologists have established themselves in several areas as appliers of knowledge. One such specialty is clinical psychology and it is very popular amongst professionals, as clinical psychologists have professional independence, prestige and money. 'Clinical Child Psychology' an emerging specialty with in the field of psychology like, Forensic Psychology and Health Psychology it (Clinical Child Psychology) is a kind of super-specialty of clinical psychology. It attempts to bring together the basic tenets of clinical psychology with a through background in child, adolescent and family development and developmental psychopathology. The Clinical Child Psychologist involves themselves in scientific research for the advancement of theoretical knowledge which may help in the understanding the normal as well as the deviant processes of children and of course the application of that knowledge for understanding, preventing, diagnosing and treating psychological, cognitive, emotional, developmental, behavioural and family problems of children. American Psychological Association recognized the importance of the issues relating to children and adolescents and the need for a separate specialty as this group has their own type of problems and need to be understood as distinct from those of adults and accepted Clinical Child Psychology as Division 53 of APA (i.e., Society of Clinical Child and Adolescent Psychology). This society represents psychologists who are active in teaching, research, clinical services, administration and advocacy in clinical child psychology to the APA and public. Several Journals and Newsletters including, "Journal of Clinical Child and Adolescent Psychology" and "Clinical Child and Adolescents Newsletter" have also been started and this indicate the growing importance of the specialty. Clinical child and adolescent psychologists employ a wide range of procedures and techniques in their work; these include assessment, intervention, prevention and consultation.

Though Clinical Child Psychology has been established as a separate specialty within psychology and clinical child and adolescent psychologists have been recognized as competent professionals as specialists in the problem of children and adolescents yet it is true only in case of the developed countries like USA, Canada, UK etc. In developing countries not to talk of Clinical Child Psychologists even the Clinical Psychologists are straggling hard for professional independence. Thus the Clinical Child and Adolescent Psychologists have to work hard for establishing themselves and for the growth of the specialty and for the welfare and well-being of the children and adolescents. The present book **"Clinical Child Psychology"** is a collection and compilation of theoretical as well as empirical articles with the aim of making the academicians and professionals working for the understanding and alleviating the problems of the children and adolescents, aware of the specific needs and problems of the children and adolescents.

In addition to an introductory chapter by Dr. Radhey Shyam, there are sixteen articles divided into four sections. Section one represents, "parenting and developmental issues" and there are six articles in it. The first article, "The 'Parenthood' of Children: the pearl of the parenting shell", by Dr. Nilanjana Sanyal has highlighted the influence of parenting style on the well-being and that of the dual personality correlates of the child and parents on the other, serves as "milestones" in the process. In the second article, "Parenting and child behaviour" Ms. Bidita Bhatacharya highlighted that the most important element in quality of care is the care giver, stimulating interaction with responsive adults as these are crucial to early cognitive; linguistic and psychological development. Dr. Debjani Mukherji and Dr. Lakshmi Krishnan in her article (article-3) examined specific aspects in semantics with focus on the active and passive voice in sentences. The study may have pedagogical implications in the area of language teaching. Values have special significance on an individual's life. Dr. O.P. Sharma and Ms. Juhi Deshmukh in their article (article-4) examined values in school children across gender and different streams. Ms. Rita Karmakar and Dr. Anjali Ghosh in their article (article-5) examined the role of maturity, gender, SES on distributive justice and cognitive ability amongst students of rural and urban areas of West Bengal and Jharkhand. Dr. Promila Batra and Ms. Dipti Arora (article-6) assessed and compared the mental ability, health and well-being of children belonging to joint and nuclear families. As the traditional joint family system is giving way to nuclear families (particularly in Indian sub-continent) it is important to understand its impact and this article may help researchers, students and all those who are concerned.

Section two of the book deals with "Childhood and Adolescent problems" and there are six articles in it. In the seventh article Dr. H.L. Kalia has taken up a very serious issue of victimization of children in schools. Taking sample from Mumbai Schools, he has been able to point out that victimization in several forms exists in Mumbai schools and it has serious implication for the children and society in general. Dyslexia is a major problem the clinical child psychologists and psychiatrists are dealing with, Dr. Azizuddin Khan (one of the editor of this book) has taken up it in his article (article-8). Dr. Sujata Satpathy has discussed and described the psychological trauma associated with disasters (article-9). Despite the advancement in various areas there are hundreds of thousands of children who do not have homes and have to live in streets, though the reasons may be very many, yet the problem is there, Dr. Veena Thakur and Ms Poonam Phogat in the 10th article has taken a sample of street children living in Delhi and examined the perception of work, stress and coping in them. HIV/AIDS is a major problem the world is facing today. In the 11th article Dr. Sandeep Singh and Sunil Kumar have reported that perceptual and attitudinal factors play a significant role in HIV risk. In the 12th article Dr. Joginder Kairo, Dr. Radhey Shyam and Dr. Priti Singh has taken up stress amongst caregivers of mentally handicapped children.

Section three of the book deals with "Assessment / diagnosis of childhood problems". Dr. Hitesh Khurana and Dr. Jyoti Kapoor have described several methods of child psychiatric assessment and have emphasized the special care the Clinical Child Psychologists/ Psychiatrists should take while assessing childhood problems (article - 13). Mr Maheshwar Satpathy has presented (article-14) a critical review of psychological tests developed for children in India. Section four deals with the "Childhood problems/disorders and intervention" and has two articles. Dr. Harpreet Kaur, Ms. Jasneet Kaur and Ms. Such Kaur in their article (article 15) described the general etiology of childhood disorders, types of disorders and have suggested several intervention techniques for treatment. In the 16th article Dr. Usha Verma Srivastava and Dr. Tanusree Dutta has described a recently developed technique 'Eye Movement Desensitization Response (EMDR)' and have examined its prospects for child psychopathology.

The editors are grateful to all the contributors for supporting their (editors) efforts to bring this book in its present form. It is with their contribution, support and encouragement that we have been able to do it. We are also thankful to the publisher and other individuals and institutions that have been of great help in bringing out this volume.

Thanks are due to Mr. Amit Bhoria, Department of Psychology, M.D. University, Rohtak, who was readily available for help. Hope this book will inspire individuals and generate interest among academicians, researchers, professionals and all other who are concerned to work for the development of the Clinical Child Psychology and for the welfare and well being of the children. The editors are not responsible for the views, opinions and suggestions made by the contributors in their articles.

April, 2009

Dr. Radhey Shyam
Dr. Azizuddin Khan

Introduction

—Radhey Shyam

Specialties, like community psychology, health psychology, behavioural medicine and neuropsychology have emerged from within the domain of clinical psychology quite early in the 20th century and have now established themselves as independent specialties and are fully developed. A few more specialties are emerging and taking independent shape from the clinical psychology. These are forensic psychology, pediatric and clinical child psychology (Trull and Phares, 2001). The commission for the recognition of specialties and proficiencies in professional psychology (CRSPPP) has defined clinical child psychology as a specialty of professional psychology which brings together the basic tenets of clinical psychology with a through back ground in child, adolescent and family development and developmental psychopathology." The CRSPPP has also defined the role of clinical child and adolescent psychologist as those who conduct scientific research and provide psychological services to infants, toddlers, children and adolescents. Division 53 of the American Psychological Association (APA) is devoted to the clinical child and adolescent psychology. The division 53, society of clinical child and adolescent psychology, represent psychologists who are active in teaching, research, clinical services, administration and advocacy in clinical child psychology to the APA and the public.[1] Thus, the research and practice of clinical child psychology are mainly focused on understanding, diagnosing, treating psychological, cognitive, emotional, developmental, behavioural and family problems of children. Moreover, their efforts are also directed towards the prevention of those problems.

Over the years, the psychologists working with the neonates, infants and toddlers are striving for a separate specialty i.e. pediatric psychology, and they have been successful in doing so. Therefore, it is pertinent here to differentiate it from clinical child psychology (as outlined above).

Though the distinction between pediatric psychology and clinical child psychology is somewhat blurred, yet the scope of clinical child psychology is more broad compared to pediatric psychology. Pediatric psychology as defined by Routh (1988) is the psychology conducted in medical settings, including hospitals, developmental clinics or medical group practice. On the contrary clinical child psychologists were more often in private practice settings or in out patient clinics in the context of traditional clinical psychologists teams in collaboration with pediatricians (Trull and Phares 2001), more often when the psychopathological symptoms have developed. The distinction can also be noticed in the orientations of pediatric psychologists and the clinical child psychologists. The clinical child psychologist's have a wide variety of orientation such as psychodynamic, family etc. whereas; the pediatric psychologists more often follow the behavioural approach. Both have differential focus in their training, research and service delivering systems, pediatric psychologists have greater emphasis on biological and medical issues whereas clinical child psychologist emphasize training on assessment, developmental process and family therapy.

Historical Development

The roots of clinical child psychology can be traced back to the Lightner Witmer's clinic where a teacher named Margaret Marguire sought help from Witmer for a boy who was a "chronic bad speller". Witmer took up the case and it became the first clinical case and Witmer became the first clinical psychologist rather the first clinical child psychologist. Witmer started a clinic (the first psychological clinic). Witner's approach was to assess the child's problem and then arrange for appropriate remedial procedures (Nietzel, Bernstein and Milich, 1994).

Characteristics of Witmer's Clinic

Nietzel et al (1994) described the following characteristics of Witmer's clinic:

1. The clients were children.
2. Diagnostic assessment was a prerequisite for recommendations for helping or remedial measures.
3. Witmer worked in a team of professionals who consulted and collaborated on a given case.

4. There was an emphasis on prevention of the problems in future.
5. Such an enterprise (clinical or clinical child psychology) would be based on scientific psychology.

Witmer described a case in the 1896 meeting of APA and as expected fellow psychologists gave him a kind of 'lead balloon' reception. It might have been because of his nature and the psychologists were scared of losing their scientific status in involving with such activities which they considered non-scientific. But later on the developments in the field of psychology particularly the development of psychological tests helped the field grow. The two World Wars (World War I and II) further necessitated the development of psychological tests particularly those of intelligence and personality. The psychologist's services were sought for proposes of recruitment, placement in different streams and of course for handling the war causalities. It gave confidence to psychologists for such kind of services. In the post war scenario there were several thousand of injured in the veteran and state hospitals (USA) and the psychologists were employed for their treatment and rehabilitation. Many more started doing private practice. Soon need was felt for a uniform standard for training and regulation of these 'new professionals'. The veteran administration (USA) appointed a committee on Graduate and Professional Training in 1947 under the chairmanship of David Shakow. The committee recommended the 'Scientist professional model' of training for clinical psychologist. It soon became the accepted model and it was followed by several universities across the United States. Several guidelines were issued by APA, and the veteran and state government's enacted laws for the regulation of this newly developed profession i.e. 'Clinical Psychology'. With the advancement in science and technology there was a rapid growth in the field of psychology in general and clinical psychology in particular. The field of clinical psychology become very popular and gave both money and prestige to the professionals, and there was a rapid growth and the scope become so wide spread and broad, that, if Lightner Witmer come out of his grave, there is all possibility that he may not recognize the field he started. Around the end of the 19th and beginning of 20th century several developments took place which invited attention toward children (Ollendick and Hersen, 1998). These include identification and care of those with mental retardation, developments in the filed of testing, growth of psychoanalysis and behaviourism, child study movement and the emergence of child guidance clinics. Not only this, changes have taken place in the classification of childhood disorders more so in the past 40-50 years. It is reflected in the diagnostic and statistical manual (DSM, published by APA). It seems that DSM I and II both have regarded childhood problems as downward extension of adult disorders, whereas DSM III, IV and now DSM IV TR have diagnostic categories which are especially relevant to children. Now several specialties have come out of this field and 'clinical child psychology' is one of these specialties. In the United States it has again on the verge of taking the shape of fully developed profession independently. APA has recognized it as the division 53rd. Division 53rd of APA (society of clinical child and adolescent psychology) represents psychologists who are active in teaching, research, clinical services, administration and advocacy in clinical child psychology to the APA and the public. It publishes the "Journal of Clinical Child and Adolescent Psychology" and the "Clinical child and Adolescent Psychology Newsletter." It also sponsors a full program at the annual APA convention.[2]

The commission for the recognition of specialties and proficiencies in professional psychology (CRS PPP)[1] has suggested certain guidelines for the preparation of clinical child psychologist, these reflects the main functions and the activities of a clinical child psychologist. These are:

1. Knowledge of normal developmental processes: the knowledge of the normal developmental process is essential for helping them to understand the behaviour of a child and to distinguish from abnormal behaviours.
2. Knowledge of normal family processes- It help him in relating the normal family processes of the child and adolescents development. It also help him in understanding the importance of family dynamics,

normal family functioning, child rearing practices on normal development and on the development of the problems.

3. Focus on child and adolescent psychopathology- It includes epidemiology and etiological models of child and adolescent psychopathology, treatment options, and treatment effectiveness for specific problems.
4. The integration of developmental psychology and clinical child and adolescent psychology reflected in developmental psychopathology.
5. Knowledge of the methods of assessment – It include the assessment of development, cognition, personality, emotion and achievement.
6. Theoretical knowledge relating to the theories and research evidence for the treatment of infant, child adolescent and family problems.
7. Prevention of child, adolescent and family disorders and it requires knowledge of normal and deviant developmental pathways as well as developmentally-informed knowledge of clinical problems.
8. Ethical and legal issues- Ethical and legal issues relating to the research and practice with children, adolescents and their families.
9. The aspiring clinical and child psychologists also require an appropriate appreciation for an understanding of principles of diversity and cultural context as they are related to appropriate professional behaviour and clinical practice.

Major Activities of Clinical Child Psychologists

The major activities are similar to those of clinical psychologist, however they perform these activities in a bit different (sometime) manner as their service seekers are children as opposed to adults. These can be grouped under the headings of assessment, treatment (intervention), prevention and almost all of them are involved in other activities like that of the clinical psychologists and these are research, teaching, consultation, and administrative work.

Assessment

Assessment of the problems of children and adolescents differs from the assessment of adults in several ways. First, unlike adults, children rarely seek help at their own. Secondly, in case of children the professional has to seek information from other sources beside the child/adolescent. These sources may include, the parents, teachers, social workers, school psychologists, physicians, and of course many others. Thirdly, for doing this the consent of the parents is required and there is a need to take the child into confidence (child's permission). It has its advantage as it help in creating an atmosphere of mutual trust and respect. There are problems because of obtaining information from multiple sources as sometime the information gathered may not agree and thus it requires greater skill on the part of the professional to analyze and synthesize it and to draw inferences from it. Besides interviewing, and use of psychological tests (specially) developed for children) behavioural observation is of special significance here. Several specific systems of observation for behavioural assessment of children and adolescents have been developed. The behavioural coding system (BCS) developed by Patterson (1971), and colleagues (Jones, Reid and Patterson, 1975), Patterson and Forgatch, 1995), and the direct observation form (DOF) developed by Achenbach's (1994), need a special mention here.

Consultation

The clinical child psychologist consult with various professional and non-professionals including parents pediatricians, medical staff, school system, welfare agencies, juvenile court systems and other health and service agencies.

Teaching

The clinical child psychologist, like the clinical psychologist is involved in teaching and training. They do this in clinical settings where they teach and train the aspiring clinical child and adolescent psychologists and in general (traditional) university/college settings.

Research

Any professional who is not in touch with the recent

developments in the field may become obsolete and therefore has to remain in touch with the journals and research magazines. Generation of knowledge is an ongoing process and in science nothing is final, therefore the clinical child psychologists are also involved in research in both the traditional university as well as in clinical settings.

Administration

Many clinical psychologist works on the administrative positions including those of director or head of the departments/ institutions in both clinical as well as in mainstream education. Treatment approaches used for children are equally diverse and generally similar to those of adults (Trull and Phares, 2001). Despite this it is pertinent to mention here that child therapy is different from that of adult as children usually do not refer themselves for treatment and lacks the capacity for introspection and self-report. Several specific therapeutic techniques (more than 230 as estimated by Kazdin, 1988) have been developed however; many of them are still to be subjected to empirical investigation for efficacy and effectiveness (Kazdin and Weisz, 1998). These therapies are psychoanalytically oriented therapies, play therapy, behaviour therapy, cognitive behaviour therapy, group and family therapies and psychopharmacological treatments etc.

Prevention

Though treatment and prevention are blended in such a manner that it is really difficult to separate them and it is revealed from the model of prevention (Caplan, 1961, 1964). The primary prevention is prevention in true sense (as its focus is on 'counteracting harmful circumstances before they have had a chance to produce illnesses). Secondary prevention is more like treatment as the focus here is an 'attacking problems' while they are still manageable and before they become resistant to treatment and the tertiary prevention is to 'reduce the duration and the negative effects of mental disorders after their occurrence'. The clinical child psychologists are involved in the development of programs to prevent the problems and disorders of children and adolescents and families. The preventive program are directed for problęms like, developmental delays (cognitive and language), antisocial behaviour, teenage pregnancy, substance abuse, delinquency etc. The prevention programs may be in the form of anticipatory guidance- use of consulting and psycho education in advance of difficulties.

Challenges for Future

As clinical child psychology is a new and emerging specialty it has the challenge to establish itself as an independent profession more so in the developing countries where even clinical psychology is yet to establish itself as an independent profession. Besides, this clinical child psychology has to deal with issues related to ethnicity, race and culture and they need to commit themselves to provide services to children and adolescents form underprivileged and underrepresented groups (Culberston, 1993). The shortage of trained professionals has to be met. The research efforts have to be strengthened and broadened to evaluate the role of ethnicity, race, culture etc in the treatment of children and adolescents. The research issues raised by Kaufman, Holden and Walker (1989), still poses challenges to the clinical child, pediatric and adolescent psychologists. These are chronic illness, prevention, cost effective, intervention, treatment effectiveness, parenting, compliance, early intervention with children at risk, child abuse, neglect, developmental psychopathology, childhood depression/ suicide, child neuropsychology etc. Another challenge before the clinical child psychologist is to develop new and innovative treatment models (Trull and Phares, 2001) as the traditional (one-to-one therapy) model may not be most effective and viable option. The conclusions of APA task force report on innovative models of mental health services for children adolescents and the families (Henggeler, 1994) need a mention here. It was suggested that:

(1) Reduce the use of impatient services and residential treatment and increase the use of home and community based services.

(2) Training providers of services in the delivery of cost effective services and to increase providers' accountability.

(3) To increase the integration of services (mental health, education, primary care etc).

(4) Provide flexible, individualized services and elicit the support of families.

One of the leading causes of death among children in injury and accident, therefore prevention of accident and injury is a challenge. Trauma, abuse (physical as well as sexual), neglect and gender discrimination are a few other factors affecting the health and well being of the children, hence need to be tackled by clinical child psychologists.

REFERENCES

Achenbach, T.M. (1994) Child behaviour checklist and related instruments. In M.E. Maruish (Ed.) *The use of psychological testing for treatment planning and outcome assessment* (pp. 517-549), Hillsdale, N.J.: Erlbaum.

Caplan, G. (ed.) (1961), *Prevention of Mental disorders in children*. New York: Basic Books.

Caplan, G. (ed.) (1964), *Principles of Preventive Psychiatry*. New York: Basic Books.

Culberston, J.L. (1993) Clinical child psychology in the 1990's broadening our scope. *Journal of Clinical Child Psychology,* 22, pp. 116-122.

Henggeler, S.W. (1994) A Consensus: Conclusions of the APA talks force report on innovative modes and mental health services for children, adolescents and their families. *Journal of Clinical Child Psychology, 23 (Suppl.), p. 6.*

Jones, R.R., Reid, J.B. and Patterson, G.R. (1975) Naturalalistic observation in clinical assessment. In P. McReynolds (Ed.) *Advances in Psychological Assessment* (Vol. 3), San Francisco: Jessey Bass.

Kaufman, K.L. Holden, E.W. and Walker, C.E. (1989). Future directions in pediatric and clinical child psychology. *Professional Psychology: Research and Practice, 20, 148-152.*

Kazdin, A.E. (1988), *Child Psychotherapy: Developing and Identifying Effective Treatments*. Elmsford, NY: Pergamon Press.

Kazdin, A.E. and Weisz, J.r. (1998) Identifying and developing empirically supported child and adolescent treatments. *Journal of Consulting and Clinical Psychology,* 66, 19-36.

Nietzel, M.T., Kazdin, A. E. and Bellack, A. S. (1983) *The Clinical Psychology Handbook*. New York: Pergamon Press.

Ollendick, T.H. and Hersen, (1998) *Handbook of Child Psychology*. (3rd ed.). Thousand oaks, CA: Sage.

Patterson, G.R. (1971) *Families: Applications of Social learning to Family Llife,* Champaign, IL: Research Press.

Patterson, G.R. and Forgatch, M.S.(1995) Predicting future clinical adjustment from treatment outcome and process variables. *Psychological Assessment, 7, 275-285.*

Pruit, S.D. and Elliot, C.H. (1992) Pediatric psychology: Current Issues and developments. In C.E.Walker and M.C. Roberts (Eds.) *Hand Book of Clinical Child Psychology* (2nd ed.) (pp. 859-872), New York: Wiley

Routh, D.K. (1988) Prevention and Lifestyle in Child Health Psychology. In B.G. Melamed, K.A. Methews, D.K. Routh, B. Stabler and N. Schneiderman (Eds.). *Child Health Psychology,* Hillsdale, NJ: Erlbaum.

Trull, T.J. and Phares, E.J. (2001) *Clinical Psychology Concepts, Methods and Profession* (6th edition) Belmont: Wadsworth/ Thomson Learning.

Notes

1. CRSPPP (Commission for the recognition of specialties and proficiencies in professional psychology) Archival description of clinical child psychology. Retrieved from *http://www.apa.org/crsppp/childclinic.html*. On 17-10-08.
2. Division 53- Society of clinical child and adolescent psychology, retrieved from *http://www.apa.org/about/division/div 53.html* on 17-10-08.

List of Contributors

1. *Anjal Ghosh,* Head, Psychology Research Unit, Indian Statistical Institute (ISI), 203, B.T. Road, Kolkata.
2. *Azizuddin Khan,* Assistant Professor, Department of Humanities and Social Sciences, Indian Institute of Technology, Bombay, Powai—400076, Mumbai, Maharashtra
3. *Ms. Bidita Bhatacharya,* Consultant Clinical Psychologist, Max Healthcare, New Delhi
4. *Debjani Mukherji,* Head Department of Psychology, St. Thomas College, Bhilai, Chhatisgarh.
5. *Ms. Juhi Deshmukh,* Assisant Professor, Department of Psychology, International College for Girls, Jaipur
6. *Ms. Dipti Arora,* Department of Psychology, M.D. University, Rohtak, Haryana
7. *H.L. Kalia,* Professor and Head, Department of Psychology, S.N.D.T. Women's University, Bombay, Mumbai.
8. *Harprit Kaur,* Lecturer, Department of Psychology, Panjabi University, Patiala, Punjab
9. *Hitesh Khurana,* Professor of Psychiatry, Department of Psychiatry, Pt. B.D.S. University of Health Sciences, Rohtak
10. *Jasneet Kaur,* Research Scholar, Department of Psychology, Panjabi University, Patiala, Punjab
11. *Joginder Kairao,* Clinical Psychologist, Department of Psychiatry, Pt. B.D.S. University of Health Sciences, Rohtak.
12. *Jyoti Kapoor,* Senior Resident, Department of Psychiatry, Pt. B.D.S. University of Health Sciences, Rohtak
13. *Lakshmi Krishnan,* Head Department of English, St. Thomas College, Bhilai, Chatisgarh
14. *Maheshwar Satapathy,* Sr. Leecturer Lovely School of Business, Lovely Professional University, G.T. Road Phagwara, Punjab
15. *Nilanjana Sanyal,* Professor of Psychology, University College of Science and Technology, Calcutta University, 92, Acharya Prafulla Ch. Road, Kolkata-700 009.

16. *O.P. Sharma,* Assistant Professor, Department of Psychology, University of Rajasthan, Jaipur, Rajasthan.
17. *Ms. Poonam Phogat,* Lecturer, Vivekananda College, University of Delhi, Delhi.
18. *Priti Singh,* Associate Professor, Department of Psychiatry, Pt. B.D.S. University of Health Sciences, Rohtak.
19. *Promila Batra,* Professor of Psychology, Department of Psychology, M.D. University, Rohtak, Haryana.
20. *Radhey Shyam,* Professor of Psychology, M.D. University, Rohtak, Haryana.
21. *Ms. Rita Karmakar,* Research Scholar, Psychology Research Unit, ISI, 203, B.T. Road, Kolkata.
22. *Sandeep Singh,* Lecturer, Department of Applied Psychology, Guru Jambeshwar University of Science and Technology, Hisar, Haryana.
23. *Sujata Satapathy,* Faculty National Institute of Disaster Management (Ministry of Home Affairs) 5-B, I.P. Esate, Ring Road, IIPA Campus, New Delhi-110029 INDIA.
24. *Ms. Such Kaur,* Research Scholar, Department of Psychology, Panjabi University, Patiala, Punjab.
25. *Mr. Sunil Saini,* Research Scholar, Department of Applied Psychology, Guru Jambheshwar University of Science and Technology, Hisar, Haryana.
26. *Ms.Tanusree Dutta,* Lecturer, Psychology Section, M.M.V., B.H.U., Varanasi-221005
27. *Usha Verma Srivastava,* Consultant Clinical Psychologist, EMDR Level I, EMDR Institute Inc. London.
28. *Veena Tucker,* Senior Reader, Department of Applied Psychology, Gargi College, Siri Fort Road, New Delhi-49.

SECTION–I : PARENTING AND DEVELOPMENTAL ISSUES

1. The "Personhood" of Children : The Pearl of the Parenting Shell
2. Parenting and Child Behaviour
3. Study of Voice Coherence in Children : A Case Study from Psycholinguistic Perspectives
4. A Study of Values Among School Children
5. Distributive Justice and Cognitive Ability Among Students of Two Regions of India
6. Mental Ability, Health and Well-Being of Children Belonging to Joint and Nuclear Families

1

The "Personhood" of Children: The Pearl of the Parenting Shell

—Nilanjana Sanyal

Continuity of human genre is the sign of perpetuating life on this earth. The universe has its manifold beauties – all ecologically balanced and co-contributing. A significant petal of this universal beauty is *"parenthood"* – the unison of two bodies and souls bringing a blooming bud to bear the torch of the natural beauty - the life with its riverine up and down flows. The hallmark of this bud is *"child,"* the child in the family, the child to carry the society to its further flows. Hence, development of his "personhood" is essential. Parent-child intimacy initiates health, happiness and splendour of warmth to glance at the world with positivity, to touch and feel the pulse of life with highest dynamicity and to create the fervour of good stay-quality. The aims and aspirations are helping the child to understand reality, being accommodative and adjustive and hence matured in his own style to enjoy life in its entirety. To understand the dynamics behind, the issue needs elaborate discussion on parenthood and parenting styles that etch its mark in framing the "personhood" of the child in the developmental sequences of life.

Parenthood and Parenting Styles

All parents want to be the best parents that they can be. Parenting is about learning from one's mistakes, not from one's successes. In a child's life, parental influences are manifold – hereditary, constitutional, social, regulative and environmental. Parents represent the most potent conditioning factor in the life of a child. In terms of personality foundation and early developments, the parents' level of emotional acceptance of the child and their resulting attitudes toward him play a leading role. The possible range of parental attitudes that affect a child's development include: genuine affectionate acceptance to hostile rejection, extreme indulgence to carefree neglect, pampered infantilization to extreme lack of mothering, complete autocracy to licensed permissiveness, multiple pressures toward acceleration to distinct nonchalance.

Being a parent involves lot of effort, adjustment and commitment. The myriad complexities of behaviour in the parents and others who surround the child inevitably tend to elicit and direct the child's behaviour into a particular pattern. Within the family matrix, a child acquires tendencies to desire or fear certain objects and situations and he learns what to do and what to avoid doing. The child also picks up from the parents the logic behind the do's and don'ts. Such learnings mould variables of his emergent personality into a specific formal structure (Way and Rossmann, 1996). Although the potentials for personality and character development exist from conception, the nucleus of personality structure seems to emerge when the infant begins to respond to external stimuli and begins to evidence *experiential learning.* Thus, when the question arises, "Why infants seem to be predisposed toward the development and exhibition of certain traits ?," the answer involves parental reactions to them, as well as the unique constitutional qualities and features which contribute to marked behavioural patterns of children.

A close-range clinical observation of childrens' behaviour reveals the following facts:

- If a child lives with criticism, he learns to condemn;
- If a child lives with hostility, he learns to fight;
- If a child lives with ridicule, he learns to be shy;
- If a child learns to feel ashamed, he learns to be shy;
- If a child lives with tolerance, he learns to be patient;
- If a child lives with encouragement, he learns confidence.
- If a child lives with praise, he learns to appreciate.

- If a child lives with fairness, he learns justice;
- If a child lives with security, he learns to have faith;
- If a child lives with approval, he learns to like himself;
- If a child lives with acceptance and friendship, he learns to find love in the world.

Hence home becomes the most salient source of learning, encouragement and support for a child and whether parents know it or not, it's their basic attitudes towards the child and definitely towards *"life"* as such that makes the most important impact. Parents render a lot of influence to build strong foundations for a successful and positive life experience for their children (Brunner, 1997). In fact, if the natural community of the family is acknowledged as the basic building block of society, then parents are acknowledged as society's first teachers of children. The natural intimacy of the parent-child relationship favours the development of the child's *"personhood,"* his/her quality of uniqueness and style, sense of self-worth and dignity to develop to its full potential of character pattern. Children see their parents as role models, specially as to their behaviour and character development (Pikunas, 1961).

Every parent aspires to raise well-rounded and confident children. To add positive flavour to the "personhood" of children, following behavioural features seem to be a must phenomenon for parents:

- *Positive attitude*—If parents tend to have positive lacing of mind, it ought to create a space in child's personhood. Parents need to send the message that the secret of success is "I can" attitude.
- *Patience*—The synonym of parenting seems patience. Although reprimanding attitudes work at times, yet it is through a patient and thoughtful approach that the lesson stays with children for a life-time.
- *Perseverance*—Right from an early age children should be encouraged and motivated to stay with a project and to give it their best attempt.
- *General ability to praise*—If parents are appreciative of many things in life, the child follows the foot-step. On

the other hand, children react to personal praise in a very positive way. It enhances their self-esteem.

- *Parents need to keep up the promise*—It creates the ambience of mutual trust and confidence.
- *Parents need to teach values*—A well-balanced development of values and virtues gives rise to matured "selfhood." The child gradually becomes equipped at his/her core of living and achieving happiness. The character fold ultimately shows "self-mastery."

It is basically the parents' attitude towards parenting, their care about it, sincerity in parenting practice together with self-values and personality integration that results in well-groomed, confident, independence-oriented children.

But before delving into the platform of dimensional aspects of parental functionality on children, the concept of *"parenthood"* or so to say, definitional characteristics of *"parents,"* need to be highlighted. This fold of analysis seems to include the following features of parents with its positive and negative tinges.

Concept of Parenthood

Parents are priviledged beings in this universe to enjoy certain benefits in life in terms of:

- It is moving a step ahead in developmental phases of life to attain and enjoy adult maturity.
- It is a context of offering tender love and care.
- Parenting is developing the canvas of self-extension and self-reflection in children.
- It is developing a bondage of warm responsibility.
- It is creating a meaning, a purpose, a goal in one's life.
- It is drafting a possible future assurance of social-emotional security.
- It is rolling down of one's hereditary line.
- Parenting is the beautification of mental drawing room and enrichment of emotionality of inner personal room.
- It is a space for adopting endeavours, folds of sacrifices of self-satisfaction, enjoying the fragrance of pains and

pleasures of life, developing a pointer to the children to be the future parents to have the experiences of similar type.

In its negative folding, parenting is:

- Stressful with its novelty, uniqueness and demands of higher quality in the context of inexperience and immaturity.
- It is taxation in terms of physical demands, emotionality and finance.
- It calls forth rearrangement of total life style and attitudinal components.
- It is suffocating at times, specially for working mothers.
- It is a pedestal of apprehension and worries.

Functionality of Parenthood

Embracing all these features in a single word of being *"parent,"* people become ready to offer their stimulating and enriching functionality to mould the temperament and character pattern of children to be the forerunner in life on the same track of future years. Hence parenthood seems to bear the fruitfulness once again in multidimensional aspects in their functional spheres like:

- Parents confer life on their children and it follows that they are primarily responsible for their education and character development.
- In fact, the responsibility for properly exercising their parenthood is the most important one people face in their life time.
- Parents who *"value"* education, formal and informal, can win the fight against all odds to ensure that their children achieve academically and be strong personally with distinctive character pattern.
- Parents are the *"lens"* for the child to view this world around to interpret it as he ponders the meaning and significance of the education and experiences received in his life.
- True education involves a training of the mind, a building up of ability to focus and concentrate at times

and to calmly ponder and contemplate at other times. Parents are the initiator of such education for children.

- Parents are the ones who necessarily convey a *fundamental view of reality* to their children that paves the way to realize the utility of value education and consequent character development in life.
- Parents stand as basic and primary role models to children, specially as to their behaviour and character development.
- Parents are the first to introduce the child to human society, to initiate the child's socialization and teach the *"how"* of living together with others.
- Parents, by word and example, are the first determiners of the child's emotional stability, character development, sense of morality and optimism about life.
- Parents introduce the child to the notion of *"rights"* and *"responsibilities"* and of the common good, social tolerance and citizenship.
- Parents lead the child into the world of human *"culture"* and *"traditions."*
- Love based parent-child intimacy creates the canvas of *unconditional emotions.* This unconditional acceptance is of immeasurable importance for the child's sense of self-worth.
- Parents are the first ones responsible for humanizing the children, understand the positive and the negative repercussions and challenges for human behaviour and human values inherent in the brave, new world their children will inhabit from their infancy.
- To reassure young parents it can be said that though parenting may seem complex and even daunting, it is simply day-to-day living with an *"educational eye open."*
- In rearing up children, the greatest demand on parents seem to teach sound habits by example and to be consistent.

The expected benefits of parenthood are gauged to be dependent on the basic attitudes of parents towards life and parenthood itself, their own temperamental qualities along with held value systems, the range of personal experiences and definitely their parenting style. In helping children to develop their self-styled temperamental frame, a brief note on different parenting styles and the consequences seems worth mentioning.

Parenting Styles

Parenting skills are generally the by-products of our earlier life experiences with our care-givers. The mechanism followed is "role modeling." But in modeling, behaviour it is just not copying our direct personal experiences, rather the road to better parenting or parenting differently from one's personal experiences, begins with a process of self-discovery. With the deeper understanding of the self on an experiential basis, adults become better equipped in identifying and recognizing the requirements of the children and hence initiate a healthy current parenting. The new step involves shedding the old patterns of parenting in favour of adopting new parenting skills. As such, the needs to follow become reminders, support and information both for what to do and what not to do. These result in parenting styles of various frames.

Parenting styles are broad patterns of child rearing practices, values and behaviours. It is a psychological construct representing standard strategies parents use in raising their children (Darling, 1999). A group of theorists has developed a typology of parenting styles, based on discipline, nurturance, reinforcement and acceptance (Becker, 1964; Dornbusch et al, 1987; Kelly, 1983; Steinberg et al., 1989). Three different parenting styles have been described by this group: authoritative, permissive and authoritarian (Baumrind, 1966; 1971; 1972; 1978; 1991).

The Authoritarian Type

Children growing up in authoritarian families do less well in school, are typically less skilled with peers than are children from other types of families, and have lower self-esteem. Some children appear subdued while others may show high aggressiveness or other indications of being out of control. Children with such parents are anxious, withdrawn, and unhappy (Kapur, 1995; Kumar, 1975; Sanyal, 2001; Baumrind, 1967). Boys are especially high in anger and defiance while girls are dependent, lack exploration and retreat from challenging tasks (Baumrind, 1971; Mehta, 1977).

The Permissive Type

Children growing up with indulgent or permissive parents also show some negative outcomes. They do slightly less well in school and are likely to be more aggressive—particularly if the parents are specifically permissive toward aggressiveness—and somewhat immature in their behaviour with peers and in school (Kapur, 1995; Sanyal, 2001; Baumrind, 1967). They are less likely to take responsibility and are less independent. They are also overly demanding and dependent on adults, and show less persistence on tasks than children of parents who exert more control (Berk, 1996).

The Neglecting Type

The most consistently negative outcomes are associated with the neglecting or uninvolved type of parenting. Such children continue to show disturbances in their relationships with peers and with adults for many years. Youngsters from neglecting families are more impulsive and anti-social and much less achievement-oriented in school (Block, 1971; Pulkkinen, 1982). Such children often show deficits in many domains, including attachment, cognition, play, and emotional and social skills (Egeland and Sroufe, 1981; Radke-Yarrow et al., 1985).

The Authoritative Type

The most consistently positive outcomes have been associated with the authoritative pattern, in which the parents are high in both control and warmth, setting clear limits but also responding to the child's individual needs. Children reared in such families typically show higher self-esteem, are more independent but, at the same time, are more likely to comply with parental requests, and may show more altruistic behaviour. They are self-confident and achievement-oriented in school and get better grades. They are more likely to use post-conventional moral reasoning (Boyes and Allen, 1993). Evidence confirms a positive association between authoritative parenting and emotional and social skills during the childhood years (Sanyal,

2001; Denham, Renwick and Holt, 1991). Such parenting is also linked with social and moral maturity, involvement in school learning and academic achievement in high school (Block, 1971; Dornbusch et al., 1987; Lamborn et al, 1991 etc.).

Setting aside these attitudinal components of parenting styles, the open behavioural features of parents at times signify the following parental forms (Baumarind, 1978):

(*a*) *The dismissing parent*—Childrens' emotions oscillate so much, and are so difficult to predict and control, that sometimes parents feel like avoiding it altogether. Habitually, dismissing or ignoring emotions could lead to difficulties in social interactions, making friends, lower achievements and overall health problems.

(*b*) *The disapproving parent*—For such parents, crying, whining, sulking, throwing tantrums are unacceptable. Instead of understanding the root of childrens' problems, they try to rectify it with punishment.

(*c*) *The neutral parent*—In such parenting, it is basically not accepting child's faults, but a sort of glossing over it. Some crucial additional emotive element seems to be missing.

(*d*) *The empathizing parent*—This involves teaching children what emotions "are" and how they "work," often in the midst of an emotionally charged event. When emotions are running high, parents need to help the child to deal with it to prevent any consequential damage.

Hence, parenting is just not adopting the role of the guardian of children, it is something extra to make its mark on the budding personalities.

In sum, children are affected by the family *"climate"* or style, which might be thought of as a set of attitudes and values that get reflected not only in the parent's behaviour but also affect the impact the parent has on the child.

Unfolding the "Person" in Children: His Character Development

Monagle (1998) defined character as *"morality of the head, the heart and the hand."* Issacs (1995) mentioned that character building is a question of developing what is most natural to an individual - the inner core of the person. This is not something new to humanity, he felt, only forgotten in the glamour-rimmed world of materialism and hence the issue of value education and character building. Character may be seen as a configuration of traits that are related to ethical and moral principles and virtues. Consistency of parental behaviour in terms of values and principles, parental discipline and the moral sense of parental responsibility are considered to be its source. Emotional identification with parents readily encompasses assimilation of parental conduct. Codification of principles and ideals commences on child's past and lead the way to character building (Bennett, 1998). Core character traits are conceived to be honesty, responsibility, respect, perseverance, loyalty, generosity, humility optimism and open-mindedness (Huffman, 1995). The conglomeration of these traits resulting in high moral value gradually gain in power to direct children's behaviour toward personally and socially desired goal objects. It paves the way toward useful roles and identifications, bringing out consistency of behaviour and conduct as external signs of internal-character structure.

Character has its roots embedded in early childhood experiences, in which the parents' influence is very strong. The experiential background of character includes most importantly the example, instruction and discipline of the parents. Here comes the issue of knowing the process or method how parents should help children in building up their character.

Character Building of Children by Parents

In the augmentation and maintenance of this process, parents need to feel that:

- Parenting is just not their *"duty,"* that is extra alertness and tension together with adoption of various efforts.
- But it is parents' *"enjoyment"* of handling a child to grow up to attend to every pulse of the experiences as facts of life and creating a track full of memories to enjoy the experiences as the *"past perfect"* relationship.

- Children should be taken as a *"human unit"* with the individual uniqueness and specificity.
- They should not be considered as *"mine and mine only"* and should not be my *"prototype."*
- They should be helped to grow according to their potentiality.
- Values need not be induced/ inflicted. They should be served in our behavioural platters. With exposures along with explanations, it is expected to be inculcated.
- Comparisons should be given up altogether. These equalities need to be encouraged and reinforced with appreciation.
- Parents should practice positive orientations in life, showing them both the sides of positivity and negativity – letting them understand negativity as limitations and not intentional harmfulness.
- Parents need to show children the means of gracefully accepting reality and being mentally sophisticated. Parents serve as significant interpreter for children of information about the world and childrens' ability.
- Parents need to show stretched limits of tolerance and help children to raise its benefits.
- Children should be given knowledge on *"object relations"* rather than making them dependent on *"emotional cushions."*
- Parents should give children exposures to enjoyment of sharing and cooperation, if needed, being alert of maintaining boundary.
- Parents should allow children the experiences of enjoying *"appreciative"* tendencies and orientations in life.
- Parents should teach children how to think positively of oneself, others and life - everyday and feel the grace of mental well-being.
- Children should be introduced to nature to follow the natural; rhythms of life.

- Children should not be asked to be like *"us,"* the parents, they should be helped to *"be"* what *"they are."*
- Through audio-visual modes, lives of country's role models should be exposed to them so that they get the chance to develop *"National philosophy"* and the power of self-prophecy.
- Parents need to look back at their childhood to prepare plans for their children to suit the real tunes of tenderhood of life.

In an overall stance, in helping children to build their character, parents should be:

- Well-organized, cohesive and expressive
- Speak their mind and manage conflicts positively
- Seek out ways to grow
- should be sociable
- make decisions through democratic negotiations
- encourage individual development
- should be emotionally engaged

In carrying on the task of character building of children, the young inexperienced parents additionally must be aware of:

- focusing on the impact of new experiences on young children
- on how to turn everyday situations into learning occasions
- on knowing their child's strengths and weaknesses
- on how to assess and analyze their child's progress
- and how to set short term, realistic goals with an eye to each developmental area.

All these they should keep within a long term context of the child growing into an autonomous, responsible and happy adult. The summation would be the attainment of a solid "personhood," the responsibility bearer of the future. In fact, the demands of parenting and what constitutes parenting is constantly changing. There can not be set rules or guide lines for parenting. To bring a completion to the task the parents need to have willingness to improve themselves too, attempting to overcome their own limitations and to become not only better parents but also better persons too. The overall message to the "personhood" of children from parents' side should include the attempts of:

- teaching the child to live from heart, not just from the logical mind;
- believing in them to instill their self-beliefs;
- helping them to be self-confident;
- showing them the benefits of flexible character pattern;
- offering them the courage to follow their dreams;
- allowing them to grow and become what they are meant to be, not what we visualize them to be;
- listening to them to learn from them too;
- to bring them up right, parents need to spend more time and less money;
- parentage should have the essence of spirituality to offer right kinds of virtues to children.

After all, today's children are tomorrow's parents. The way we weave the design of parenting, its bearing is going to be decided.

REFERENCES

Baumrind, D. (1966). Effects of authoritative parental control on child behaviour. *Child Development,* 37, 887-907.

Baumrind, D. (1967). Child care practices anteceding three patterns of preschool behaviour. *Genetic Psychology Monographs, 75,* 43-88.

Baumrind, D. (1971). Current patterns of parental authority. *Developmental Psychology Monograph*, 4 (1, Part 2).

Baumrind, D. (1972). Socialization and instrumental competence in young children. In W.W. Hartup (Ed.), *The young child: Reviews of research* (Vol. 2, pp. 202-224). Washington, DC: National Association for the Education of Young children.

Baumrind, D. (1978). Parental disciplinary patterns and social competence in children. *Youth and Society*, 9, 239-275.

Baumrind, D. (1991). The influence of parenting style on adolescent competence and substance use. *Journal of Early Adolescence*, 11, 56-59.

Becker, W.C. (1964). Consequences of different types of parental discipline. In M.L. Hoffman and L. Hoffman (eds.), *Review of child development research*, pp. 169-208. Vol 1. New York: Sage.

Bennett, W.J. (1998). *The Death of Outrage.* New York: The Free Press.

Berk, L.E. (1996). *Child Development*, 3rd edition, New Delhi: Prentice Hall.

Block, J. (1971). *Lives through time.* Berkeley, CA: Bancroft Books.

Bloiv, K. (1997). *Parenting that promotes resilient urban African-American families: Scholars describe the characteristics of their parents' parenting behaviours.* Paper presented at the Annual Conference of the National Council on Family Relations, Arlington, VA.

Boyes, M.C., and Allen, S.G. (1993). Styles of parent-child interactions and moral reasoning in adolescence. *Merrill- Palmer Quarterly, 39,* 551-570.

Brunner, E. (1997). Stress, biology and inequalities. *British Medical Journal,* 314, 1472-1476. *Bulletin,* 94, 68-99.

Darling, N. (1999). *Parenting style and its correlates.* Eric Digest Campaign: Eric Clearinghouse on Elementary and Early Childhood Education. University of Illinois.

Denham, S.A., Renwick, S.M., and Holt, R.W. (1991), Working and playing together: Prediction of preschool social-emotional competence from mother-child interaction. *Child Development, 62,* 242-249.

Dornbusch, S.M., Ritter, P.L., Leiderman, P.H., Roberts, D.F., and Fraleigh, M.J. (1987). The relation of parenting style to adolescent school performance. *Child Development, 58,* 1244-1257.

Egeland, B., and Sroufe, L.A. (1981). Developmental sequelae of maltreatment. In R. Rizley and D. Ciccheti (Ed.). *New directions for child development (No.11, pp.77-92).* San Francisco: Jassey-Bass.

Huffman, H.A. (1995). The unavoidable mission of character education. *The School Administrator.* 8, 6-17.

Issacs, D. (1995). *Character building.* Dublin: Four Courts Press.

Kapur, M. (1995). *Mental Health of Indian Children,* New Delhi: Sage.

Kelly, C.G.G. (1983). Adolescents' perception of three styles of parental control. *Adolescence,* 18, 567-571.

Kumar, K. (1975). Social climate in school and characteristics of pupils. *Indian Journal of Clinical Psychology, 2,* 163-172. (IPA, 10: 146).

Lamborn, S.D., Mounts, N.S., Steinberg, L., and Dornbusch, S.M. (1991). Patterns of competence and adjustment among adolescents from authoritative, authoritarian, indulgent, and neglectful families. *Child Development, 62,* 1049-1065.

Mehta, P. (1977). "Political behaviour and processes," in Pareek,U. (Ed.) *Survey of Research in Psychology*, Vol. 2, ICSSR, Bombay: Popular Prakasan.

Monagle, V. (1998). *Changing families, challenging futures.* Paper presented in 6th Australian Institute of Family Studies Conference. Melbourne, 25-27 November.

Pikunas, J. (1961). *Psychology of Human Development.* New York: McGraw Hill.

Pulkkinen, L. (1982). Self-control and continuity from childhood to late adolescence. In P.B. Baltes and O.G. Brim, Jr. (Eds.), *Life-span development and behaviour* (Vol.4, pp. 63-105). New York: Academic Press).

Radke-Yarrow, M., Cummings, E.M., Kuczinski, L., and Chapman, M. (1985). Patterns of attachment in two- and three-year-olds in normal families with parental depression. *Child Development, 56*, 884-893.

Reasoning in adolescence. *Merrill-Palmer Quarterly, 39*, 551-570.

Sanyal, N.(2001). Socio-economic status and child abuse: Clinical observations. *In Socio-Economic Development in India, Vol.1* (Edited by Prof. B.N. Roy), New Delhi: Mohit Publications, (pp. 150-157).

Schneider, A.A. (1960). *Personality development and adjustment in adolescence.* Milwanke: The Bruce Publishing Co.

Steinberg, L. Elmen, J.D. and Mounts, N.S. (1989). Authoritative parenting, psychosocial maturity, and academic success among adolescents. *Child Development,* 60, 1424-1436.

Way, W.L., and Rossmann, M.M. (1996*). Learning to work: how parents nurture the transition from school to work. Family matters in school to work transition.* Burkeley, CA: National Centre for Research in Vocational Education.

2

Parenting and Child Behaviour

—Bidita Bhattacharya

"Despite the fact that most people become parents and every one whoever lived has had parents, parenting remains a mystifying subject about which almost everyone has opinions, but about which few people agree. Freud once listed bringing up children as one of the three "impossible professions" – the other two being governing nations and psychoanalysis". (Bornstein, 1995)

This quote is from the editor preface to a four volume- 'Handbook of Parenting' (Bornstein, 1995a). Parenting seems mysterious and difficult; it makes sense that over the centuries, many have attempted to provide guidance for parents.

Merriam- Websters 'Collegiate Dictionary (1994) provides an acceptable starting place. Parenting is defined as "the raising of a child by its parents; the act of caring for some one in the manner of a parent". Bornstein (1995a) described four essential functions of care giving:

(a) Nurturant care giving meets the physical requirements of the child;

(b) Material care giving constructs and organizes the child's physical world;

(c) Social care giving includes the variety of behaviours parents use in engaging their children in interpersonal exchanges; and

(d) Didactic care giving consist of the variety of strategies parents use in stimulating children to engage in and understand the world outside the parent-child dyad.

The central task of parents, then, is not simply to keep their infants alive or to provide appropriate discipline but to create the conditions in which children can develop to their fullest capacity both inside and outside the family. This view provides a broad perspective on parenting. First, Bornstein's description of parenting as a set of functions does not limit the focus of discussion to biological parents; other biological relatives and caretakers who are unrelated to the child may also be centrally engaged in parenting. The assumption that mothers as primary caregivers have the most powerful effects on their children's development is open to question and empirical investigation. Second, Bornstein makes the point that parenting is a relationship that unfolds over time. Third, he emphasizes the responsibilities of parents to socialize children to help them become well functioning members of the culture in which they live. Fourth, he defines parenting not solely by what parents' belief about child rearing or how they behave towards their children – but to a consideration of how parents create family environments that foster children's development. Some studies have highlighted potentially beneficial consequences of early childcare, especially of high-quality care on social functioning, as well as on cognitive – linguistic development (Burchinal et al., 2000; Peiser-Feinberg et al., 2001). Parenting quality significantly predicted all the developmental outcomes and much more strongly than did any of the child-care predictors. Higher levels of parenting quality predicted better performance in reading, math and vocabulary in fifth grade. This study also showed lesser levels of teacher-rated externalizing problems and conflict and higher levels of social skills, social-emotional functioning, and work habits in sixth graders (Belsky et al., 2007).

There are almost as many ways of conceptualizing and assessing parent-child relationships, as there are researchers and authors. Some investigators think about parenting in global dimensions that are typically called "parenting style"- the emotional climate in which parenting bahaviours are expressed. Other look at more micro analytic "parenting practices"- specific socialization behaviours can be observed when parents interact with their children. A third related approach emphasizes the different "parenting roles'" of mothers and fathers in their children's lives – as nurtures, disciplinarians, gate keepers, and so on. Ladd and Hart (1991) have suggested that parents influence their children not only by what they do but also by the role they play in structuring the physical and social environment. In their role as arrangers of the child care, activities, lessons and visits with friends, parents function as "gate keepers" who restrict or encourage their children's access to the world outside the family. There is some evidence to suggest that when parents expose young children to a wider variety of these experiences, the children show higher levels of social adaptation (e.g. Bryant, 1985).

Child Rearing Practices in Indian Context – Ancient Studies

In the ancient Indian law, attitude expressed towards child is of protective nurturance. The protective indulgences shown to the child is clearly expressed in Manu's work on the disciplining of children. Children are only to be beaten with a rope or a bamboo stick split at the end. Also this is to be done only on the back not on the head or chest (Buhler, 1998).

Ayurvedic texts (c/f Ganguli, 2005) have detailed instructions on how to take care of the young child. It considers feeding practices as central to the formation of the personality of the child and breast-feeding as important for the mental and physical development of the child. It speaks on diverse topics on when a child should be encouraged to sit up or specification of toys with regards to the shape, size, and colour. The practice of persuading the child to stop crying by conjoining up threatening vision of ghosts, they tell us to avoid because of its harmful effects. Also child should not be awakened from sleep suddenly, should not be snatched or thrown up arms, should not be irritated and should be kept happy at all costs as this is crucial for his psychological development and future well being.

In context to the Ayurveda, Mahabharata considers child rearing practices and the environment of the early rearing cannot alter basic nature of the child, which has received a strong biological stamp. The child centeredness as Mahabharata states is limited to boys. Also Mahabharata put emphasis on mother's role in child rearing (Ganguli, 2005). Indian tradition is indifferent if not hostile to the development of girls.

PARENTING MODELS

Erikson's Model:

Erikson's theoretical formulations (Erikson, 1963, 1968) are exclusively concerned with ego development. In his views, an individual would become more competent in dealing with the environment over the course of development. Erikson introduces a new perspective concerning the person's relationship to parents and the cultural contexts in which the family is located. Erikson (1963) partitioned the life span into eight separate stages of psychosocial ego development, colloquially "the eight stages of man".

Oral Sensory Stage: Infancy:

The first psychological stage corresponds to Freud's oral stage and encompasses the first year of life. For Erikson, a general sense of trust is the cornerstone of a healthy personality, while others regard this same characteristic as 'confidence'. In Erikson's view, if the mother acts in a loving and consistent way, the infant is likely to develop a sense of basic trust. An infant with a basic sense of 'inner certainty' experiences the social world as a safe, stable place and people as nurturant and reliable. Erikson believes that the degree to which infants are able to acquire a sense of trust in other people and in the worlds depends upon the quality of maternal care that they receive.

A sense of trust depends on the mother's ability to give her child a sense of familiarity, consistency and sameness of experience. Erikson stresses the fact that infants must trust not only the external world but the internal world as well. Such behaviour is shown when the infant can tolerate the mother's absence without suffering undue "separation" anxiety. A sense of basic mistrust, however, is created if the mother acts as in an unreliable, aloof and rejecting way. This fosters in the infant a psychosocial attitude of fear, suspicion, and apprehension toward the world in general and people in particular that will manifest its ill effects in later stages of personality development.

Finally, parents who display divergent patterns of childcare, who lack self-confidence in their role as parents, and who have value system conflicting with the culture's dominant life style may create an atmosphere of ambiguity for the child, resulting in feelings of distrust. The behavioural consequences of a seriously defective development of basic trust, according to Erikson, are acute depression in infants and paranoia in adults.

The psychosocial strength, or virtue, gained from successful resolution of the *trust versus mistrust conflict* is termed ***hope*** by Erikson. Trust, in other words, becomes the infant's capacity for hope, which, in tern, is the foundation of the adult's faith in some form of institutionalized religion. Hope as the first ego strength also serves to maintain the person's belief in the meaning and trustworthiness of a common cultural world.

Muscular – Anal Stage: Early Childhood:

In this stage acquisition of a sense of basic trust sets the stage for the struggle to attain a certain degree of autonomy and self control and to avoid shame, doubt and humiliation. During this period, the child's muscles begin to mature, and he/she starts to learn to have a control over them. For Erikson, through interaction with parents during toilet training, the child discovers the difference between holding as a form of caring and holding as a destructive form of restraint. The child also learns to distinguish between letting go in the sense of relaxed "letting it be", and letting go as a form of destructive release. This stage, therefore, becomes decisive for the ratio of goodwill and willfulness. A sense of self-control without loss of self-esteem is the ontogenetic source of confidence in free will; a sense of over control and loss of self-control can give rise to a lasting propensity for doubt and shame (Erikson, 1968).

As children rapidly gain neuromuscular maturation, language, and social discrimination, they begin to explore and interact with their environment more independently. In particular, they feel pride in their newly discovered locomotor skills. There is a tremendous desire to explore, choose, and manipulate coupled with an attitude toward parents of "let me do it" and "I am what I will".

In Erikson's view, satisfactorily meeting the psychosocial crisis of this stage depends primarily on the parents' willingness to gradually allow children freedom to control those activities that affect their lives. Autonomy does not mean giving the child unrestricted freedom; rather it means that parents must maintain "degrees of freedom" over the child's growing capacity to exercise choice. Erikson believes that the attainment of a stable sense of autonomy adds substantially to the child's sense of trust. He also believes that parents must convey a deep and abiding commitment to justice and a respect for the rights and privileges of others if their children are to be prepared to accept a limited autonomy in adulthood.

Locomotor – Genital Stage: Play Age:

Initiative versus guilt is the final psychosocial conflict experienced by the preschool child during what Erikson calls the "play age". This is when the child's social world challenges him or her to be active, to master new tasks and skills, and to win approval by being productive children also begin to assume additional responsibility for them and for that which defines their world. Whether children will leave this stage with their sense of initiative favorably outbalancing their sense of guilt depends largely upon how parents react to their self-initiated activities. Children who are encouraged to undertake their own activities have their sense of initiative reinforced. Initiative is further facilitated when parents acknowledge their children's curiosity and do not ridicule or inhibit fantasy activity.

A sense of guilt in children is caused by parents who are unwilling to allow them the opportunity of completing tasks on their own. A sense of guilt is also fostered by parents who employ excessive amounts of punishment in response to the child's urge to love and be loved by the opposite sexed parent.

Latency Stage: School Age:

The fourth psychosocial period occurs from about 6 to 12 years of age, and corresponds to the latency period in Freudian theory. Here for the first time the child is expected to learn the rudimentary skills of the culture via formal education. This period of life was associated with the child's increased powers of deductive reasoning and self-discipline as well as the ability to relateto peers according to prescribed rules. The child's love for the parent of the opposite sex and rivalry with the same-sexed parent are typically sublimated and expressed by an inner desire to learn and to be productive.

According to Erikson, children develop a sense of ***industry*** when they begin to comprehend the technology of their culture through attending school. For Erikson, industry includes a feeling of being interpersonally competent – the confidence that one can exert positive influence on the social world in quest of meaningful individual and social goals. The psychosocial strength of competency thus underlies the basis for effective participation in the social-economic-political order.

The danger of this stage lies in the potential development of a sense of inferiority or incompetence. A sense of inferiority may develop if children discover that their gender, race, religion, or socio-economic status – rather than their own skill and motivation – is what determines their worth as persons. The result is that children may lose confidence in their ability to function effectively in the working world.

Adolescence: Ego Identity Vs. Role Confusion:

The new psychosocial dimension that appears during adolescence has *ego identity* at the positive end and *role confusion* at the negative end. The task confronting adolescents is to consolidate all the knowledge they have gained about themselves and integrate these various self-images into a personal identity that shows awareness of both a past and a future. Erikson (1982) stresses the psychosocial nature of ego identity, with the focus not on conflicts between psychic structures but rather on a conflict with the ego itself, namely of identity versus role confusion.

Early Adulthood: Intimacy Vs. Isolation:

The sixth psychosocial stage marks the formal beginning of adult life. This is generally a period in the life cycle when a person becomes involved in courtship, marriage, and early family life. It extends from the adolescence until early adulthood. Early attainment of personal identity and the involvement in productive work that mark this period give rise to a new interpersonal dimension with intimacy at one extreme and isolation at the other. Healthy resolution of the intimacy-versus-isolation crisis promotes the psychosocial strength of *love*. The social institution linked with this stage of the life cycle is ethics. For Erikson, an ethical sense emerges as we recognize the value of committing ourselves to lasting friendships and social obligations – as well as the importance of honoring such commitments even if they require personal sacrifice. People who lack such a ethical sense are ill-equipped to face the next stage in psychosocial development.

Middle Adulthood: Generativity Vs. Stagnation:

Seventh stage of development corresponds to middle years of life and focuses on the issue of *generativity* versus *stagnation*. Generativity occurs when a person begins to show concern not only for the welfare of the next generation but also for the nature of the society in which that generation will live and work. Generativity then represents the older generation's concern to establish and guide those who will replace them. if the capacity of adults for generativity surpasses their sense of stagnation, the virtue that emerges is care (Erikson, 1982).

Late Adulthood: Ego Integrity Vs. Despair:

The final psychosocial stage (65to death) marks the closing of people's lives. The sense of ego integrity arises from the person's ability to glance back on his or her life in full perspective and humbly but assuredly affirm, "I am satisfied". Erikson (1982) concludes that old people must become involved in such activities as grand parenting, politics and fitness programmes if they are to maintain vitality in the face of declining physical and mental abilities.

ADLER'S MODEL

Adler emphasized on the social context of personality development and focused attention on birth order as a major determinant of life style, attitudes. Specifically he reasoned that even tough children have the same parents and grow up nearly the same family setting, they do not have identical social environments. The experiences being older or younger than one's siblings and of being exposed to parental attitudes and values that vary as a result of the arrival of more children create unique conditions in childhood that profoundly influence the formation of the life style.

The First Born (Oldest) Child:

According to Adler, the first-born child is in the enviable position for a time of being an "only child". Adler often referred to the first born as a "dethroned monarch", and noted that this might be a very traumatic experience seeing that a younger sibling is winning the contest for parental attention and affection, the oldest child's natural inclinations is to fight back in order to regain his or her former supremacy in the family. Eventually the child learns that the parents are too busy, too harassed, or too unconcern to tolerate infantile demands. Then, too, the parents exercise far more power than the child exercises and are likely to counter troublesome "attention getting" behavior with punishment. The final outcome of this family struggle is that the first born child "trains himself for isolation" and masters the strategy of surviving alone and independently of the need for anyone's affection or approval. Adler (1927) further suggested that the oldest child is likely to be conservative, power-oriented, and predisposed toward leadership. Therefore, he or she often becomes the upholder of family attitudes and moral standards.

The Only Born Child: Single Child:

The only child is in the unique position of not having other siblings with whom to compete. This fact coupled with a vulnerability to being pampered by the mother, often leads an only child into an intense rivalry with the father. She or he thus becomes "tied to the mother's apron strings" and expects pampering and protection from all others too. Dependency and self-centeredness are the leading qualities of this life style. Such a child continues to be the focus of family attention throughout childhood.

In later life however, a rude awakening occurs the discovery that he or she is no longer the centre of attention. The only child never had to share the centre stage not to compete with other siblings for it. The only child often has difficulty interacting with peers (Alder, 1927).

The Second Born (Middle) Child:

The second child has, from the very beginning, pacesetter in the form of an older brother or sister and is thus stimulated, or perhaps challenged, to out do the older child's exploits. This spurs the second born often generating a faster rate of development than the first born exhibited. The second born is characterized by being highly competitive and ambitious. Her life style is one of constantly trying to prove that she os better than her older sibling. Thus, the middle child is characterized by being achievement-oriented using both direct and devious means to surpass the older sibling.

The Last Born (Youngest) Child:

The situation of the last-born is unique in several ways. First, the child never experiences the shock of dethronement by another sibling and may be pampered not only by the parents, but particularly in large families by older siblings as well. Second, if the parents are economically strapped this child may be relegated to the role of "tag-along kid" who has nothing of his own and must get by on hand-me-downs from other family members. Third, with older role models that set the pace, all of whom are bigger and more privileged than he is, he is likely to experience strong feelings of inferiority along with a lack of independence.

Nonetheless, the last born possesses one advantage a high motivation to surpass older siblings. As a result, this child often becomes the fastest swimmer, the best musician, the most talented artist, or the most ambitious student in the family. Adler sometimes spoke of the "fighting youngest child" as the child most likely to become a revolutionary. (Adler, 1927)

Each of the above examples represents a stereotypic description of the "typical", oldest, only, middle and youngest child – not every child in each of these categories will fit the general life-style descriptions proposed by Adler. Adler's interest in birth order relationships was nothing more than an attempt to discover the kinds of problems faced by children and the kinds of solutions they might develop in trying to cope with these problems.

CAUSAL MODEL

Parenting includes stable biological and personality characteristics of each parent as they are revealed in interaction with the child: collectively these qualities shape the environment of the developing child. Until recently, both public and scientific discourse about the impact of parents on children used the language the language is causality: certain behavior in the parent leads to or causes certain outcomes in the child.

A (Parent Behaviour) ⟶ B (Child Outcome)

Causal relationships are generally very difficult to establish. In this case, it would need to determine that (a) when antecedent A is present, outcome B is present, (b) when antecedent A is absent, out come B is absent, (c) that B is not traceable to factors other than A (e.g. factors within the culture rather than within the family) (Cowan, Powell, and Cowan; 1988).

In studies of parent-to-child effects, causality is virtually impossible to determine. Because almost all studies of parents and children are correlational in design, it is not possible to establish whether parent's behaviours are affecting the child' behavior is a product of the parent-child relationship, or the child's behavior is attributable to familial and extra familial factors that are separate from parenting (Cowan, Powell, and Cowan; 1988).

RISK MODEL

Instead of beginning with specific child behaviour as outcome and attempting to determine its cause, it can begin by focusing on parent behaviour. It acts as a risk factor with respect to a given outcome and attempts to map the paths of development of children at greater and lesser risk. Risk, a term originally developed by insurers of ships and adopted as a central construct in the theory and practice of public health, refers to the probability of a negative outcome in a population given a specific antecedent factor (Cowan, Cowan, and Schulz, 1996; Rutter, 1987).

The origins of risk analysis are interwoven with the aims of action and intervention. Patterson and Capaldi (1991) have shown that when parents of adolescents are not effective "monitors" (knowing where their children are and setting limits on being away from home) their children are at risk for aggression and delinquency.

Risks do not always produce negative outcomes. Some families in which parents fail to monitor their adolescents have children who are not aggressive and delinquent. In the framework of causal analysis, this finding disconfirms the hypothesis that parents' behaviour is linked with children's behaviour (Cowan, Powell, and Cowan; 1988). By contrast, in the framework of risk models, the exceptions inform us about fruitful avenues for further investigation because they reveal potential buffers or protective factors that reduce negative outcomes despite the presence of risk. For example, parents who are ineffective monitors of their children may enroll them in schools that provide structured programmes to encourage prosocial behaviour. Grandparents or neighbours who live nearby may be functioning as effective parent surrogates who provide structure and positive encouragement to teens who might otherwise get into trouble with unsupervised peers(Cowan, Powell, and Cowan; 1988).

In some cases, risks fail to produce the expected negative effects not because of the presence of protective or buffering mechanisms but because the child is resilient. Some formulations of resilience imply a kind of "inner Teflon" in the child that prevents risks from producing negative effects, where as others view resilience as the outcome of a process in which risks present challenges that stimulate highly adaptive responses (Garmezy, Masten and Tellegen, 1984).

In some families, the effects of risk are magnified by vulnerabilities (genetic, temperamental, intrapsychic, and experiential). Without one or more of these vulnerabilities, the risks would not be expected to produce such problematic outcomes. As Rutter (1987) argued a decade ago, risks are not static events. Rather they set in motion a series of mechanisms that link the risks with a variety of outcomes. It may not be possible to change a risk or vulnerability factor such as genetic inheritance, but it may be possible to modify some of the consequences of genetic inheritance that have a disruptive impact on parent-child relationship.

PARENTS' ROLE:

Childcare practices and patterns of interaction vary greatly around the world, depending on the culture's view of child's nature and needs. Patterns of parent child interaction greatly depend upon parent's role.

Mother's Role: Mother's role was shown in different studies and has been discussed in several ways. A pioneering experiment conducted by *Harry Harlow* and his colleagues (Harlow and Harlow,1962; Harlow and Zimmerman, 1959) on rhesus monkeys. These monkeys were separated from their mothers six to twelve hours after birth and raised in a laboratory. The infant monkeys were put into cages with one of two kinds of surrogate "mothers": a plain cylindrical wire – mesh form or a form covered with terry cloth. Some monkeys were fed from bottles connected to the wire "mothers"; others were nursed by the warm, cuddly cloth ones. The difference in responsiveness to this 'pseudo' mother figure was astonishing. When the monkeys were allowed to spend time with either kind of mother, they all spent more time clinging to the cloth surrogates, even if they were being fed only by the wire ones. In an unfamiliar room, the babies raised by cloth surrogates showed more natural interest in exploring than those "raised" by wire surrogates, even when the appropriate "mothers" were there. It is hardly surprising that a dummy mother would not provide the same kinds of stimulation and opportunities for development as a live mother. These experiments show that feeding is not the only, or even the most important thing babies get from their mothers. Mothering includes the comfort of close bodily contact and, in monkeys, the satisfaction of an innate need to cling. Human infants also have social needs that must be satisfied if they are to grow up normally.

Father's Role: The father's role, like the mother's entails emotional commitments, and often direct involvement in the care and upbringing of children. Still, while father's involvement varies greatly, women are children's primary caregivers in most cultures. A father's frequent and positive involvement with his child, from infancy on, is directly related to the child's well being and cognitive and social development (Cabrera et al., 2000). At the same time, many fathers are not even present in the household. In those cases, father's absence may affect a child in many ways, from economic loss to psychological distress (Cabrera et al., 2000). The responsible fathering means a father's active involvement in meeting his child's financial, physical and emotional needs. Factors may include his motivation and commitment, his beliefs about fathering, his confidence in his parenting skills, his success as a breadwinner, his relationship with the mother, and the extent to which she encourages his involvement (Coley, 2001; Doherty Kouneski and Erickson, 1998).

Parents role in developing gender role: Being male or female affects how people look, how they move their bodies, and how they work, play and dress. It influences what they think about themselves and what others think of them. All those characteristics are included in the word *gender*, which means to be male or female.

Measurable differences between baby boys and girls are few. Males are physically more vulnerable than females from conception on. On the other hand, baby boys are a bit longer and heavier than baby girls and may be slightly stronger. New born boys and girls react differently to stress, possibly suggesting genetic, hormonal, or temperamental differences (Davis and Emory, 1995). An analysis of a large number of a studies found baby boys more active than baby girls, though this difference is not consistently documented. The two sexes are equally sensitive to touch and tend to teethe, sit up and walk at about the same ages (Maccoby, 1980).

Parental shaping of boys' and girls' personalities appears to begin very early. Fathers, especially, promote gender-typing, the process by which children learn behaviour that their culture considers appropriate for each sex (Bronstein and Cowan, 1988). Father treat boys and girls more differently than mothers do, even during the first year. During the second year, fathers talk more and spend more time with sons than with daughters (Lamb, 1981). Mothers talk more, and more supportively to daughters than to sons. Overall, fathers are less talkative and supportive – but also less negative – in their speech than mothers are. These differences are especially pronounced with toddlers, whose mothers typically spend much more time with them than fathers do (Leaper, Anderson and Sanders, 1998). Fathers of toddlers play more roughly with sons and show more sensitivity to daughters (Kelley, et al., 1998).

Parents role in developing attachment: Attachment is a reciprocal, enduring emotional tie between an infant and a caregiver, each of whom contributes to the quality of the relationship. Attachments have adaptive value for babies, ensuring that their psychosocial as well as physical needs will be met. According to ethological theory, infants and parents are biologically predisposed to become attached to each other, and attachment promotes a baby's survival (Papalia, Olds, and Feldman; 2005).

Ainsworth (1967) observed one-year-olds in the strange situation and at home, they found three main patterns of attachment: Secure (the most common category into which 66% of US babies fell) and two forms of anxious, or Insecure, attachment: Avoidant (20% of US babies) and Ambivalent, or Resistant (12%).

Babies with *secure attachment* cry or protest when the mother leaves and greet her happily when she returns. They use her as a *secure base*, leaving her to go off and explore but returning occasionally for reassurance. They are usually cooperative and relatively free of anger. Babies with *avoidant attachment* rarely cry when the mother leaves, and they avoid her on her return. They tend to be angry and do not reach out in time of need. Babies with *ambivalent (resistant) attachment* become anxious even before the mother leaves and are very upset when she goes out. On mother's return, they show their ambivalence by seeking contact with her while at the same time resisting it by kicking or squirming. These three attachment patterns are universal in all cultures in which they have been studied – cultures as different as those in Africa, China and Israel – though the percentage of infants in each category varies (van Ijzendoorn and Kroonenberg, 1988; van Ijzendoorn and Sagi, 1997).

Other research (Main and Solomon, 1986) has identified a fourth pattern, *disorganized-disoriented attachment*. Babies with the disorganized pattern often show inconsistent, contradictory behaviours. They greet the mother brightly when she returns but then turn away or approach without looking at her. They seem confused and afraid. This may be the least secure pattern and is most likely to occur in babies whose mothers are insensitive, intrusive, or abusive (Carlson, 1998).

Several studies had indicated problems related to the difficulty in developing attachment. There are number of studies which reported that disorganized attachment predicts later child psychopathology (Green and Goldwyn,2002). In a pioneering study Main and Hesse (1990) found an association between unresolved loss or trauma in parents' state of mind and disorganized behaviour in their infants. Some studies found evidence that 'frightening' or 'frightened' parental behaviour mediates unresolved mental representation of attachment and children's disorganization (Abrams, 2000; True, Pisani and Oumar, 2001). Extreme insensitive parental behaviour has frightening aspects triggering disorganized attachment behaviour in children (Juffer, and Bakermans-Kranenburg, 2005).

DISCIPLINING

Discipline refers to methods of teaching children character, self-control and moral values and behaviour. It can be a powerful tool for socialization with the goal of developing self-discipline. Different researchers have different views about forms of discipline, which work best. Following is a brief sketch of various prevalent techniques:

Behaviourist techniques: reinforcement and punishment:

Parents sometimes punish children to stop undesirable behaviour, but children usually learn more from being reinforced for good behaviour. External reinforcements may be tangible (candy, money, toys or gold stars) or intangible (smile, a word of praise, a hug, extra attention or a special privilege). Whatever the reinforcement the child must see it as rewarding and must receive it fairly, consistently after showing the desired behaviour. Eventually, the behaviour should provide its own internal reward: a sense of pleasure or accomplishment. Still, at times punishment—such as isolation, or denial of privileges – is necessary. Some times a child is will fully defiant. In such situations, punishment, if consistent, immediate and clearly tied to the offense may be effective. It should be administered calmly, in private, and aimed at eliciting compliance, not guilt. It is most effective when accompanied by a short, simple explanation (AAP Committee on Psychosocial aspects of child and family health 1998: Baumrind,1996, 1996a). However, some punishment can be counter productive. Children who have punished harshly and frequently may have trouble interpreting other people's actions and words; they may attribute hostile intentions where none exists. Young children who have been punished harshly may later act aggressively, even though the punishment is intended to stop what a parent sees as purposely aggressive behaviour (Nix et al., 1999). On the other hand, such children may become passive because they feel helpless. Children may become frightened if parents lose control and may eventually try to avoid a punitive parent, undermining the parents' ability to influence behaviour (Grusec and Goodnow, 1994).

Corporal punishment: Corporal punishment has been defined as "the use of physical force with the intention of causing a child to experience pain, but not injury, rather for the purpose of correction or control of the child's behaviour" (Straus, 1994, p.4). it can include spanking, hitting, slapping, pinching, shaking (which can be fatal to infants), and other physical acts. Corporal punishment is a pervasive part of the socialization of many children. Many people believe that it is more effective than other remedies and harmless if done in moderation by loving parents. However, a growing body of evidence suggests that these beliefs are untrue, that corporal punishment can have serious negative consequences, and that it should not be used (Straus, 1999; Straus and Stewart, 1999).

Power assertion, induction and withdrawal of love: Looking at reinforcement and punishment alone may be an over simplification of how parents influence behaviour. Contemporary research has focused on three broader categories of discipline: power, assertion, induction, and temporary withdrawal of love. *Power assertion* is intended to stop or discourage undesirable behaviour through physical or verbal enforcement of parental control; it includes demands threats, withdrawal of privileges, spanking and other punishments. *Inductive techniques* are designed to encourage desirable behaviour (or discourage undesirable behaviour) by reasoning with a child; they include setting limits, demonstrating logical consequences of an action explaining, discussing, and getting ideas from the child about what is fair. *Withdrawal of love* may include ignoring, isolating, or showing dislike for a child. The choice and effectiveness of a disciplinary strategy may depend on the parents' personality, the childs' personality and age, and the quality of their relationship, as well as on culturally based customs and expectations (Grusec and Goodnow, 1994).

Induction is usually the most effective method, and power assertion the least effective, of getting children to accept parental standards (McCord, 1996). Inductive reasoning tends to arouse empathy for the victim of wrongdoing, as well as guilt on the part of that individual (Krevans and Gibbs, 1996). Kindergarteners whose mothers reported using reasoning were more likely to see the moral wrongness of behaviour that hurt other people (as opposed to merely breaking rules) than children, whose mothers took away privileges. It may be because removal of privileges encourages children to focus on themselves and their own feelings rather than on the way, their behaviour affects others (McCord, 1996).

The child's cognitive level, temperament, and emotionality may affect the child's response (Grusec et al., 2000). Gentle guidance seems particularly suited to temperamentally fearful or anxious children, who tend to become upset when they misbehave. Such a child will readily internalize parental messages with a minimum of prodding: displays of power would merely make the child more anxious (Kochanska, 1995, 1997). shame tends to arise when parents are angry or rejecting and do not use appropriate discipline of any kind (Eisenberg, 2000). Children in such situations may feel unworthy of their parent's attention.

The effectiveness of parental discipline may hinge on how well the child understands and accepts the parents' message, both cognitively and emotionally (Grusec and Goodnow, 1994). The child has to recognize the message as appropriate: so parents need to be fair and accurate, and clear and consistent about their expectations. They need to fit their actions to the misdeed and to the child's temperament and cognitive and emotional level. The child may be more motivated to accept the message if the parents normally are warm and responsive, if they arouse the child's empathy for someone harmed by the misdeed, and if they make the child feel less secure in their affections as a result of the misbehavior. It may help if parents deliver the message in humorous or indirect terms.

Because a child interprets and responds to discipline in the context of an ongoing relationship with a parent, some researchers have looked beyond specific parental practices to overall styles or patterns of parenting.

PARENTING STYLES

In pioneering research, Diana Baumrind (1996) studied 103 preschool children from 95 families. She measured how the children were functioning, where she identified three parenting styles, and described typical behaviour patterns of children raised according to each. However, Baumrind's work and the large body of research it inspired have established strong associations between each parenting style and a particular set of child behaviour.

Authoritarian parents, according to Baumrind, value control and unquestioning obedience. They try to make children conform to a set of standard of conduct and punish them arbitrarily and forcefully for violating it. They are more detached and less warm than other parents are. Their children tend to be more discontented, withdrawn and distrustful.

Permissive parents value self-expression and self-regulation. They make few demands and allow children to monitor their own activities as much as possible. When they do have to make rules, they explain the reasons for them. They are warm, noncontrolling and undemanding. Their preschool children tend to be immature-the least self-controlled and the least exploratory.

Authoritative parents value child's individuality but also stress social constraints. They have confidence in their ability to guide children, but they also respect children's independent decisions, interests, opinions and personalities. They are loving and accepting, but also demand good behaviour, are firm in maintaining standards, and are willing to impose limited, judicious punishment when necessary, with in the context of a warm, supportive relationship. They explain the reasoning behind their stands and encourage verbal give-and-take. Their children apparently feel secure in knowing that they are both loved and firmly guided. Preschoolers with authoritative parents tend to be the most self-reliant, self-controlled, self-assertive, exploratory and content.

Eleanor Maccoby and John Martin (1983) added a fourth parenting style – *Neglectful or Uninvolved* – to describe parents who, sometimes because of stress or depression, focus on their own needs rather than those of the child. Neglectful parenting has been linked with a variety of behavioural disorders in childhood and adolescence (Parke and Buriel, 1998). In authoritarian homes, children are so strictly controlled that often they can not make independent choices about their own behaviour. In permissive homes, children receive so little guidance that they may become uncertain and anxious about whether they are doing right thing. In authoritative homes, children know when they are meeting expectations and can decide whether it is worth risking parental displeasure to pursue a goal. These children are expected to perform well, fulfill commitments, and participate actively in family duties as well as family fun.

When conflict arises, an authoritative parent can teach the child positive ways to communicate his or her own point of view and negotiate acceptable alternatives. Internalization of these broader set of skills, not just of specific behavioural demands, may well be a key to the success of authoritative parenting (Grusec and Goodnow, 1994). Children become better able to regulate their own thoughts, emotions and behaviours they develop. Disruption in the process of self-regulation contribute to the development of behavioural problems (e.g aggression, conduct problems) in childhood and adolescence (Eisenberg and Morris, 2002; Hill, 2002). Parenting and parent-child relationship are critical parts of these regulatory processes. Contemporary theories of socialization emphasize dyadic mutuality – the formation and maintenance of emotionally warm, mutually responsive and well-synchronized interactions – as being a fundamental component of these parent-child relationship mechanisms (Harrist and Waugh, 2002). This is a well-known fact that there was an association between lower levels of mother-child mutuality and higher levels of child behaviour problems. In a recent study Deater-Deckard and Petrill (2004) examined mutuality in mother child pairs in a novel sample of school-aged children living in adoptive families. They found mother-child mutuality is child specific within families, which again indicated that lower levels of maternal mutuality and higher levels of child behaviour problems.

THE CHILD IN THE FAMILY

Family environment, its atmosphere and its structure or composition is an extremely important area to understand a child's behaviour. As Bronfenbrenner's bioecological theory (Bronfenbrenner; 1979, 1986) describes, additional layers of influence – including parent's work, socioeconomic status and societal trends (such as organization, changes in the family size, divorce and remarriage). These contribute in shaping the family environment and, thus, childrens' behaviour.

Family atmosphere

The most important influences of the family environment on children's development come from the atmosphere with in the home.

Parenting issues: coregulation and discipline:

As children's lives change, so do the issues between them and their parents, and the ways in which issues are being resolved. During the course of childhood, control of behaviour gradually shifts from parents to child. Middle childhood is the transitional stage of coregulation in which parent and child share power. Parents oversee but children exercise moment-to-moment self-regulation (Maccoby, 1984). Children are more apt to follow their parents' wishes or advice when they recognize that the parents are fair and are concerned about the child's welfare.

The way parents and children resolve conflicts may be more important than the specific outcomes. If family conflict is constructive, it can help children see the need for rules and standards of behaviour. They also learn what kinds of issues are worth arguing about and what strategies can be effective (Eisenberg, 1996).

As children become preadolescence and they are striving for autonomy becomes more insistent the quality of family problem solving and negotiation often deteriorates. The shift to coregulation affects how parents handle discipline. Parents of school-age children are more likely to use inductive techniques that include reasoning.

Effects of parents' work:

The impact of mother's work depends on many factors. It includes the child's age, sex, temperament and personality. The nature of the mother's work (i.e. whether the mother works full or part time), why she is working, and how she feels about her work; whether she has a supportive or unsupportive mate, or none; the family's socioeconomic status; and the kind of care the child receives before and/or after school (Parke and Buriel, 1998). Another factor is whether there are two parents or only one in the household. The more satisfied a mother is with her employment status, the more effective she is likely to be as a parent (Parke and Buriel, 1998). School-age children of employed mothers tend to live in more structured homes than children of full time homemakers, with clear-cut rules giving them more house hold responsibilities. They are also encouraged to be more independent, and they have more egalitarian attitudes about gender roles (Parke and Buriel, 1998).

There are several studies, which indicated how mother's employment affects school achievement. Both boys and girls in low-income families seem to benefit academically from the more favourable environment a working mother's income can provide

(Goldberg, et al., 1996). In middleclass families however, sons of working mothers tend to do less well in school than sons of homemakers, where as daughters usually do as well or better when mothers work (Goldberg, Greenberger and Nagel,1996). These gender differences in middleclass families may have to do with boys' greater need for supervision and guidance.

Some children of employed mothers are supervised after school by their fathers, grand parents, other relatives, or baby sitters. Some go to structured programmes, either at school or in childcare settings. Like good childcare for preschoolers, good after school programmes have relatively low enrollment, low child staff ratios and well-educated staff (Posner and Vandell, 1999).

Poverty and parenting:

Poverty can harm children's development through its impact on parent's emotional state and parenting practices and on the home environment, they create. Ecological analysis of the effects of poverty traces a route that leads to adult psychological distress, to effects on child rearing, and finally to emotional, behavioural and academic problems in children. Parents who live in poor housing (or have none), who have lost their jobs or do not have any job, who are worried about their next meal, and who feel a lack of control over their lives are likely to become anxious, depressed or irritable. They may become less affectionate with, and less responsive to, their children. They may discipline inconsistently, harshly, and arbitrarily. They may ignore good behaviour and pay attention only to misbehavior. The children, in turn, tend to become depressed themselves, to have trouble getting along with peers, to lack self-confidence, to have behavioural problems, and to engage in antisocial acts (Mistry et al., 2002). In Indian scenario, also it is applicable. This linkage of poverty, family stress, and children's social and emotional problems exists among rural, low-income group people. A father's involvement with his children tends to be related to his economic success; when a father feels like a failure as a breadwinner, his demoralization is likely to carry over his fathering role and to negatively affect his relationship with his children.

FAMILY STRUCTURE

Adoptive families

Adoption is found in all cultures throughout history. It is not only for infertile people, older people, single people, gay and lesbian couples; but adoption occurs in people who already have biological children have become adoptive parents. Adopting a child carries special challenges. Besides the usual issues of parenthood, adoptive parents need to deal with integrating the adopted child into the family, explaining the adoption to the child, helping the child develop a healthy sense of self and perhaps eventually helping the child to contact the biological parents. Children adopted in infancy are least likely to have adjustment problems. Any problems that do occur seem to surface around the time of sexual maturation (Sharma, McGue and Benson, 1996).

Divorce

Influence of divorce on a child's adjustment depends on the the child's age or maturity, gender, temperament, and psychological and social adjustment before the divorce. Younger children are more anxious about divorce, have less realistic perceptions of what caused it, and are more likely to blame themselves. However, they may adapt more quickly than older children, who better understand what is going on. School-age children are sensitive to parental pressures and loyalty conflicts; like younger children, they may fear abandonment and rejection. Boys generally find it difficult to adjust than girls do. However, this difference may be less significant than was once thought and may depend largely on how involved the father remains (Hetherington, Bridges and Insabella, 1998). Emotional and behavioural problems may stem from parental conflict, both before and after divorce, as well as from the separation itself (Furstenberg and Kiernan, 2001). If parents can control their anger cooperate in parenting, and avoid exposing the children to quarreling the children are less likely to have problems. Unfortunately, the strains of divorce make it harder for a couple to be effective parents.

One-Parent Family

One-parent families result from divorce or separation, unwed parenthood or death. Children in one-parent families tend to do less well socially and educationally than children in two parent families, partly because one-parent families are more likely to be poor (Seltzer, 2000). Children in one-parent families are more on their own than children living with two parents. They tend to have more household responsibility, more conflict with siblings, less family cohesion, and less support, control or discipline from fathers, if the father who is absent from the household. Divorced mothers particularly tend to have trouble with school age sons. However, poor outcomes are far from inevitable. Not only the fathers involvement, but also the child's age and level of development, the parents' financial circumstances, whether or not there are frequent moves and other aspects of the family situation affect how children turn out (Seltzer, 2000).

Stepfamily

Stepfamilies often start out of cohabiting families, when a single parent brings a new partner into the house (Seltzer, 2000). A child's loyalties to an absent or dead parent may interfere with forming ties to a stepparent. Adjustment is harder when there are many children, including those from both the man's and woman's previous marriages, or when a new child is born. Findings on the impact of remarriage on children are mixed. Some studies have found that boys – who often have more trouble than girls in adjusting to divorce and single parent living, usually with the mother – benefit from a stepfather. A girl on the other hand may find a new man in the house a threat to her independence and to her close relationship with her mother and may be less likely to accept him.

CONCLUSION

It is a well-established fact that early life experiences have a significant role in the development of personality and it regulate our behaviours. Our early life experiences are solely dependent on parenting and/or caregivers in the beginning years of our life. Effects of the early childcare may depend on the type, amount, overall quality, and stability of care, as well as the age at which children start receiving it. The most important element in quality of care is the caregiver, stimulating interactions with responsive adults are crucial to early cognitive, linguistic and psychosocial development. It should not be surprising that what look on the surface like effects of childcare often may be effects of family characteristics. After all stable families and favourable home environments are more able, and therefore more likely, to place their children in high-quality care.

REFERENCES

Abrams, K.Y. (2000). *Pathways to disorganized attachment.* Unpublished doctoral dissertation, University of California at Berkeley.

Adler, A. (1927). The practice and theory of individual psychology. New York: Harcourt, Brace.

Ainsworth, M.D.S. (1967). *Infancy in Uganda: Infant care and the growth of love*. Baltimore: Johns Hopkins University Press.

American Academy of Pediatrics (AAP) Committee on Psychosocial Aspects of Child and Family Health (1998). Guidance for effective discipline. *Pediatrics*, 101, 723 – 728.

Baumrind, D. (1996). A blanket injunction against disciplinary use of spanking is not warranted by the data. *Pediatrics*, 88, 828-831.

Baumrind, D. (1996a). The discipline controversy revisited. *Family Relations*, 45, 405-414.

Belsky, J., Burchinal, M., Mc Cartney, K., Vandell, D.L., Clarke-Stewart, K.A. and Owen, M.T. (2007). Are there long term effects of early child care?. *Child Development*, 78, 681-701.

Bornstein, M.H, (1995). Introduction to handbook of parenting. In M.Bornstein (E.D.), *Handbook of parenting* (Vol.1, pp. xxiii – xxiv). Hillsdale, N J: Erlbaum.

Bornstein, M.H, (1995a). Parenting infants. In M. H. Bornstein (E.d.), *Handbook of parenting* (Vol.1, pp. 3 -39). Hillsdale, N J: Erlbaum.

Bornstein, P., and Cowan, C. P. (Eds.) (1988). *Fatherhood today: Men's changing role in the family*. New York: Wiley.

Bronfenbrenner, U. (1979). *The ecology of human development*. Cambridge, M.A: Harvard University Press.

Bronfenbrenner, U. (1986). Ecology of the family as a context for human development: Research perspectives. *Developmental Psychology*, 22, 723 – 742.

Bryant, B. (1985). The neighborhood walk: Sources of support in middle childhood. *Monograph of the Society for Research in Child Development*, 50 (3,Sl No 210).

Buhler, G. (1998). *Indian History Sourcebook: The laws of Manu*, c. 1500BCE. Chapters 8 and 9. http://www.fordham. edu/ halsall/india/manu-full.html

Burchinal, M.R., Roberts, J.E., Riggins, R., Zeisel, S., Neebe, E., et al. (2000). Relating quality of centre child care to early cognitive and language development longitudinally. *Child Development*, 71, 339-357.

Caberera, N.J., Tamis-LeMonda, C.S., Bradley, R.H., Hofferth, S., and Lamb, M.E. (2000). Fatherhood in the twenty-first century. *Child Development*, 71, 127-136.

Carlson, E.A. (1998). A prospective longitudinal study of attachment disorganization/disorientation. *Child Development*, 69, 672-691.

Coley, R.L. (2001). (In)visible men: Emerging research on low-income, unmarried, and minority fathers. *American Psychologist*, 56, 743-753.

Cowan, P.A., Cowan, C.P., and Schulz, M. (1996). Risk and resilience in families. In E.M. Hetherington and E. Blechman (Eds.), *Risk and resilience: Advances in family research* (Vol.5, pp.1-38). Hillsdale: N J. Erlbaum.

Cowan, P.A., Powell, D., and Cowan, C.P. (1988). Parenting interventions: A family systems perspective. In Damon, W (Ed). *Handbook of child psychology* (4th vol.). New York: John Wiley and Sons, Inc.

Davis, M., and Emory, E. (1995). Sex difference in neonatal stress reactivity. *Child Development*, 66, 14-27.

Deater-Deckard, K., and Petrill, S.A. (2004). Parent-child dyadic mutuality and child behaviour problems: An investigation of gene-environment processes. *Journal of Child Psychology and Psychiatry*, 45, 1171-1179.

Doherty, W.J., Kouneski, E.F., and Erickson, M.F., (1998). Responsible fathering: An overview and conceptual framework. *Journal of Marriage and the Family*, 60, 277-292.

Eisenberg, A.R. (1996). The conflict talk of mothers and children: Patterns related to culture, SES, and gender of child. *Merrill-Palmer Quarterly*, 42, 438 – 452.

Eisenberg, N. (2000). Emotion, regulation and moral development. *Annual Review of Psychology*, 51, 665 – 697.

Eisenberg, N., and Morris, A.S. (2002). Children's emotion-related regulation. In R.Kail (Ed.), *Advances in child development and behaviour* (Vol.30.,pp.189-229). San Diego, CA: Academic Press.

Erikson, E.H. (1963). *Childhood and society* (2nd. ed.). New York: Norton

Erikson, E. H. (1968). Life cycle. *In International Encyclopedia of the Social Sciences* (vol. 9, pp. 286 – 292). New York: Crowell Collier and Macmillan.

Erikson, E. H. (1982). *The life cycle completed.* New York: Norton.

Furstenberg, F.F., and Kiernan, K.E. (2001). Delayed parental divorce: How much do children benefit? *Journal of Marriage and the Family*, 63, 446 – 457.

Ganguli, K.M. (2005). *The Mahabharata of Krishna-Dwaipayana Vyasa*. Vol.4. Section LXXXVI. 5477.htm" http://infomotions.com/etexts/gutenberg/dirs/1/5/4/7/15477/15477.htm

Garmezy, N., Masten, A.S., and Tellegen, A. (1984). The study of stress and competence in children: A building block for developmental psychopathology. *Child Development*, 55, 97-111.

Goldberg, W.A., Greenberger, E., Nagel, S.K. (1996). Employment and achievement: Mothers' work involvement in relation to children's achievement behaviours and mothers' parenting behaviours. *Child Development*, 67, 1512 – 1527.

Green, J., and Goldwin, R. (2002). Annotation: Attachment disorganization and psychopathology: New findings in attachment research and their potential implications for developmental psychopathology in childhood. *Journal of Child Psychology and Psychiatry*, 43, 835-846.

Grusec, J.E., and Goodnow, J.J. (1994), Impact of parental discipline methods on the child's internalization of values: A reconceptualization of current points of view. *Developmental Psychology*, 30, 4-19

Grusec, J.E., Goodnow, J.J., and Kuczynski, L. (2000). New directions in analyses of parenting contributions to children's acquisition of values. *Child Development*, 71, 205 -211.

Harlow, H.F., and Harlow, M.K. (1962). The effect of rearing conditions on behaviour. *Bulletin of the Menninger Clinic*, 26, 213-224.

Harlow, H.F., and Zimmerman, R.R., (1959). Affectional responses in the infant monkey. *Science*, 130, 421-432.

Harrist, A.W., and Waugh, R.M. (2002). Dyadic synchrony: Its structure and function in children's development. *Developmental Review*, 22, 555-592.

Hetherington, E.M., Bridges, M., and Insabella, G.M. (1998). What matters? What does not? Five perspectives on the association between marital transitions and children's adjustment. *American Psychologist*, 53, 167 – 184.

Hill, J. (2002). Biological, psychological, and social processes in the conduct disorders. *Journal of Child Psychology and Psychiatry*, 43, 133-164.

Juffer, F., and Bakermans-Kranenburg, M.J. (2005). The importance of parenting in the development of disorganized attachment: Evidence from a preventive intervention study in adoptive families. *Journal of Child Psychology and Psychiatry*. 46, 3, 263 – 274.

Kelley, M.L., Smith, T.S., Green, A.P., Brendt, A.E., and Rogers, M.C., (1998). Importance of fathers' parenting to African-American toddler's social and cognitive development. *Infant Behaviour and Development*, 21, 733-744.

Kochanska, G. (1995). Children's temperament, mothers' discipline and security of attachment: Multiple pathways to emerging internalization. *Child Development*, 66, 597 – 615.

Kochanska, G. (1997). Multiple pathways to conscience for children with different temperaments: From toddlerhood to age 5. *Developmental Psychology*,33, 228 – 240.

Krevans, J., and Gibbs, J. C. (1996). Parents' use of inductive discipline: Relations to children's empathy and prosocial behaviour. *Child Development*, 67, 3263 – 3277.

Ladd, G.W., and Hart, C.H. (1991). Parents' management of children's peer relations: Patterns associated with social competence. *Paper presented at the 11th meeting of the International Society for Behavioural Development*, Minneapolis, MN.

Lamb, M.E. (1981). The development of father-infant relationships. In M.E. Lamb (Ed.), *The role of the father in child development* (2nd ed.) New York: Wiley.

Leaper, C., Anderson, K.J., and Sanders, P. (1998). Moderators of gender effects on parents' talk to their children: A meta-analysis. *Developmental Psychology*, 34(1), 3-27.

Maccoby, E. (1980). *Social development*. New York: Harcourt Brace Jovanovich.

Maccoby, E.E. (1984). Middle childhood in the context of the family. In W.A. Collins (Ed.), *Development During Middle Childhood*. Washington, DC: National Academy.

Maccoby, E.E., and Martin, J.A. (1983). Socialization in the context of family: Parent-child interaction. In P.H. Mussen

(Series Ed.) and E.M. Hetherington (Vol. Ed.), *Handbook of Child Psychology*: Vol 4. *Socializatoin, personality, and social development* (pp. 1 – 101).

Main, M., and Hesse, E. (1990). Parents' unresolved traumatic experiences are related to infant disorganized attachment status: Is frightened and/or frightening parental behaviour the linking mechanism? In M.T. Greenberg, D. Cichetti, and E. Cummings (Eds.), *Attachment in the preschool years: Theory, research, and intervention* (pp. 161-182). Chicago: University of Chicago Press.

Main, M., and Solomon, J. (1986). Discovery of an insecure, disorganized/ disoriented attachment pattern: Procedures, findings, and implications for the classification of behaviour. In M. Yogman and T.B. Brazelton (Eds.), *Affective development in infancy*. Norwood, NJ: Ablex.

McCord, J. (1996). *Unintended consequences of punishment, Pediatrics*, 88, 832-834.

Merriam – *Webster's Collegiate Dictionary* (1994). Springfield, MA: Merriam – Webster.

Mistry, R.S., Vendewater, E.A., Huston, A.C., and McLoyd, V. (2002). Economic well-being and children's social adjustment: The role of family process in an ethnically diverse low income sample. *Child Development*, 73, 935 – 951.

Nix, R.L., Pinderhughes, E.E., Dodge, K.A., Bates, J.E., Pettit, G.S., and McFadyen-Ketchum, S.A. (1999). The relation between mothers' hostile attribution tendencies and children's externalizing behaviour problems: The mediating role of mothers' harsh discipline practices. *Child Development*, 70(4), 896-909.

Papalia, D. E., Olds, S. W., and Feldman, R. D. (2005). Psychosocial development during the first three years. *In Human Development* (9th Ed.) (pp. 186 – 223). New Delhi: Tata McGraw-Hill Publishing Company Limited.

Parke, R.D., and Buriel, R. (1998). Sociallization in the family: ethnic and ecological perspectives. In W. Damon (Series Ed.) and N. Eisenberg (Vol.Ed.), *Handbook of Child Pshycology:*

Vol.3.Social, emotional, and personality development (5th ed.,pp.463-552). New York: Wiley.

Patterson, G.R., and Capaldi, D. (1991). Antisocial parents: Unskilled and vulnerable. In P.A. Cowan and M.E. Hetherington (Eds.), *Family transitions: Advances in family research* (Vol. 2, pp. 195-218). Hillsdale, N J: Erlbaum.

Peiser-Feinberg, E.S., Burchinal, M.R., Clifford, R.M., Culkin, M.L., Howes, C., et al. (2001). The relation of preschool child-care quality to childrens' cognitive and social developmental trajectories through second grade. *Child Development*, 72, 1534-1553.

Posner, J.K., and Vandell, D.L. (1999). After school activities and the development of low income urban children: A longitudinal study. *Developmental Psychology*, 35 (3, 868-879)

Rutter, M. (1987). Psychosocial resilience and protective mechanisms. *American Journal of Orthopsychiatry*, 57, 316-331.

Seltzer, J.A. (2000). Families formed out side of marriage. *Journal of Marriage and the Family*, 62, 1247-1268.

Sharma, A.R., McGue, M.K., and Benson, P.L. (1996). The emotional and behavioral adjustment of United Sates adopted adolescence, Part II: Age at adoption. *Children and Youth Services Review*, 18, 101-114.

Straus, M.A. (1994). *Beating the devil out of them: Corporal punishment in the American families.* San Frnsisco, CA: Jossey-Bass.

Straus, M.A. (1999). The benefits of avoiding corporal punishment: New and more definitive evidence. Submitted for publication in K.C. Blaine (Ed.), *Raising America's Children.*

Straus, M.A., and Stewart, J.H. (1999). Corporal punishment by American parents: National data on prevalence, chronicity, severity, and duration, in relation to child and family characteristics. *Clinical Child and Family Psychology Rev ɛw* 2, 55-70.

True, M.M., Pisani, L., and Oumar, F. (2001). Infant-mother attachment among the Dogon of Mali. *Child Development*, 72, 1451-1466.

van IJzendoorn, M.H., and Kroonenberg, P.M. (1988). Cross-cultural patterns of attachment: A meta-analysis of the strange situation. *Child Development*, 59, 147-156.

van IJzendoorn, M.H., and Sagi, A. (1997). Cross-cultural patterns of attachment: Universal and contextual dimensions. In J. Cassidy and P. Shaver (Eds.), *Handbook of attachment theory and research*. New York: Guilford Press.

3

Study of Voice Coherence in Children: A Case Study from Psycholinguistic Perspectives

—*Debjani Mukherji and Lakshmi Krishnan*

"Out of the abundance of the heart the mouth speaketh". Thus it is written in the New Testament (*Matthew, XII, 34*). However, the science of modern psycholinguistics has proved that it is not the heart but a combination of psychological and neurobiological factors which is the source of speech and which enable humans to acquire, use and understand language. Psycholinguistic studies have moved from the realm of the philosophical to that of the scientific as more cohesive data on how the human brain functioned was acquired (Chomosy, 2000, Harley, 2008).

Thus psycholinguistics today includes the study of the cognitive and perceptual processes which make it possible to put together the units (words) according to the rules (grammar) and generate sentences, discourses and texts within the structure of language. One of the various branches of psycholinguistics is developmental psycholinguistics, where children's ability to learn language is studied. The psychological aspect of psycholinguistics studies the impact of the psychological features like motivation, intellegence, anxiety, memory etc. in language learning and production.

Psycholinguistics is interdisciplinary in nature and is studied by people in a variety of fields such as psychology, cognitive science and linguistics (Harley, 2008). This area studies the mental processes of thought and concept formation and their articulation in language and how the human brain understands meanings, how it links syntax (word order) and memory and how it decodes and stores messages. There are several subdivisions within psycholinguistics that are based on the components that make up human language (Harley, 2008, Steinberg and Sciarini, 2006, Chomosky, 2000). Some of them are:

1. Phonetics and phonology are concerned with the study of speech sounds. Phonetics studies language at the level of sounds : how sounds are articulated by the human speech mechanism and how they are received by the auditory mechanism. Phonology studies the combination of sounds into organised units of speech, the formation of syllables and larger units. Phonological classification is made on the basis of the phoneme, i.e a distinctive, contrasted sound unit, eg: /m/, /t/, /p/. These distinct sounds combine with others and form meaningful units. The rules for combination are different in different languages. Within psycholinguistics, research focuses on how the brain processes and understands these sounds.
2. Morphology is the study of word structures, especially the relationships between related words (such as cat and cats) and the formation of words based on rules (such as plural formation). A morpheme is the smallest sound unit which makes sense; it cannot be further broken up because if it is, it will no longer make sense. For example, a morpheme 'cat' is made up of three sounds: /k/ /ae/ and /t/. This combination carries the meaning of 'cat' but if it is broken up, it will no longer carry the meaning. Morphology studies the formation of the combination of sounds into these minimal distinctive units of meaning called morphemes.
3. Syntax is the study of the patterns which dictate how words are combined together to form sentences. At this level, we study how words combine to form phrases, phrases combine to form clauses and clauses combine to form sentences. The study of syntax also involves the description of the rules of positioning of elements such as the subject, verb, object, adverbials, prepositions etc.

Syntactic changes can alter the entire meaning of a sentence.

4. Semantics deals with the meaning of words and sentences. Where syntax is concerned with the formal structure of sentences, semantics deals with the actual meaning of sentences.
5. Pragmatics is concerned with the role of context in the interpretation of meaning. For example, if, on a hot day, a visitor comes home and comments, "This scorching weather makes one so thirsty!", this statement can be contextually interpreted to mean, "I would like to have something cool to drink!"
6. The study of word recognition and reading examines the processes involved in the extraction of orthographic, morphological, phonological, and semantic information from patterns in printed text.

Generally, the methodology in experimental psycholinguistics is in the form of behavioral experiments. In such studies, subjects are presented with some form of linguistic input and asked to perform a task (e.g. make a judgment; reproduce the stimulus, read a visually presented word aloud). Reaction times and proportion of correct responses are the most often employed measures of performance.

In such experiments the tasks may be, for example, asking the subject to convert nouns into verbs; e.g., "pen"suggests "to write," "milk" suggests "to drink," and so on. Another experiment might present an active sentence such as "Ravi gave the book to Anil" and a passive equivalent, "The book was given to Anil by Ravi" and then ask the question, *"Who gave the book?"* We might then conclude (as is the case) that active sentences are processed more easily (faster) than passive sentences. More interestingly, we might also find out (as is the case) that some people are unable to understand passive sentences; we might then make some tentative steps towards understanding certain types of language deficits.

Cognitive psychology explores the phenomena of perception and understanding in human beings. The present study is concerned with a specific aspect in semantics, focusing on the usage of active and passive voice in sentences. The cognitive aspect in psychology is involved here to discover which of the two voices is more easily perceived, and an attempt has been made to throw light on the reasons for this. From a pedagogical point of view, it is hoped that this study will be useful in the area of language teaching and will help teachers to understand error production and individual differences among the learners so that appropriate syllabi and material can be devised for them.

In the present research dealing with semantics, two children were randomly identified for the experiment: Subject A (boy, age 10) and Subject B (girl, age 11). Both subjects A, (a student studying in grade 4) and subject B (a 5th grader) were familiar with the English language being students of English medium public school. Each was given the same two sets of sentences in active and passive voice and their task was to identify the subject in each sentence and answer certain questions put to them to gauge their level of comprehension.

Set 1 (Active)

1. Brutus stabbed Caesar.
   (Subject {S}-verb {V} (simple past)-Object)
2. The people will make him king.
   (S-V(future)-O + Indirect object)
3. Who taught you grammar?
   (S-V(simple past)-O-Interrogative)
4. The Mughals expected to conquer the Deccan.
   (S-V(simple past)-O+ Prepositional complement)
5. Give the order.
   (S (implicit)-V (simple present)-O (Imperative)
6. His behaviour angers me sometimes.
   (S-V (simple present)-O+Adverbial
7. The police were taking the thief away.
   (S-V-(past continuous)-O+ Adverbial
8. One should obey one's parents.
   (S-Auxiliary-Verb-determiner-Object)
9. They have pulled down the old house.
   (S (generalized)-V (past perfect)- O)

10. I have been studying hard.
    (S-V (past perfect continuous + Adverbial)
11. You must endure what you cannot cure.
    (S-auxiliary-V- O)
12. Call the police.
    (S (implicit)-V-O-Imperative).

The following questions on the above set were put to each child:

1. What is the subject?
2. Who is "doing" the verb?
3. Who is the verb being "done" to?

Subject identification was difficult in sentences 5, 6, 8 and 12, showing that sentences with generalized subjects, implicit subjects and imperative verbs were more difficult to identify. In all the other sentences, it posed no problem and elicited immediate responses.

In all the above active voice sentences, questions 2 and 3 elicited the correct responses, once the subject had been successfully identified. Responses to sentence 1, 2, 4, 6, 7, 10 and 11 were relatively quicker (15 seconds response time) in comparison to sentences 3, 5, 8, 9 and 12 (25 seconds response time).

Variation in tense was not a factor in response.

Set 2 (Passive)

1. The ball was hit by John.
   (S-V (simple past)-agent)
2. Honey is made by bees.
   (S-V (present perfect)-agent)
3. Let the order be given.
   (Imperative-S-V (present perfect)-understood agent)
4. The Prime Minister's speech was loudly cheered.
   (S-V (simple past)-adverb in mid position-understood agent)
5. He was being taken to prison by the police.
   (S-V (past perfect continuous)-prepositional phrase-agent)

6. It was expected that he would come first in class.
   (S-V (simple past) + subordinate clause)
7. Promises should be kept.
   (S-auxiliary+ verb- understood agent)
8. He was chosen leader.
   (S-simple past-complement-understood agent)
9. Why should I be suspected by you?
   (Split interrogative-S-V(present perfect)-agent)
10. The telephone wires have been cut.
    (S-V (present perfect)- understood agent)
11. We shall be blamed by everyone.
    (S-V (future)-Agent)
12. Stones should not be thrown by those who live in glass houses.
    (S-auxiliary + verb-agent)

The same set of questions was put to each child after this set of passive sentences:

1. What is the subject?
2. Who is "doing" the verb?
3. Who is the verb being "done" to?

Question 1 (subject identification) was done by both children in the sentences which had the subject as the initial word. However, in sentences 3, 4, 7 and 9, neither child could identify the subject.

Question 2 elicited correct responses in sentences 1, 2, 5 and 11, where the agent is explicitly stated. However, in sentences 9 (explicitly stated agent + initial interrogative) and 12 (explicitly stated agent couched in a subordinate clause), the respondents could not answer the question, "Who is 'doing' the verb?" Sentences 3, 4, 6, 7, 8 and 10, where the agent is to be implicitly understood, either no responses or incorrect responses were given.

Question 3 got correct responses in sentences 1, 2, 5 and 11. The other sentences, with understood agents and/or subjects qualified by adjectival phrases and imperative sentences did not get correct responses.

The difference in understanding the active and passive sentence is subtle at first, but easy to master once the grammarian understands the basics. Examine the *subject* and the main verb of the two sentences below:

(A) The girl threw the stone.

(B) The stone was thrown. (Or, the stone was thrown by the girl).

In sentence A, the question arises, who does the throwing? The answer is the subject, ***girl***. That subject is *actively* performing the verb; it is actively "doing" the verb threw to a direct object, the stone. This sentence is an example of active voice.

In sentence B, if we ask ourselves what is the subject? (***stone***.) What is the subject doing? (Nothing.)

The subject is not throwing anything else. So who exactly is doing the verb? It is not clear unless we place a prepositional phrase "by the girl" at the end of the sentence. The subject is *passively* sitting, doing nothing, while some outside agent performs the action (throwing). Since the subject of the sentence is passive grammatically, the sentence is a passive voice sentence.

Note: Sometimes the passive voice sentence is necessary when the speaker wants to hide the agent or obscure what occurs. For instance, a political party leader up for reelection might say, "Last election ***taxes*** were raised over the course of the year." The passive voice sentence hides the actor. It would be uncomfortable for him to teli potential voters, "Last election, ***I*** raised taxes over the course of the year." In that last sentence, the one who did the action is painfully clear! This type of situation is one of the few times that passive form proves useful, albeit in a somewhat deceptive way. In almost all other cases, it is better rhetoric to use active voice. It is a better choice for several reasons:

1. Active voice sentences are often more compact than passive voice. Expressing the same idea in passive voice frequently takes 35% to 45% more words:

The fighter punched Ali and dodged the uppercut. (Active voice—8 words)

Ali was punched by the fighter, and then an uppercut was dodged by him.

(Passive voice—14 words, about 40% longer)

In the last generation, the family built a new house and raised a new brood of children. (Active voice: 17 words)

In the last generation, a new house was built by the family, and a new brood of children was raised by them. (Passive voice—25 words, about 30% longer)

2. The passive voice clause can be confusing or unclear, especially in long sentences.

   My car has been driven to Mumbai. (By whom? By the speaker? By a car-thief?

   Fifty dosas were consumed in one sitting.

   (Who is consuming the dosas?)

   Five army jawans entered the room, and the terrorist was flattened against the wall.

   (Does that mean the five army jawans flattened the terrorist against the wall? Or does it mean when the five army jawans entered the room, the terrorist had flattened himself against the wall? Or did someone else entirely flattened the terrorist against the wall before the army jawans arrived? It is impossible to tell with passive voice structure in the last clause.)

3. Passive voice uses more "weak" words. Abstract words like *is / am / are / was / were / being / been*, the demonstrative pronoun "*the*," and prepositions like "*by*" and "*of*" are dull and colorless in comparison to "strong" words. Strong words include concrete nouns, powerful verbs, and vivid adjectives. To make clear who is doing what, writers who use passive voice often have to tag unwieldy phrases at the end of clauses, such as "by so-and-so." For instance:

   The car was driven(by the driver).

   The chocolates were eaten (by the boy).

> In the starry night, the waltz was danced (by the couple).
>
> The *to-be* verbs and the prepositions do not add much to the sentence in terms of color. It would be far more *active* to simply write the following:
>
> The driver drove the car.
>
> The boy ate the chocolates.
>
> In the starry night, the couple danced the waltz.
>
> The heart of the sentence beats within its strong verbs, concrete nouns, and vivid description. Prepositions and articles are dead weight.

It is significant that native English speakers are better able to remember material they read in the active voice rather than the same material in the passive voice. This is possibly because the English speaker's mind has internalized the Subject-Verb-Object pattern ("the adjectival noun verbed the direct object adverbially" as opposed to, say, the same sentence in French which would be "the noun adjectival verbed adverbially the direct object". The passive voice inverts this pattern which the English speaker's mind is accustomed to, thereby derailing the mental process of retention. Thus, use of the active voice in English may better enable the reader to remember what he/she has read. Moreover, better mental retention of the written material on the part of the reader would give the writer a better chance of creating an argument that would hold water and change the reader's way of thinking

REFERENCES

Chomsky, N. (2000) *New Horizons in the Study of Language and Mind.* Cambridge: Cambridge University Press.

Harley, T. (2008) *The Psychology of Language: From data to theory (3rd. ed.)* Hove: Psychology Press. (Earlier editions 2001, 1995.)

Piattelli-Palmarini, Massimo. (ed.) (1980) *Language and learning: the debate between Jean Piaget and Noam Chomsky*. Cambridge, Mass.: Harvard University Press.

Pinker, S. (1994) *The Language Instinct*. New York: William Morrow.

Psycholinguistics From Wikipedia, the free encyclopedia.

Rayner, K. and Pollatsek, A. (1989) The Psychology of Reading. New York:Prentice Hall.

Steinberg, Danny, D. and Sciarini, N. (2006) *Introduction to Psycholinguistics (2nd edition)*. London: Longman.

Syal, P. and Jindal, D.V. (1998) An introduction to linguistics: Language, Grammer and Semantic. New Delhi: Prentice Hall of India.

Verma S.K, Krishnaswamy N.K (1989), *Modern Linguistics. An Introduction.* New Delhi: Oxford University Press.

4

A Study of Values Among School Children

—Sharma O.P. and Deshmukh J.

Jacob (1957) defines values as "preferences, criteria, or choices of personal or group conduct." In two separate works, one by Athos and Coffey (1968) and the other by Scheibe (1970), the authors described personal values as ideas and questions about what is good, desirable, or preferable for individuals in situations in which they are faced with alternative courses of actions. Feldman and Newcomb(1969) defined values as "a cluster of attitudes organized around a conception of the desirable." According to Rokeach (1959), values are "abstract ideas, positive or negative, not tied to any specific situation, representing a person's beliefs about modes of conduct.

Rokeach (1971) differentiated between values and attitudes by saying that "an attitude represents an organization of interrelated beliefs that are all focused on a specific object or situation, while Values are generalized standards of the means and ends of human existence that transcend attitudes towards specific objects and situations."

In this respect, England (1967) observes that a person's value structure is "a relatively permanent perceptual framework which shapes and influences the general nature of an individual's behaviour. Values are similar to attitude but are more ingrained' permanent and stable in nature." Thus values are general principles that guide an individual's decisions. These principles have an inherent organization to them, a rational basis and impute worth to objects and other individuals.

Studying numbers of individuals, Spranger (1928) found that almost everyone had some consistency in reaction to similar situations. Furthermore, people's reactions were based upon some rational set of criteria that had a hierarchical structure associated with it. And these criteria were more important in the decision-making processes than others. He classified individuals into six major types, and called the types of attitudes. Later authors and researchers called them values. The six types that Spranger found were:

1. *Theoretical*- This type of person's primary interests are the discovery of truth and the systematic ordering of knowledge. To pursue his or her goals, the theoretical person will take a "cognitive" approach, will look for identity and differences, will disregard the beauty or utility of objects in judgments, and will seek only to observe and to reason.

2. *Economic*- The economic person characteristically values what is. useful and practical. Their decisions are dominated by the expected economic and practical results. They judge things primarily by their tangible utility.

3. *Aesthetic*-The aesthetic person places the highest value in beauty, form and harmony. They judge things from the standpoint of grace, symmetry and fitness.

4. *Social*-The highest value for the social person is other humans in terms of altruistic or philanthropic love. The social person values love as the most important component of a human relationship. They view other people as "ends", not "means". They are kind, sympathetic and unselfish.

5. *Political*- The political person values power and influence. They like competition and the "struggle". They desire positions of leadership and popularity.

6. *Religious*- The highest value for the religious person is unity. They seek to comprehend and understand the cosmos as a whole and their place within it. Their mental activity is constantly directed toward creating the highest and most satisfying values in experience.

This classification of values can still be appropriate today. We can measure the relative importance of these values to the individual, rather than the "absolute" importance of each value. A high preference for certain values must always be at the expense of the other values.

Over the years, a numbers of researchers have examined the influence of personal value structure on behaviour and in making decisions. Gilligan (1982) found that women responded differently than men to moral dilemmas. As values are codes or general principles guiding action, enrollment decisions to subjects have been found related with subjective value (Feather, 1988) and group membership (Gari, Mylonas and Kasagianni, 2005) of students. In order to take on these variables in relation to study the values, the present investigation aims to study value-pattern of school students with reference to their faculties and gender.

Hypotheses

For the present study following null hypotheses were framed :

1. The mean scores of corresponding personal values will not differ in boys and girls.
2. The mean scores of personal values will not differ among all students of different faculties.

METHOD

Sample

For testing the hypotheses a sample of 180 school students from different schools of Jaipur city were randomly selected. These students were selected from three different stream of arts, science and commerce, 30 male and 30 female from each stream. All subjects were in the age range 15-18 yrs.

Tools

For the purpose of data collection 'Study of Values' by Dr. R.K. Ojha was used as a tool. This scale is based upon Sprangeris Types of men (1928). The scale is self-administrating. The test has two parts: first part consists of 30 items with two alternative answers and second part consists of 15 items with four alternative answers. Roughly 20 alternative answers belong to each of the six values. The scale is efficient instrument for measuring values of school students or for adults who have had some school education.

Procedure

The aim of the present investigation was to study the values of school students. To fulfill this purpose 'Value scale' was adminstered to the subjects in a group of 5. After establishing a good rapport, test was introduced to subjects and they were asked to follow the instructions written above the test-booklet. As test comprises two types of questions, distinction was made clear to them.

After the proper instructions it was ensured that each of them has understood method. At the time of taking booklet back, it was confirmed that subject has responded to each item. After collecting the whole data, scoring was done as guided by manual.

Statistical Analysis

1. Mean scores of six personal values computed for all students, in order to compare the ranking of the personal values among the different faculties and among male and female students.
2. Simple analysis of variance was employed to compute overall differences in personal values among all students of each faculty.

RESULTS AND DISCUSSION

For the overall population of the study, a group of personal values with different degrees of relative importance was

TABLE 1: Personal value hierarchies of the male and female students, ranked by mean score

Rank	*Whole Population*		*Male*		*Female*	
	Personal Value	*Mean Score*	*Personal Value*	*Mean Score*	*Personal Value*	*Mean Score*
1.	Economic	43.76	Theoretical	43.52	Economic	44.05
2.	Social	42.93	Economic	43.48	Social	42.67
3.	Theoretical	42.53	Social	43.20	Theoretical	41.53
4.	Political	38.60	Political	39.63	Aesthetic	37.95
5.	Aesthetic	36.06	Religious	34.99	Political	37.56
6.	Religious	35.48	Aesthetic	34.16	Religious	35.97

observed. These personal values were rank ordered and could be presented in a hierarchy of priorities based on the degree of the relative importance (mean score) attached to each of them.

TABLE 2: ANOVA for personal value scores of male and female students showing significance of mean difference (df 1,178)

Dependent Variable	*Sum of Squares*	*Mean Squares*	*F*
Theoretical	198.63	198.63	7.65*
Economic,	17.39	17.37	.35
Aesthetic	666.03	666.03	12.87**
Social	13.89	13.89	.37
Political	198.97	198.97	8.87*
Religious	48.06	48.06	1.05

** $p < 0.01$; * $P < 0.05$ Independent variable – Gender

For the population as a whole, the ranking of personal values were from highest to lowest, economic, social, theoretical, political, aesthetic and religious. As presented in table 1, male and female students have totally different value pattern. Though theoretical, economic and social values remain the leading ones; priorities were different for both groups (table 1). Economic value was the dominant personal value for whole population; but it has a higher degree of relative importance for female students, it was second preference for boys. Theoretical value was found as dominant for male students, but less preferred by females. Boys were found to have aesthetic value as least preferred value. Religious values were emerged as least preferred among girls and for whole population in the study. Results are in accordance with earlier studies (Ojha, 1959; Lubinsky Schmidt and Bennow, 1996; Simadi, 2006), suggesting different value patterns among boys and girls.

Results of ANONA (Table 2) revealed that the boys and girls differed significantly on scroes of three types of values viz. theoretical, aesthetic and political and thus the first hypothesis was rejected. Boys scored higher mean scores (mean = 43.52) then the girls (Mean=41.53). The means differed significantly (F=7.65).

TABLE 3: Personal value hierarchy's of the students of different faculties, ranked by mean score

Rank	*Science*		*Arts*		*Commerce*	
	Personal Value	*Mean Score*	*Personal Value*	*Mean Score*	*Personal Value*	*Mean Score*
1.	Theoretical	44.98	Social	43.83	Economic	45.30
2.	Social	43.08	Economic	43.40	Social	41.89
3.	Economic	42.60	Theoretical	42.68	Theoretical	39.93
4.	Political	38.85	Political	39.46	Aesthetic	37.86
5.	Aesthetic	35.54	Religious	35.35	Political	37.48
6.	Religious	34.42	Aesthetic	34.76	Religious	36.68

TABLE 4: ANOVA for personal value scores of the students of different faculties showing significance of mean difference (df 2,177)

Dependent Variable	*Sum of Squares*	*Mean Squares*	*F*
Theoretical	777.632	388.816	14.974**
Economic	237.520	118.760	2.391
Aesthetic	330.365	165.183	3.191 *
Social	121.402	60.701	1.598
Political	126.721	63.361	2.823
Religious	156.077	78.038	1.709

** $p < 0.01$; * $P < 0.05$ Independent variable – Faculty

Personal value preferences for students of different faculties also suggest difference in their scores (table 3). Science students were found more theoretical, whereas art students were found having more social values with them.

Commerce, students have appeared as economic men in present study. Social value was second preferred value for science and commerce groups, but art students place economic value here. Aesthetic and religious values were least preferred values for Science and in comparison to other two groups, arts students, whereas commerce students were least influenced by political and religious values. Similarly difference in value patterns was also found significant in university students of business, social sciences and technology (Myyry and Helkama, 2001).

Thought results (Table 3) suggest variations in scores of three groups, ANOVA (Table 4) confirms that there was no significant difference among scores for economic, social, political and religious values. But difference in theoretical value scores was highly significant; science students were found more theoretical difference among scores of aesthetic value was also found significant (Table 3). Thus our hypothesis (2) was rejected.

As a conclusion it can be said that gender of a person has significant influence on personal value preferences. The difference in values of different faculty students can be because of the fact that different faculty students carry different value patterns; it may be due to their personal value preferences that they go for different streams, as *Feather* (1988) found in his study.

REFERENCES

Athos, A. G. and Coffey, R. E. (1968). *Behaviour in Organization: A Multidimensional View:* Englewood Cliffs, NJ: Prentice-Hall.

Cox, S. C. (1988). A longitudinal study of values in preferences changes as an index of adult development in Berea school students and alumini. *Paper presented at the Annual. Meeting of the American Educational Research Association (New Orleans, LA, April 5-9).*

England, George, W. (1967). Personal Value Systems of American Managers. *Academy of Management Journal.* March, 53-68.

Feather, N.T. (1988). Values, valances, and course enrollment: Testing the role of personal values within and expectancy-valance framework. *Journal of Educational Psychology, 80,* 381-391.

Feldman, K., and Newcomb, T. (1969). *The impact of school on students.* San Francisco: Jossey-Bass.

Gari, A., Mylonas, K. and Karagianni, D. (2005). Political and religious group membership, value priorities and educational values. *Journal of Belief and Values, 26,* 301-310.

Gilligan, C. (1982). *In a different voice: Psychological theory and women's development.* Cambridge; MA: Harvard University Press.

Jacob, P. (1957). *Changing values in school: An exploratory study of the impact of school teaching.* New York: Harper and Row.

Lubinsky, D., Schmidt, D. B. and Benbow, C.P. (1996). A 20-year stability analysis of the study of values for intellectually gifted individuals from adolescents to adulthood. *Journal of Applied Psychology,* 81, 443-451.

Myyry, L. and Helkama, K. (2001). University students' value priorities and emotional empathy. *Educational Psychology,* 21, 25-40.

Ojha, R. K. (1959). *Manual for Study of values.* Rokeach, M. (1959). The role of Values in Public Opinion Research. *Public Opinion Quarterly.* 32, 124.

Rokeach, M. (1971). Long-range experimental modification of values, attitudes and behaviour. *American Psychologist, 26,* 453-459.

Scheibe, K.E. (1970). *Beliefs and Values,* New York : Holt, Rinehart and Winston.

Simadi, FA (2006). The United Arab Emirates youths (UAEU) between modernity and traditionalism. *International Journal of Sociology and Social Policy, 26,* 172-184.

Spranger, E. (1928). *Types of men: The psychology and ethics of personality.* New York: Johnson.

5

Distributive Justice and Cognitive Ability Among Students of Two Regions of India

—*Rita Karmakar and Anjali Ghosh*

Distributive justice is concerned with fair allocation of resources among diverse members of community. It determines what is just or right with respect to the allocation of goods in a society. Distributive justice expressed as reward allocation has been examined mainly by comparing the preference for equity (merit) and equality, or equity, equality and need as allocation rules (Adams, 1965; Deutsch, 1975; Homans, 1961). Piaget and Kohlberg have pointed out the characteristics of various developmental stages and considered justice as a central theme in moral development. In discussing the moral development, Piaget (1932) made a number of observations regarding the developmental sequences of distributive justice. He characterized early forms of justice as motivated by obedience to authority, later forms of justice as fundamentally equalitarian, and mature justice as conforming to equity. Damon (1980, 1981) has described the development of distributive justice by incorporating both cognitive and moral development. According to him, the development of distributive justice follows an orderly stage sequence, which are as follows:

Level 0-A is characterized by any rule that the person wishes to adopt, and can be justified only on the basis of self-interest.

At *Level 0-B*, the distributive justice decision is solely based on some external characteristics. For example, the eldest and tallest child should get more than the other children.

Level 1-A is characterized by a preference for equality, mainly as a way to avoid interpersonal conflict and foster positive social relationship. For example, everybody should get the equal amount of resources.

At *Level 1-B*, the ideas of merit, deserving and reciprocity emerge that means those who work harder or contribute more should get more.

Level 2-A is characterized by an acknowledgement of individual differences in the perception of what is fair, and therefore, deviations from both equality and merit are accepted. Special circumstances such as recipient's need etc, are considered in judging fairness. For example, one who needs more should get more in resource allocation system.

At *Level 2- B*, co-ordination is evident between equality and merit/ reciprocity as justice criteria, there is also sensitivity to situational requirements. Thus there may be deviations from equality, but explanations are given for the chosen rule. This stage is the combination of Level 1-B and Level 2-A.

Research studies have supported the trend suggested by developmental theories. Studies by Enright and his collaborators using the Distributive Justice Scale of Enright, Franklin and Manheim (1980) have presented evidence for Damon's developmental stages of distributive justice (Enright, Enright and Lapsley, 1981; Enright, Enright, Manheim and Harris, 1980). Hook and Cook (1979) observed that younger children more commonly follow the equality rule in reward allocation whereas older follow the equity rule. Study done by Sigelman and Weitzman (1991) revealed that equality was more commonly preferred by younger children, but there was greater variation in justice rule preferences among older children, depending on the situation, but it is not a general equity preference.

A few studies have shown departures from the trends suggested by the developmental theories, which can be attributed to situational variables. Studies conducted by Lerner (1974) and Anderson and Butzin (1978) have shown the transition from equality to ordinal equity to proportional equity sequence. In a series of three experiments they asked children of 4 to 11 years of age to distribute rewards based on information, need, work, and both need and work about pairs of story characters. Their results showed that the majority of 4-year-olds consistently used the need and work information in allocating rewards. Nelson and Dweck (1977) found that 4-year-olds also followed the equity rule when given the appropriate instructions. The investigators explained the findings in terms of motivational and competence related factors. Studies done by Krishnan (1987, 1995) showed no significant age difference in actual allocation. In both the studies equality was adopted significantly more frequently than equity (merit) by younger and older children. Mishra and Mishra (as quoted in Mishra, 1991) did a study on a modified version of the Distributive Justice Scale (DJS) designed by Enright, Franklin, and Manheim (1980) to assess the developmental "levels" with regard to positive allocation and found that both younger and older Indian subjects tended to exhibit behavioural and psychological reciprocity, as well as equality more often than other considerations such as recipient's need. The investigators also found that age and gender interacted significantly to influence allocation judgements. In general, girls showed more maturity in their allocation judgements than boys, and this gender difference was greater at the younger age levels. Enright et al., (1980) conducted a study on distributive justice among children of lower and middle socio economic status and suggested that children from lower socioeconomic status showed lower levels of distributive justice development than children from middle socioeconomic status. According to them, the possible reason for this type of finding is that society is unfair to lower socioeconomic status children with regard to equal distribution of goods and this group of children also get lack of opportunities for participation in distributive decision which make them incompetent in their distributive justice reasoning than the children from middle socioeconomic status. To determine the role of cultural variation on moral judgement, a cross cultural study by Miller and Bersoff (1992) revealed that Indians give more priority to interpersonal relations in moral situation relative to justice consideration, in comparison to American group. But it is to be kept in mind that Indian culture is not a uniform one. In India, there exists unity in diversity. So not only the cross cultural variation but also regional variation within Indian culture is needed to be taken into consideration while studying the effect of culture on the development of distributive justice.

There are considerable evidences that moral understanding is the key aspect of a child's development of cognitive ability. Shaffer (1993) claimed that moral understanding complements a child's intellectual development. According to Kohlberg (1976) "cognitive ability is the corner stone of moral reasoning". Cognitive skills also help people to identify situations that have moral component (Rest, 1986). But there is almost no research study regarding the relationship between distributive justice and cognitive ability especially in the Indian context. Study done by Lynn and Irwin (2004) showed no significant gender differences in cognitive ability as measured by Raven's Standard Progressive Matrices (SPM) and Advanced Progressive Matrices (APM) among children. It was also revealed that males obtained higher scores on cognitive ability from the age of 15 years through old age. Studies conducted by Hernstein and Murray (1994) and Rushton et al., (1996) revealed that socioeconomic status correlated significantly with scores on tests of cognitive ability, and higher socioeconomic status group scoring better than the lower socioeconomic status group. Another study by Anand (1973) revealed significant differences in non-verbal and verbal cognitive ability among students of different socioeconomic status and the high socioeconomic status group scored highest. Jachuck and Mohanty (1974) also observed that subjects with a high socioeconomic status performed better on Raven's Progressive Coloured Matrices test than the students of low socioeconomic status.

Reviews of pertinent studies indicate that maturity, gender and socioeconomic status play an important role in the development of distributive justice and cognitive ability. But very few Indian studies were conducted for exploring the effect of these demographic variables on the development of distributive justice and cognitive ability. The present study is an effort to determine the role of maturity, gender and socioeconomic status on the development of distributive justice and cognitive ability in students from two different states of Eastern India, namely, West Bengal and Jharkhand. Though these two states are from Eastern India, still there exist differences with respect to beliefs, values and customs which may influence the development of idea of fairness and cognitive ability in an individual. The study also intended to find out whether the students from rural and urban area vary with respect to distributive justice and cognitive ability, that is why the students from both rural and urban locations were selected randomly from one district of Jharkhand, namely Giridih and two districts of West Bengal, namely, Kolkata and Murshidabad.

Keeping in mind the research gaps stated earlier, the present study aims to find out:

1. The role of maturity, gender, socioeconomic status (SES), rural and urban background and regional variation in the development of distributive justice and cognitive ability of school students, and
2. The pattern of relationship between distributive justice and cognitive ability.

METHOD

Participants

Participants consisted of 238 students (boys = 119, and girls =119) randomly selected from one district of Jharkhand and two districts of West Bengal. Students were randomly selected from rural and urban background of both the states. The socioeconomic status (SES) of the students ranged from middle to lower socioeconomic status. The age range of the students was 9-16 years with a mean age of 12.08 years (Standard Deviation 2.02). As students varied widely with respect to their ages, the total group of students were divided into two groups based on their mean age i.e. younger (below mean age) and older (above mean age).

The design of the study is given in the following figure:

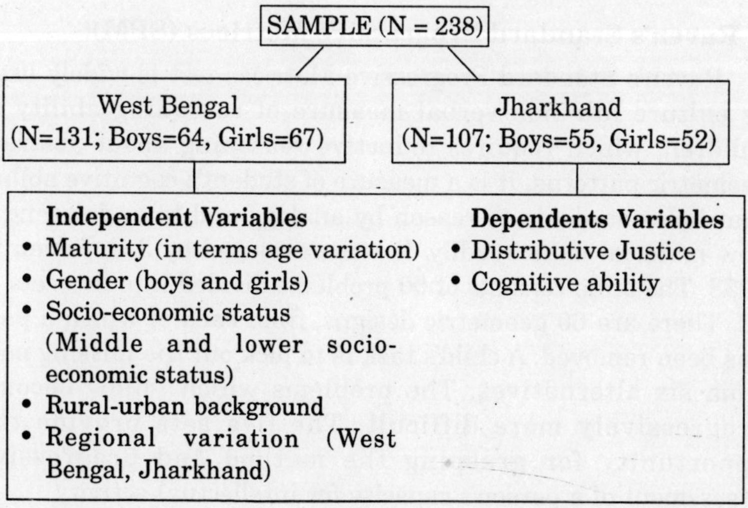

Tools used:

1. Distributive Justice Scale (DJS):

For assessing distributive justice of the children, Distributive Justice Scale (DJS) of Enright, Franklin, and Manheim (1980) was used in this study. DJS is a standardized and objectively scored paired-comparison test. Two dilemmas are presented in the test, and after each one the child is presented with 15 pairs of pictures and statements. Each picture and its accompanying statement represents a stage of distributive justice development. For each pair of pictures, the child is asked which picture (stage) better ends the story. The order of picture pairing is randomized, and within each pair, the decision as to which stage would be presented first was randomized to control for order effects. Besides the 15 pairings per dilemma, 3 pairs are repeated to check for consistency. The repeated pairs are presented in reverse order of their original pairings to control for primacy or recency effects. Total administration time is approximately 15 minutes per child. Some minor modifications with the permission of the author were made in the scale to suit in Indian culture. This scale generally assesses six stages of distributive justice: Stage 0, Stage 0.5, Stage 1.0, Stage 1.5, Stage 2 and Stage 2.5. These six stages are similar to the stages of distributive justice proposed by Damon (1980, 1981).

2. Raven's Standard Progressive Matrices (SPM):

Raven's Standard Progressive Matrices test is widely used as culture fair non-verbal measure of reasoning ability of children, which requires inductive reasoning about abstract geometric patterns. It is a measure of student's cognitive ability that helps students to reason by analogy and to understand a new material more readily. It was developed by J.C. Raven in 1938. The scale consists of 60 problems divided into five sets of 12. There are 60 geometric designs, from each of which a part has been removed. A child's task is to pick out the missing part from six alternatives. The problems which follow become progressively more difficult. The five sets provide the opportunity for grasping the method and progressive assessment of a person's capacity for intellectual activity.

3. General Information Schedule:-

General information schedule was given to know the age, gender, socio-economic status, rural and urban background and regional variation of the students.

All the tools were administered on all the students in one session in their respective schools.

RESULTS AND DISCUSSION

For the analysis of data, 2×2×2×2×2 factorial design ANOVA (maturity in terms of age variation, gender, socioeconomic status, rural-urban background and regional variation) was carried out on distributive justice and the significant F-ratios are presented in Table 1.

TABLE 1: Summary of ANOVA for maturity, gender, socio-economic status, rural-urban background and regional variation on Distributive Justice of students (df = 1,205)

Source	*SS*	*MS*	*F-ratio*
Maturity	3.48	3.48	15.76**
SES	1.60	1.60	7.24**
Maturity C SES	2.47	2.47	11.18**
Maturity C SES C Regional variation	1.41	1.41	6.34*
Error	205	46.69	.221

** Significant at 0.01 level.
* Significant at 0.05 level.

From the results (Table 1) it is revealed that maturity and socio-economic status as well as their interaction play a significant role in the development of distributive justice of students whereas the main effect of gender, rural-urban background and regional variation do not play significant role in the development of distributive justice of students. ANOVA results also revealed a significant interaction between maturity, socio-economic status and regional variation, but considering the main effects, there is no such significant effect of regional variation on distributive justice of students. It may be due to the fact that we have collected data from two neighbouring states of Eastern India. Further scrutiny of the data revealed that younger students are close to stage 1-A which represents the preferences for equality and older students are close to stage 1-B (which gives emphasis on the preferences for merit at the time of allocating resources) according to Damon's theory (1980, 1981). Both younger and older students from middle socioeconomic status show more maturity than their low SES counterparts. This finding is being supported by the study of Enright, et al., (1980). Significant interaction effect of maturity, gender and regional variation indicates that younger and older students of middle socioeconomic status from different states of Eastern India i.e. Jharkhand and West Bengal show more maturity at the time of allocating resources than the other groups. This result shows the prominent effect of maturity, and SES because the preferences of choosing different modes of distributive justice differ with respect to maturity and SES but not with regional variation.

To determine whether maturity, gender, socioeconomic status, rural urban background and regional variation play any significant role on the development of cognitive ability of students, again 2×2×2×2×2 factorial ANOVA was computed and the significant F-ratios are given in Table 2.

TABLE 2: Summary of ANOVA for maturity, gender, socio-economic status, rural urban background and regional variation on Cognitive Ability of students (df = 1, 211)

Source	*SS*	*MS*	*F-ratio*
Maturity	1502.233	1502.233	16.35**
Gender	443.642	443.642	4.83*
SES	1254.767	1254.767	13.66**
Maturity C Gender	644.293	644.293	7.01**
Maturity C Gender C SES C Regional variation	390.571	390.571	4.25*
Error	19385.897	91.876	

** Significant at 0.01 level.
* Significant at 0.05 level.

Results (Table 2) indicate that maturity, gender, socioeconomic status as well as the interaction of maturity and gender play important role in the development of cognitive ability of students. Other two independent variables such as regional variation and rural urban background do not play any salient role in the development of cognitive ability. Interaction effect of maturity, gender, socio-economic status and regional variation is also found to be significant. Closer scrutiny of the data indicates that younger students scored significantly lower than older students on SPM. Both younger and older boys scored significantly higher than girls on SPM. Younger and older students from middle socio-economic status scored higher than the students from lower socioeconomic status. This finding is partially supported by the findings of Hernstein and Murray (1994) and Rushton and Ankney, (1996) who observed that children from high socioeconomic status scored better than the children from lower socioeconomic status. Significant interaction effect of maturity, gender, SES and regional variation reveals that younger (boys and girls) and older (boys and girls) students of middle socioeconomic status from West Bengal and Jharkhand scored significantly higher than their low SES counterparts with a exception that the older boys of West Bengal belonging to middle socioeconomic status scored slightly lower on SPM than those from lower socioeconomic status. Again the results indicate that maturity, gender, socio-economic status are the deciding factors in the development of cognitive ability and also regional variation combined with other independent variables (e.g. maturity, gender, socio-economic status) play a significant role in the development of child's cognitive ability.

We have already determined the significant role of maturity and socio-economic status and gender on distributive justice and cognitive ability of students. For further analysis, separate t-tests of three significant independent variables (maturity, socio-economic status, gender) on distributive justice and cognitive ability of students have been computed and the results are presented in Tables 3, 4, and 5.

TABLE 3: Means, Standard Deviations (SDs) and t ratios of DJS and RPM scores of younger and older students irrespective of their regional variation

Variables	*Age Group*	*N*	*Mean*	*SD*	*t-ratio*
DJS	Younger	110	1.37	.47	5.82**
	Older	128	1.75	.52	
RPM	Younger	110	24.58	11.04	8.42**
	Older	128	36.23	10.27	

** Significant at 0.01 level.

TABLE 4: Means, SDs and t ratios of DJS and RPM scores of younger and older students of middle and lower socio-economic status irrespective of their regional variation.

Variables	*Age Group*	*SES*	*N*	*Mean*	*SD*	*t-ratio*
DJS	Younger	MSES	22	1.54	.41	2.20*
		LSES	88	1.33	.48	
	Older	MSES	47	1.89	.52	2.22*
		LSES	81	1.69	.51	
RPM	Younger	MSES	22	31.68	9.10	3.54**
		LSES	88	22.80	10.80	
	Older	MSES	47	40.85	9.05	4.10**
		LSES	81	33.55	10.02	

** Significant at 0.01 level

* Significant at 0.05 level.

MSES= Middle socio-economic status and LSES= Lower socio-economic status.

It is revealed from results (Table 3) that the mean DJS and RPM scores of older students is significantly higher than younger students. It indicates that changes occur significantly in the pattern of distributive justice and cognitive ability with the progression of age. In distributive justice younger students generally prefer equality as a justice rule to avoid interpersonal conflict whereas older students generally prefer merit, reciprocity as a justice rule. In case of cognitive ability, student's ability to reason properly also increased significantly with their level of maturity.

TABLE 5: Means, SDs and t ratios of DJS and RPM scores of male and female students of two different age groups irrespective of their regional variation

Variables	*Age Group*	*SES*	*N*	*Mean*	*SD*	*t-ratio*
DJS	Younger	Boys	61	1.35	.46	.61
		Girls	49	1.40	.49	
	Older	Boys	58	1.71	.54	1.07
		Girls	70	1.81	.49	
RPM	Younger	Boys	61	27.09	12.18	2.16*
		Girls	49	22.69	9.20	
	Older	Boys	58	38.48	11.06	2.31*
		Girls	70	34.20	9.52	

* Significant at 0.05 level.

From the results (Table 4) it can be seen that socio-economic status plays an important role in the development of distributive justice and cognitive ability. Students from middle socio-economic status scored significantly higher than the students of lower socioeconomic status on both distributive justice and cognitive ability. This finding is favoured by the findings of Enright et al., (198C), which suggested that children from middle SES showed higher levels of distributive justice than their lower SES counterparts. The possible reason for this finding is that children from lower SES generally experience unfair treatments from other members of the society and get little chance to participate in distributive decision which inhibits their concept of fair judgement. The role of socioeconomic status is much more prominent in cognitive ability than distributive justice. The results also indicate that in case of cognitive ability the difference between the students of two socioeconomic status increased with age and the same trend was also present in case of distributive justice, but the difference was much more prominent only in case of cognitive ability. This finding is being supported by the study of Feinstein (2003), which stated that the disparity in cognitive ability due to socio-economic status increased with age. The possible reason for this finding may be that with the passage of time i.e. with maturity, children are much more aware of their family's financial background which influences their cognitive ability. The effect of SES is much more prominent in case of cognitive ability because children from lower SES get less or no stimulation regarding cognitive tasks like solving analogy, use reasoning in solving problems etc. from their parents because in most of the cases parents of lower SES are either not enough educated to teach their children or they don't have sufficient time to spend with their children as because both the parents are busy enough in their daily activities.

Findings (Table 5) indicated that gender play a significant role in the development of cognitive ability. Boys of two different age groups scored significantly higher than girls and this difference is more prominent in case of older students. This finding is partially supported by the findings of Lynn and Irwin (2004) which revealed that males obtained high scores on cognitive ability from the age of 15 years and above. The possible explanation for this finding may be that as SPM requires inductive and abstract reasoning to solve its' problems, boys performed well as they tend to prefer abstract activities more than girls, and girls generally prefer concrete activities (Bartlett and Ferber, 1998). With the passage of time (i.e. maturity), the ability to solve the abstract problems generally increases among boys and for this reason the difference in SPM scores is much more prominent among older students. No significant effect of gender on distributive justice has been found out but it is seen that girls of two different age groups scored slightly higher than boys which indicates that girls showed a bit more maturity in distributive justice. This result partially support the findings of Mishra (1991) which stated that girls showed more maturity in their allocation rule preferences than boys. Closer scrutiny of the data reveal that older girls are close to Stage 2 than older boys. This indicates that older girls generally prefer recipient's need at the time of allocating resources. This may be due to the fact that in our culture the socialization processes differ with respect to gender of children. Generally, girls are taught to consider the needs of others while distributing resources. Besides this explanation, some biological factors may play role in this finding. It is a general belief that in most of the cases girls are much more soft hearted and considerate than boys.

One of our objectives was also to find out the pattern of relationships between distributive justice and cognitive ability for different groups of school students. Therefore, the correlations between DJS and SPM scores for younger boys and girls, older boys and girls and total group of students were calculated and the results are presented in Table 6.

TABLE 6: Correlation of coefficients between DJS and SPM scores.

Group	*Gender*	*N*	*r - value*
Younger students	Boys	61	0.10
	Girls	49	0.24
Older students	Boys	58	0.10
	Girls	70	0.27*
Total group	Boys	119	0.26**
	Girls	119	0.36**

** Significant at 0.01 level.

* Significant at 0.05 level.

It was found (Table 6) that the correlation between distributive justice scores and SPM scores was significant in both boys and girls in the total sample. This reveals that students with higher level of cognitive ability generally prefer higher stages of distributive justice i.e. both need and merit at the time of allocating resources. The result also indicates (Table 6) that the positive relationship between DJS and SPM is significant only in case of older girls. The probable cause for this may be that older girls generally showed more cognitive reasoning at the time of allocating resources than older boys.

CONCLUSION

It may be concluded from the above findings that-

- Maturity as well as socioeconomic status are the deciding factors of both distributive justice and cognitive ability of students. Generally younger students prefer equality to avoid interpersonal conflict whereas older students prefer merit, reciprocity as a justice rule. Older students are also capable to reason well in non-verbal measure compared to younger students. Students from middle socioeconomic status scored higher on both distributive justice and cognitive ability than the students from low socioeconomic status.

- Gender plays an important role in the development of cognitive ability of students, with boys scoring higher than girls, but it does not have any effect in case of distributive justice but still girls show a bit more maturity in their allocation judgement than boys. Girls are more need oriented than boys.
- No significant effect of regional variation on both distributive justice and cognitive ability was observed. It may be due to fact that values, cultural norms, behaviours etc. are more or less similar in these two neighbouring states of Eastern India.
- The positive relationship between distributive justice and cognitive ability of students reveals that students with higher levels of distributive justice also show higher levels of cognitive ability. The relationship between cognitive ability and distributive justice becomes stronger with further maturity and this is more prominent in case of girls.

The results of the present study have significant implication. From the above study it is clear that maturity and socio-economic status are the most important factors which can influence the distributive justice as well as cognitive ability. But the finding of the present study need to be replicated on larger samples taking students/participants from varied cultural groups, before being generalized.

REFERENCES

Adams, J.S. (1965). Inequity in social exchange. In L. Berkowitz (Ed.), *Advances in Experimental Social Psychology* (Vol. 2, pp. 267-99). New York: Academic Press.

Anand, C.L., (1973). A study of the effect of socio-economic environment and medium of instruction on mental abilities and the academic achievement of children in Mysore State, Ph.D., (Unpublished), Mysore University.

Anderson, N.H., and Butzin, C.A. (1978). Integration theory applied to children's judgements of equity. *Developmental Psychology*, 14, 593-606.

Bartlett, R.L. and Ferber, M. A. (1998). Humanizing Content and Pedagogy in Economics Classrooms. In W. B. Walsted and P. Saunders, (Eds.) *Teaching Undergraduate Economics: A Handbook for Instructors*. Irwin: McGraw-Hill.

Damon, W. (1980). Patterns of change in children's social reasoning: A two-year longitudinal study. *Child Development*, 51, 1010-17.

Damon,W. (1981). The development of justice and self-interest during childhood. In M.J. Lerner, and S.C. Lerner (Eds.) *The Justice Motive in Social Behavior* (pp. 57-72). New York and London: Plenum Press.

Deutsch, M. (1975). Equity, equality, and need: What determines which rule will be based as the basis of distributive justice? *Journal of Social Issues*, 31, 137-149.

Enright, R.D, Franklin, C., and Manheim, L. A. (1980). Children's distributive justice reasoning: A standardized and objective scale. *Developmental Psychology*, 1980, 16, 193-202.

Enright, R.D, Enright, W.F., and Lapsley, D.K. (1981). Distributive justice development and social class: A replication. *Developmental Psychology*, 17, 826-832.

Enright, R.D., Enright, W.F., Manheim, L., and Harris, B. (1980). Distributive justice development and social class. *Developmental Psychology*, 16, 555-563.

Feinstein, L. (2003). 'Inequality in the Early Cognitive Development of British Children in the 1970 Cohort,' *Economica*, 70, 73-97.

Hernstein, R.J., and Murray, C. (1994). *The Bell Curve*. New York: Free Press.

Homans, G.C. (1961). *Social Behavior: Its Elementary Forms*. New York: Harcourt, Brace and World.

Hook, J.G., and Cook, T.D. (1979). Equity theory and the cognitive ability of children. *Psychological Bulletin*, 86, 429-445.

Jachuck, K. and Mohanty, A.K. (1974). Low socio-economic status and progressive retardation in cognitive skills – a test of cumulative deficit hypothesis. *Indian Journal of Mental Retardation*, 7, 36-45.

Kohlberg, L. (1969). Stage and Sequence: the cognitive–developmental approach to socialization. D. Golsin, (Ed.) *Handbook of Socialization Theory and Research*, (pp.347-480). Chicago: Rand-Mcnally.

Kohlberg, L. (1971). From is to ought: How to commit the naturalistic fallacy and get away with it in the study of moral development. In T. Mischel (Ed.), *Cognitive Development and Epistemology* (pp. 151-284). New York: Academic Press.

Kohlberg, L. (1976). The cognitive-developmental approach to moral education. In T. Lickona (Ed.), *Moral Development and Behavior: Theory, Research and Social Issues*. New York: Holt, Rinehart and Winston.

Krishnan, L. (1987). Equality and equity in reward distribution in an Indian setting. *Psychological Studies*, 32, 97-103.

Krishnan, L. (1995). The effect of age, amount of resources, and small/large input by allocator on equal or equitable allocation. *Working paper, ICSSR Project*, Indian Institute of Technology, Kanpur.

Lerner, M.J. (1974). The justice motive: "Equity" and "parity" among children. *Journal of Personality and Social Psychology*, 29, 539-550.

Lynn, R. and Irwin P. (2004). Sex differences on the Progressive Matrices: A meta-analysis. *Intelligence*. 32, 481-498.

Miller, J.G. and Bersoff, D.M. (1992). Culture and moral judgment: How are conflicts between justice and interpersonal responsibilities resolved? *Journal of Personality and Social Psychology*, 62, 541-554.

Mishra, G. (1991). Socio-cultural influence on moral behavior. *The Indian Journal of Social Work*. LII (2), 179-194.

Nelson, S.A., and Dweck, C.S. (1977). Motivation and competence as determinants of young children's reward allocation. *Developmental Psychology*, 13, 192-197.

Piaget, J. (1932). *The Moral Judgement of the Child*. Gabain, M. (trans). New York: Free Press.

Raven, J.C. (1938). *Progressive Matrices: A Perceptual Test of Intelligence*. London:H.K. Lewis.

Rest, J. R. (1986). Moral development in young adults. In Mines, R.A. and Kitchener, K.S. (Eds.), *Adult Cognitive Development: Methods and Models*. NY: Praeger: 92-111.

Rushton, J.P., and Ankney, C.D. (1996). Brain size and cognitive ability: Correlations with age, sex, social class, and race. *Psychonomic Bulletin and Review*, 3:21-36.

Shaffer, D.R. (1993). *Developmental Psychology*. (5th Ed.) USA: Brooks/ Cole

Sigelman, C.K., and Weitzman, K.A. (1991). The development of distributive justice orientations: Contextual influences on children's resource allocations. *Child Development*, 62, 1367-78.

6

Mental Ability, Health and Well-being of Children Belonging to Joint and Nuclear Families

—*D. Arora & P. Batra*

Health, well-being and mental ability of the children are an important concern for any kind of family whether it is a joint or nuclear family. Health and well-being is a broad concept. Health has become a widely accepted state of general well being that includes both physical and psychological components. (Wheeler and Miyake, 1992). Physical health involves having a sound disease free body with good cardiovascular performance, sharp senses, vital immune system and the ability to withstand physical injury. Certain psychosocial factors that affect the health of an individual are socioeconomic status, gender, race, employment, and acute and chronic stress, social support versus isolation, anger and depression. Psychological health refers to being able to think clearly, having good self-esteem and enjoying general feeling of well-being. It involves creativity, problem solving skills and emotional stability. Emmons and Kings (1998) have mentioned that general well being is conceptually related to health. Well-being is a broad category of phenomenon that includes people's emotional responses, domain satisfaction and global judgments of life satisfaction (Diener, Suh, Lucas, and Smith, 1999). Diener and Diener (1996) and Lykkon and Tellegen (1996) defined general well being as the subjective feeling of contentment, happiness and satisfaction with life experiences and of one's role in world of work, sense of achievement, utility, belongingness and no distress, dissatisfaction or worry. The person reporting low well being means that he or she is not having complete or harmonious functioning of whole personality in relation to physical or mental health. Health and well being of an individual have been shown to affect the mental ability as it is not only the genetic capacity rather it has been shown to develop with environmental factors, for example, nutrition, health etc. can affect the mental ability of an individual. Mental ability can be defined as the power to learn or retain knowledge, the ability to understand the facts and significance of behavior. It is the composite of several functions required for the survival and advancement in the world of work consisting of combination of various abilities such as verbal, reasoning or numerical etc. Mental ability is the capacity to deal with a variety of different tasks, in which one has to adjust to different kinds of performance in quick succession. In other words, it is the way to assess the mobility in the level of performance among different types of tasks (Jalota, 1984). The parents and the family play a great role in determining the status of a child on all the above-mentioned interrelated concepts of health, well-being and the mental abilities. Studies related to parenting, parental role, and parental relationships are found in abundance (Buijzen, and Valkenburg, 2003, Flouri, Eirini and Buchanan, 2002) but the studies related to influence of joint families on the upbringing of children are a few.

Today's scenario is filled with competitive spirits that has generated a stress among both the children and the parents. The students in the school are overburdened and the amount of competition amongst them is a little too high. Neck to neck competition has made the survival difficult leading to a lot of anxiety and tension. Therefore, the children need more attention, at least in terms of being affectively attended by the parents, so as to share their experiences and problems to get proper guidance. Unfortunately, the picture is just the reverse kind. In the present scenario, due to economic pressure, a majority of the women are working. It is often seen that the parents are in a neurotic hurry and they are not able to provide that social support, attention and affection to the children, which are necessary for complete growth and development of a child. So both the physical and mental nurturance of children are in damage.

Following section is an attempt to understand the family and its role in the above-mentioned constructs. Family, a smaller and vital part of the society, is complex and dynamic institution in India/world. Family denotes a group of "People" people affiliated by consanguinity, affinity, or co-residence. The primary function of the family is to perpetuate society, either biologically, socially, or both. It is a social group where a child learns how to interact, behave or react with other members, along with the norms, values, traditions or customs of the family. Family and community networks profoundly influence individual values and attitudes in ways that one is not even conscious of.

From the perspective of children, the family is a family of orientation; the family serves to locate children socially, and plays a major role in their "Enculturation" and socialization. From the point of view of the parents, the family is a family of procreation, the goal of which is to produce and enculturate and socialize children (Murdock,1949). Families have a major and long lasting effect on children's lives. The home and the family is the first environment of learning for the child, where the acquisition of knowledge, competencies, attitudes and values first begins (Berk, 2000). The child learns many skills including language skills, social skills and emotional skills. Families are expected to care for and nurture children, financially provide for them and transmit cultural and moral values to them (Bowes and Watson, 1999). That's why more number of the members in a family has been paralleled with environment enrichment.

Formally family types in India have been classified as nuclear or joint families. The term nuclear family was developed in western world to distinguish the family group consisting of parents and their children from what is known as extended family. Nuclear family can be of any size, as long as the family can support itself and there are only parents and children. According to Census of India (Ministry of Home Affairs, 1991), Indian families comprise largely of nuclear family structure with joint families forming about a fifth of the total households. In its most usage, the term "nuclear family" refers to a household consisting of a father, a mother and their children, where as, joint families are like microcosms of an entire world.

As already discussed, families are the first training grounds where people learn interpersonal skills. Although all families are the ground for first and foremost learning and one learns in the family till later stages of life, yet a distinction has been made by the psychologist and sociologist about what and how the children learn in different types of families. In the nuclear families, as the members are less, the total time spent with the family is lesser than the time given by various members in the joint families. The nature of interaction and its quality also differs especially if both members in a nuclear family are working. Generally the habit patterns of children also differ in the nuclear and joint families and degree of exposure may also vary.

Although every member of the family has his/her own contribution, yet joint families have been shown to play an importantly different role in the development of children, especially the role played by grandparents has been paid attention. The role being played by the grandparents in children's development became an increasingly recognized phenomenon in the U.S. as well as other developed nations at one point of time (Fogarty, 2008). Fuller, and Minker (2000), wrote, "There has been a recent, steep increase in grandparents serving as surrogate parents to their grandchildren. The increase has been attributed to a number of dire conditions affecting parents/ children of grandparents such as (1) death, divorce, child abuse, drug use and incarceration (Edwards; Daire, 2006) and (2) grandparents are the most willing of any family member to take grandchildren into their home (Edwards, 1998). Beyond the influence, grandparents have on their grandchildren while they raise them such as academic success and psychological well being (Edwards, 2003), grandparents also affect grandchildren even when they do not live under the same roof. While living together the members are very culturally rooted and have a tradition of their own which guarantees a good upbringing with good values (Sinha, 2008). Therefore joint families may be better and may also affect the mental ability, health and well being of children.

But it is unfortunate that family system is slowly giving way to nuclear families (Taqui; Itrat; Qazi; and Qidwai, 2008).

The industrialization and subsequent urbanization are the major reasons of such divergence. The relationship patterns in these families are certainly different exerting a different kind of influence on the children in the family. The explorations of these unique and extraordinary family relationships encompass new and uncommon dimensions that should become the focus of research to human experience. (Mckay and Suzzane, 2004). Keeping this in mind, it was decided to investigate into the following problem.

Problem

To assess and compare the mental ability, health and well being of the children in nuclear and joint families.

Design

Two groups design was used. One group consisted of children belonging to joint family and the other group consisted of children belonging to nuclear family.

Hypotheses

- Health of the children raised in joint families would be significantly better than the children raised in nuclear families.
- Children raised in joint families would possess significantly better well being than the children raised in nuclear families.
- Mental ability score would be significantly higher amongst the children raised in joint families than the children raised in nuclear families.

METHOD

Sample

Total sample consisted of 155 children (67 from joint families and 88 from nuclear families). These children were students of 9th standard having age range of 13-14 years. The sample was purposively selected from six high schools of Rohtak city. Besides this, the sample was equated in terms of various socio-demographic variables such as occupation of parents and socioeconomic status and on the continuum of healthy relationships by using a personal data sheet.

Tools

Jalota's Mental Ability Scale: It was developed by S. Jalota in 1951 then revised in 1984. It measures the global as well as three aspects of mental ability of an individual viz verbal, numerical and reasoning. There are total 100 questions in this scale, each having different alternatives. Its spilt half reliability ranges from .87 to .97.

PGI Health Questionnaire (N-1): It was developed by Verma, Wig and Pershad, (1985). It has further two divisions i.e. physical and psychological. It consists of total 38 statements, 16 related to Area A (Physical) and 22 related to Area B (psychological). Its test-retest reliability is 0.88 and spilt-half reliability is 0.86.

PGI General Well Being Scale: It was developed by Verma and Verma (1989). It is a 20-item scale, measuring the well being of a person. Its reliability by KR-20 formula was 0.98, by test-retest 0.91 for English version and 0.86 for Hindi version.

In addition to these tools, a personal data sheet and a semi-structured interview were administered to check the relationship of children with their grandparents and parents.

Procedure

Total 250 participants were approached in the different schools of the Rohtak City. Having established rapport and ensuring confidentiality, the subjects were informed about the purpose of the study and the informed consent was taken. Now the subjects filled a personal data sheet. They were individually interviewed on about their relationship with all others present in family. Only those children were retained for investigation who had a normal, healthy and good relations with their parents/grandparents. Their co-operation was elicited and confidentiality was again assured, that their responses would be used for research purposes only. The answer sheets of the test were attached together and the measures were administered. Relevant instructions for each test/scale were given uniformly to all the children. It took participants about 40 minutes to complete the given work. Participants were told to ask if they had any questions in their mind regarding all this.

At the time of collecting back the answer sheets, these were checked, for any omission and the respondent's doubts were clarified. Now the scoring was done and the results were tabulated.

Results and Discussion

The present study aimed at assessing and comparing the health, well being and mental abilities of the children belonging to joint and nuclear families. For this purpose, means and standard deviations on all variables for both the groups were calculated. For further analyses of the scores, t for independent sample means was applied. All these values have been shown in Table-1, 2 and 3.

TABLE 1: showing the mean scores obtained by nuclear and joint family children on health, along with standard deviation and t-values (df=153)

Components of health	*Mean (standard deviation)*		*t-value*
	Joint family	*Nuclear family*	
Total	11.70 (6.82)	12.86 (6.82)	0.28 ns
Physical health	3.74 (2.43)	4.13 (3.07)	0.39 ns
Psychological health	7.71 (4.46)	8.72 (4.49)	0.17 ns

ns = Non-Significant.

The results (Table 1) revealed that the total scores on health dimension were higher in nuclear families. Similarly the scores on physical health for nuclear family children (4.13) were higher than the mean for joint family i.e. 3.74. Even the mean for psychological health was also higher in case of nuclear family (8.72) as compared to the mean score (7.71) of joint families. So, the trend was just opposite of the predicted results for overall health. When tested for t-test none of the values i.e. for physical, psychological and overall health were found to be significant. Thus the first hypothesis that health of the children raised in joint families would be significantly better than the children raised in nuclear families was not verified here.

The obtained results are contradictory to earlier studies. For example Resnick, Bearman, Blum, Harris and Jones et. al.,

(1997), reviewed adolescent risk behaviors that pose the main threat to adolescent's health. The key finding of the study was that being connected with their parents and families and with their schools protects teens against the health risk in the field of emotional health, violence and substance use. It is expected that in present scenario, when both parents are busy, grandparents could be a good source of giving a feeling of connectivity. Not only this, they can better take care of the food being served as they have all time presence. It has been conveyed when Murthy, Ramnath, Vijayaraghavan and Rao (1985) studied the nutritional profile of joint and nuclear families children. The mean intake of protein and calories among joint family was higher than that of the nuclear families, and the nutritional status of young children in joint families also tended to be better. No doubt nutrition has very high correlation with health. Similar finding have been obtained in relation to the mental health component. For example Taqui, Itrat, Qadri, and Qidwai (2007) conducted a study on depression and found that residing in a nuclear family system is a strong predictor of depression, although the subject taken here were the elderly. They found that transition in family system towards nucleation might have a major deleterious effect on physical and mental health of the elderly. These and many other such results lead to the idea of a positive role of joint families in health. However, nothing of such kind seems to have influenced the growth and nurturance of the children. The following section may perhaps be a little more revealing.

Research on adolescent development has indicated that a relationship with at least one caring adult, not necessarily a parent, is perhaps a single most element in protecting young people who have multiple risks in their lives (Carnegie council on adolescent development, 1992; National commission on children, 1991; Wynn, Costello, Halpern and Richman, 1994). Similarly the emphasis in Resnick et al's (1997) study is also 'on being connected with'. This 'with' could be anyone. It seems from the results of the present study that the quality of connectivity is more important than the person whom one looks at for feeling attached and secured. May be the attachment itself is enough to enable the child to take care of himself /herself. Following section reveals the results obtained on well being component.

TABLE 2: Showing the mean scores obtained by nuclear and joint family children on well being, along with standard deviation and t-values (df = 153)

Components of health	*Mean (standard deviation)*		*t-value*
	Joint family	*Nuclear family*	
PGI general well-being	14.37 (4.46)	15.35 (3.87)	0.14 ns

ns = Non-Significant.

Results (Table 2) revealed that the mean score of well being of nuclear family (15.35) was higher as compared to joint family mean score (14.37) and again the trend is just reverse of the predicted results. The higher mean scores of nuclear family indicate that subjects experienced a feeling of satisfaction, contentment and happiness. However, when t-test was applied for testing the significance of difference, it was found to be non-significant. Thus the hypothesis that well-being would be better amongst children in joint families than the children in nuclear families was also not verified. Thus the findings of the study are contradictory to the earlier studies, which show that the well being of joint families' children was be better than the children in nuclear families. Munshi, Iqbal, Rafique and Ahmad (2008) conducted a study to see the morbidity pattern in Kashmir valley and depression level in relation to family support in geriatric population and concluded that the joint family system and strong family ties have some positive effect on the well being of the elderly. Here being elderly could be an important factor in a sense that in that age the feelings of insecurity increases and every act of the family members particularly sons and daughters is interpreted negatively. Actually the basic reasons underlying such a prediction was the relationship between health and well-being. As discussed in the introductory part, these two variables are directly correlated. Thinking in the same way as about health, the following study is quite revealing. Love, Keisha and Murdock (2004) in their study compared the individuals from biologically intact families and stepfamilies and evaluated attachment to parents as possible explanation for discrepancies in psychological well-being. The results confirm that attachment was a significant predictor of well-being. Thus the obtained results can be explained in terms of attachment.

The results (Table 3) clearly indicate that the mean verbal mental ability score for nuclear family children (21.93) was higher than the mean for joint family i.e. 21.49. Similarly the mean for reasoning ability was also higher in case of nuclear family i.e. 22.23 as compared to joint family children mean i.e. 21.91. So the trend was just reverse of the predicted results for these two abilities. However, for numerical abilities the results trend was same as predicted the means being 8.97 and 8.36 for joint and nuclear families respectively. When tested for significance upon t-test, none of the four values i.e. that for total mental ability as well as for verbal, reasoning and numerical ability were found to be significant.

TABLE 3: Showing the mean scores obtained by nuclear and joint family children on mental abilities, along with standard deviation and t-values. (df = 153)

Components of health	*Mean (standard deviation)*		*t-value*
	Joint family	*Nuclear family*	
Mental ability (total)	52.40 (15.11)	52.60 (15.27)	0.92 ns
Verbal	21.49 (5.70)	21.93 (5.72)	0.63 ns
Numerical	8.97 (6.76)	8.36 (6.90)	0.58 ns
Reasoning	21.91 (5.60)	22.23 (5.73)	0.72 ns

ns = Non-Significant.

Agarwal, Upadhyay, Agarwal and Tripathi (1989) studied the mental functions of 388 (6-8 years of age) rural primary school children matched for social and educational status. The subjects were assessed in relation to anemia and nutritional status. They were also assessed for intelligence, immediate and delayed memory with arithmetic test. Observation showed that malnutrition and anemia were well associated with lower levels of attention and concentration and with both type of memory performance.

Parental rejection is associated with diminished intelligence and memory during the early school years (Hurley, 1965). Grossly deprived environments seem to retard the intellectual growth. The home and educational environments are conducive to intellectual development of children (Meenal, Praveen and Aneja, 2000). Research that examined the components of support was marked by more behavioral coping and academic competence and less tolerance for deviance and uncontrolled behavior (Wills and Cleary, 1996). It is clearly shown in the above mentioned and many other studies in the past literature that the health and well-being affect the mental abilities in a negative way. However, as there is no impact of the presence of the grandparents on health and well being, the mental abilities also not expected to be affected.

These results are congruent with the findings of Poonam and Balda (2001) that among the larger families the performance IQ was found to be lesser. In that case the question that arises here is that, are mental abilities, health and well being innate? It is well established in the literature of psychology that even the mental abilities depend on the environment enrichment (Skeels, 1966, Scarr and Weinberg, 1976). As already mentioned, it seems convincing that actually it is not the presence of any significant others, rather the quality of relationship and the resultant interaction and communication that is responsible for better growth of mental abilities. What matters is exposure, and increased interest in the surroundings and academics due to enriched resources. It seems that in the nuclear families, now the parents have gone conscious and are moving towards better style of parenting.

Before concluding it is important to have a careful look at the difference in nuclear and joint family in order to understand both the prediction and outcome in this study. In the present scenario, when joint family system is eradicating day by day, the value system, morale, etc of the individuals are also deteriorating. This is because of the fact that parents are so overburdened with their work and responsibilities, that they have no time for their children. They are not able to provide that support, affection, values and morale to their children which are necessary for their upbringing or development, for example when a child needs help with studies, the parents are not able to provide that help because of the lack of time and arrange tuitions for their child and after that they will not bother about the studies of their child. In a nuclear family, everyone is busy in his/her own life and doesn't have time for anyone else and crave for individual space. Everyone seems to follow a different time for lunch or dinner, thus, doesn't have time to sit together and enjoy. As a result there is no intimate bonding among the family members (Sinha, 2008). In a nuclear family, the responsibility of the culture, traditions and values that a child grows up with, lies on the parents. Many a times, due to lack of time, parents are unable to devote enough time to this aspect of child rearing. This problem is not faced in a joint family set-up, where culture, tradition and values get transmitted from a whole range of people to children and everyone spends a lot of time with other members of the family. Joint family system ensures a greater bonding between the members of the family. Everyone is there for one another. Children of such a system grow up together, so mostly they do not learn to be selfish or jealous of each other and become very understanding and cooperative individuals. They eat together, play together, study together, and go to school together. This system helps to inculcate in the members respect for others, especially for the elders in the family. People in joint families learn lessons of patience, tolerance, cooperation and adjustment. They also learn what it means to take collective responsibility. "One for all and all for one." In a joint family a child learns and is reared by a number of people, thus dividing work, saving time and creating a spectrum of exposure and awareness. In a joint family, authority and respect for elders are paramount, and the family unit controls members in all areas of their lives. Traditionally, all familial, emotional, professional, financial, or health-related difficulties are handled within the family.

However no such effect has been observed, indicating that either our children have been able to get adapted to this new changed system or the deteriorated value system itself may be responsible for such results. Now that the children don't want anyone to interfere much with their matters, the presence of grandparents or more family members seem to be perceived as a factor curtailing their independence. They have not observed their parents being obedient and they don't value the obedience and discipline. They feel disturbed by the imposition of these and such others values regarding various do's and don'ts by the family members. Najam and Kausar (1992) identified differences in adjustment pattern and general satisfaction of housewives living in joint and nuclear family system. The finding indicated that the housewives living in nuclear families are significantly well adjusted and satisfied as compared to housewives in joint families. The present generation has its roots in reality orientation and practicality. The roles of parents have changed. Maybe, they want to enjoy the freedom of nuclear family. For this, they don't mind bearing the stress of bearing and rearing their children. They look for, and have learnt to grab every opportunity. After all, it is a question of survival. Darwin's 'survival of the fittest'. Therefore, the new roles have evolved and adaptations have to be there. However, the contributions of the schools in giving more opportunities to students and children's own consciousness due to extra burden of parents as well as use friendly technology and media development could also be the reasons for the role of grandparents. As mentioned by McKay and Suzanne, (2004) it is the time to explore the variables in relation to nuclear and joint families. However, the study doesn't challenge what the grandparents can do. May be the children and parents are paying some hidden cost to compete the race of time, without the grandparents. Yet it certainly is a reflection upon the fact that help can be extended only if the other person wants trust, confides and has faith in the helping agency. The study also suggests the further exploration of the role of grandparents on these and such other variables.

REFERENCES

Agarwal, D.K., Upadhyay, S.K., Agarwal, K.N., and Tripathi, A.M. (1989). Anaemia and mental functions in rural primary school children. *Annual Trop Paediatrics*, *9*, 194-198.

Berk, L. (2000). *Child Development.* Boston: Allyn and Bacon.

Bowes, J. M., and Watson, J. (1999). Families as a context for children. In Bowes, J. and Hayes, A. (Eds) *Children, Families, and Communities.* Oxford: Oxford University Press.

Buijzen, M. and Valkenburg., P.M.(2003). The unintended effects of television advertising: A parent child survey. *Communication Research*, *30*, 483-503.

Carnegie Council on Adolescent Development. (1992). *A matter of time: Risk and opportunity in the non-school hours*. Washington, DC: Author.

Diener, E., and Diener, C. (1996). Most people are happy. *Psychological Sciences*, *7*, 181-185.

Diener, E., Suh, E., Lucas, R. E., and Smith, H. (1999). Subjective well-being: Three decades of progress. *Psychological Bulletin*, *125*, 276-302.

Edwards, O.W. (1998). Helping grandchildren raised by grandparents: Expanding psychology in the schools. *Psychology in the Schools*, *35*, 173-181.

Edwards, O.W. (2003). Living with grandma: A grand family study. *School Psychology International*, *24*, 204-217.

Edwards, O.W., and Daire, A.P. (2006). School-age children raised by their grandparents: Problems and solution. *Journal of Instructional Psychology*, *33*, 113-119.

Emmons, R.A., and King, L.A. (1998). Conflict among personnel striving: Immediate and long term implications for psychological and physical well being. *Journal of personality and social psychology*, *54*, 1040-1048.

Flouri., Eirini., and Buchanam., A. (2002). The protective role of parental involvement in adolescent suicide. *Crisis*, *23*, 17-22.

Fogarty, K. (2008). *Research news you can use: The Protective Role of Grandparents*. Florida : University of Florida.

Fuller-Thomson, E., and Minkler, M. (2000). America's grandparent caregivers: Who are they? In B. Hayslip Jr. and R. Goldberg-Glen (Eds.), *Grandparents raising grandchildren: Theoretical, empirical, and clinical perspectives* (pp. 3-21). New York: Springer.

Hurley, W.F. Jr. (1965). The effect of monetary incentive in paired associative learning using an absolute method. *Psychonomic Science, 3,*141-142.

Jalota, S. (1984). *Group Test of General Mental Ability* (Hindi), Chandigarh.

Love., Keisha, M., and Murdock, T.B. (2004). *Attachment to parents and psychological well being: an examination of young adult college students in intact families and stepfamilies, 18,* 600-608.

Lykken, D., and Tellegan, A. (1996). Happiness is a stochastic phenomenon. *Psychological sciences, 7,* 186-189.

Mckay, V.C., and Suzanne., C.R.(2004). The nature of family relationships between and within generations: relations between grandparents, grandchildren and siblings in later life *Handbook of communication and aging research.* Lawrence Erlbaum Associates, Manwah, NJ. *92,* 251-271.

Meenal J., Praveen, K., and Aneja, A. (2000). Performance intelligence and socio-economic correlates. *Indian Journal of Applied Psychology, 37,*10-14.

Ministry of Home Affairs _ Social Studies Division. (1991). Census of India (Occasional paper no. 1). New Delhi: Author.

Murthy, P.S., Ramnath, T., Vijayaraghavan, K., and Rao, N.P. (1985). Nutritional profile of joint and nuclear families in rural Andhra pradesh. *Journal of Family Welfare, 32,* 80-87.

Murdock, G.P. (1949). *Social Structure, 13.* New York: Macmillan Co. ISBN-0-02-922290-7.

Mushi, Y.I., Iqbal, M., Rafique, H., and Ahmad, Z. (2008). Geriatric Morbidity pattern and depression in Relation to family support in aged population of Kashmir Valley. *The Internet Journal of Geriatrics and Gerontology, 4.* Internet Scientific Publication. LLC.

National Commission on Children. (1991). *Beyond rhetoric: A new American agenda for children and families.* Washington: Author

Najam, N., and Kauser, S. (1992). A comparative study of Pakistani females living in joint versus nuclear family system. *Journal of Indian Academy of Applied Psychology, 18,* 61-66.

Poonam, and Balda, S. (2001). Effect of family factors on children's intelligence. *Indian Psychological Review, 56,* 8-11.

Resnick, M.D., P.S. Bearman, R.W. Blum, K.M. Harris, J. Jones, et al. (1997). Protecting adolescents from harm: Findings from the National Longitudinal Study on Adolescent Health. *Journal of the American Medical Association, 278,* 823-832.

Scarr, S., and Weinberg, R.A. (1976). IQ test performance of black children adopted by white families. *American Psychologist, 31,*726-739.

Sinha, S. (2008) *Joint family system.* http:// www.google.com.

Skeels, H.M. (1966). Adult status of children with contrasting early life experiences: A follow-up study. *Child Development Monograph, 31*,105.

Taqui, A.M., Itrat, A., Qadri, Z., and Qidwai, W. (2007). *Depression in elderly : Does family system play a role ? A cross sectional study.* Aga Khan.

Taqui, A.M., Itrat, A., Qazi, F., and Qidwai, W. (2008). *Family Systems: perception of patients and their attendents presenting at a university hospital in karachi.* Aga Khan.

Verma, S.K., Wig, N.N., and Pershad (1985). P.G.I. Health Questionnaire N-1. Agra : National Psychological Corporation.

Verma, S.K., and Verma, A. (1989). *PGI General Well-being Measure.* Lucknow: Ankur Psychological Agency.

Wheeler, L., and Miyake, K. (1992). Social comparison in everyday life. *Journal of Personality and Social Psychology, 62*, 760-773.

Wills, T.A., and Cleary, S.D. (1996). How are social support effects mediated? A test with parental support and adolescent substance use. *Journal of Personal and Social Psychology, 71*,937-952.

Wynn, J., Costello, J., Halpern, R., and Richman H. (1994). *Children, families, and communities: A new approach for social services.* Chicago: University of Chicago.

SECTION II : CHILDHOOD AND ADOLESCENT PROBLEMS

7

Victimization of Children in Mumbai Schools

—H.L. Kalia

In the past and also present, the schools have come under a sharp review and focus for the ways they have treated children with differing abilities and potentials. The media has reflected quite a bit on the performance of schools time and again building up pressure and stress on the growing-up children. Recently suicides have been reported frequently among school age children. How do we save our children from worst schools is a big question, this study attempts to address this socially relevant issue?

Child abuse in school, particularly 'within the four walls of classroom' have gone unnoticed, and the children have felt miserable so much so that they have developed inexpressiveness over the concerns that are close to their hearts, and they could rarely learn to express their creativity in school. A teacher is teaching lesson on non-violence with a stick-in-hand, pouring her / his own stress on children, and mouthing off insulting language on children. Authorities at all levels have shut their ears and eyes, probably not aware of the magnitude of the child's pain. Overall and in general the schools are not the temples of learning any more but readily hand over worst experiences to children at every grade; a few schools are changing due to the sensitivities prevailing at the leadership of the top management. The races of competition and commercial inclinations have ruined the fundamental values of education in schools. And what we achieved is that the children suffered mentally and physically, when the WHO emphasized mind-body relationship on World Mental Health Day, 2005 (Kalia, 2007).

Sample

The Sample of the study consisted of 966 students (600 male and 366 female) in the age range of 16-22 years. The students were selected on non-random basis from 14 educational institutions in different locations of Mumbai. The students reported the nature and extent of their traumatic events while in school.

Method

The Student Alienation and Trauma Survey (SATS) questionnaire developed by Hyman and Shook (2000) was used to collect data from school and college students of Mumbai and around. The scale has two parts with 58 items on worst experiences of children in schools and 105 items on how do they cope up. All the items were to be rated on 5 point scale.

RESULTS AND DISCUSSION

Some Worst experiences of Mumbai school children

Here are the narratives of some of the 'worst experiences happening to children in their school time' that were stated by the students themselves during this study.

1. I was hit with a ruler, paddle, or something else

A student said, "I was in standard 10th and my science journal was incomplete, so the Miss had put me and my friends out of the class. And at the same time our principal was on a round. He started inquiring about the matter and hit us". Another student said, "When in 6th standard I had taken new admission in school, and no one talked with me. One girl teased me and showed me her shoe and hit me with it and I cried but no one helped or talked to me. Later on my mom spoke to teacher and everything is fine now". Overall, the findings revealed that 34.1% of male students and 18% of female students expressed that they were hit with a ruler, paddle, or something else a few times. The percentage of male students reporting worst experience in school was much more than female.

2. I was not allowed to go to the bathroom

In the words of a student, "I wanted to go to the bathroom urgently but I was not allowed. I was upset as the teacher thought I was lying". In all there were about 11.3% of male students and 6.6% of female students were not allowed to go to the bathroom a few times.

3. I wished I were dead

The author wont be surprised if in the coming years, every school reports suicide cases as 9.7% of students (nearly one out of every 20) reported a few times that 'I wished I were dead' and its impact lasted for more than a month amongst 4% (nearly one out of every 25) students.

4. I was picked last

A student said, "During the inter-school contest I was picked as a substitute to other student despite my good show in the studies. And I thought myself as a scholar so it hurt me that I was picked up as a substitute. This was the worst experience of my school days". Another student said, "I felt very hurt when I was picked last because the person who ignored me was supposed to be one of the close friends. Now, it so happened that a teacher came to our classroom and asked each one individually about our papers because it was our exam that day. But she completely ignored me, I felt very hurt as well as depressed because at that time my friend was also not speaking to me. This happened many times to me that whosoever became my close friends, they started taking me for granted and when I protested they stopped talking to me but I always could cope up with it within a month. But this time it took me 1 year". About 9.7% of male students and 7.8% of female students expressed similar feelings that they were picked last a few times.

5. Someone talked about sex and I didn't like it

A student said, "the worst experience was the one, which related to a friend talking to me about sex. At that juncture, I was focused on my studies and during the spare time occupied in sports. The untimely conversation disturbed me greatly". In all about 17.0% students in school experienced one time that someone talked about sex and they didn't like it. However, the percent of those reporting such thing to have had occured more than once was a little less (10.40%)

6. Sexual comments were made about me

Five point two percent of the sampled students in school experienced that sexual comments were made about them a few times. A student said, "Someone wrote sexual comments to me on notes and I felt really embarrassed and did not tell anyone about it and forget the whole thing in few days".

7. I was touched sexually

A student said, "One of my uncle's friends who become my uncle, used to try to have a sexual touch with me". Another student said, "A senior student sexually touched me during the extra lecture time. I felt little bit upset and different at that time but I didn't react to it, as I did not know anything about sex. I did not come to know what he was doing and was it right or wrong. But later when I passed 12th standard and came in Degree College and heard about sex I remembered this incident and then felt guilty about it". Overall, 5.6% students reported sexual touch one time in the school. However about 3.4% students stated that they were touched sexually a few times.

8. I was forced to have sex

In all about 1.9% students were forced to have sex one time and 1.3% students reported it to have happended a few times. A student said, "My worst experience was that I was sexually harassed first when I was in Sr. KG. This occurred in the school. The person tried to catch my hand. Touched on the parts, forced me remove my clothes. The same incident also occurred when I was kept at baby sitter. It was her son who was a quiet boy above 20 yrs. He forced me remove my clothes and thus harassed me forcibly when there was no one at home.

9. I was locked in a closet or small room

One out of every twenty students were locked in school one time in a closet or small room. It was more in case of boys (6.9%) than the girls (4.7%).

10. I was given a punishment that was not fair

A student said, "The worst experience in school was when I was punished for no fault of mine. Other girls were shouting and misbehaving in the class and when teacher came, they gave my name and she shouted at me and wrote a note to my parents and teacher asked me a question to be answered as a punishment. After sometime they started to tease, and harass me in the class". Another student said, "In 10th standard I had an awful dictator as a principal who drove away very good and experienced teachers with whom we also had emotional attachment. We were given punishments that were not fair like our Perfect's day was about to be cancelled. Due to that principal I still have a slight bad patch in my memory about school life". About 28.0% of boys and 15.1% of girls experienced a few times that they were given a punishment that was not fair.

11. I was beaten up

A student said, "when I was in 10th standard my science teacher had beaten me a lot because I made a minor mistake in the answer paper and because of this, most of my marks were deducted, and I was afraid of my teacher. After beating, the teacher explained me how I wrote the paper. I felt that if she told me this before, I would have understood more". A total of 19.2% of male students and 13.1% of female students stated that they were beaten up a few times.

12. I was slapped

A student said, "one of my friend slapped me during the class and that two in front of everyone for no reason whatsoever. I got angry but I controlled my anger. But after few days things were back to normal". Another student said, "When I was in 9th standard I had also joined tuition class after the school. One day on my way to the class after the school, I took an apple and part of it stuck between my teeth as I was entering the class I was trying to remove that piece by my tongue and just at that time the teacher entered the class and she thought that I was making faces on her and she immediately slapped me. I could not understand what was my fault that she had to slap me hard and I will never forget her face for the rest of my life". Results revealed that the boys had experienced such incidents more often as the percent of boys reporting that they were slaped was 18.40 as compared to that of girls, i.e., 6.30.

13. Reflections and Interventions

Teachers victimize students in order to discipline their classroom, as they don't know better ways of managing the classroom. Teachers are not aware as to how they harm emotional health of children. Peers bully their friends as they seek fun and thrill, they are not aware as to how they are affecting their friends emotionally.

Largely in the Indian schools scenario, the children are not allowed to speak out or raise their voices. They don't speak out in the classroom, and teachers also don't let them speak out. In the Indian society where for the name sake democracy persists but in reality it is not practiced in schools. Children become the victim in such situations. The school principals are not aware of the magnitude of children being victimized in school premises and the effects of victimization on children.

Victimization of children is a crime; it needs to be curbed. Some teachers have continued punishing or harassing children over the years, even to an extent that a father said, "this teacher has not changed, she used to ask me to stand on the bench, and now she is asking my son to do the same, isn't it disgusting".

The major factor that triggers such misbehaviors of teachers was that they are not equipped or trained with knowledge or wisdom on how to manage the class without affecting an emotional health of children. Peer education has a critical role to play in order to stop teasing or harassment among students, which has mental health implications.

Ask any child or adult (regardless of their background), she/ he would tell us as to how she / he was victimized or bullied by their teachers or peers while in school. This indicates that victimization has been there for decades and it has gone unexamined and unquestioned. If we can check and stop it, we can certainly improve the mental health of our growing-up children in our society. Findings of the study clearly reveal how children have been exposed to maltreatment in school. The policy makers need to take note of this phenomenon and take necessary action.

Victimization in school is brewing unhealthy children and giving way to an ill society. We need to make teachers aware about the worst experiences of children in school, and ask them, what would they do or how would they intervene to correct this situation in school for creating an 'emotional health of children' a value and concern in educational institutions.

It is pertinent here to mention that the positive experience can be taken up and reiforced us to counter sands negative ones. Beside victimization, two students expressed positive notes as follows: "I was not giving due attention to the study, so during the month of November, teacher advised me to study hard not for you but also for your parents. I did try my best and passed with good marks and I felt proud of my teacher". Another student said, "There was a boy in my class, who lied that I've an affair with him. It made me little upset, but after talking to my class teacher, I felt relaxed". Only one student out of 966 students categorically wrote, "I have good experience in school and my school is very good".

Sometimes students may also victimize teachers; as one student said, "one of my favourite teacher was made to cry just because of some of the senior students were taunting her for the way she looks...And she literally cried for that". Hence there is need for 'total mental health programme in school system'. Teacher's mental health is equally important so that they can adequately take care of students.

The 'victimization' is in the attitudes and behaviors of teachers, peers and the school climate. This scenario and situation is not going to change until we take informed steps to correct these attitudes and behaviors. The schools need to invest on teachers to upgrade their mental software to deal effectively with the emotional health concerns of children. And it may take a few years to achieve a change in this direction for improved mental health of children. We definitely need healthy minds for better economies of our nations.

Though male students received victimization (such as slapped, pushed, shaken) significantly more than the girls, the girls seem to be more affected (such as getting angry, nervous) than the boys as a result of worst experience in school.

Democracy in Schools

It is felt that classroom is the most undemocratic place in the world. An Australian child was asked, how do you feel in a democratic school, he replied, "I am accepted here, I asked what do you mean, he added, my personality is accepted here in this school". Sharon, a democratic school teacher from South Africa was asked, what is the syllabus in your school, she answered, "each child is a syllabus". Sharon was again asked what you mean by democratic school, she narrated, "Once a teacher from France visited her school for two months, she asked Sharon, what I can teach to your students, Sharon being a democratic teacher said, you may ask students what they wish to learn from you. Teacher from France went to the classroom, introduced herself and asked the students, what they wish to learn from her, the students replied, since you are from France, we would love to learn French language from you. She taught French language to the students for two months. While going back, she went back to Sharon and asked, now since I am going back, how you would manage teaching French language, Sharon said; I would ask children, let them decide. Children said, it's enough of French language, now we would like to learn something else". In a democratic school, children are empowered with decision making on matters that matter to them (Kalia, 2007).

Democracy in schools means an experience of Love, Inspiration, Freedom, and Enjoyment (LIFE) by children, teachers, parents and everyone. Does school provide LIFE is a big question mark? While working with schools in India, what is being increasingly realized is that it is crucial to change 'teachers' view on children' through interactive discussion and dialogues as a measure to reform schooling to be experienced by children as promoting their natural potentials and creativity.

Indian schools are so much adult and authority driven, syllabus-pressurized and marks-oriented that they don't even see whether democracy in schools is what the children are wanting. The school teachers here are quite open to change. My most important observation is that teachers are also seeking democracy in schools but the school system is so deeply vicious and complex that they fall short to change it. Though teachers and children both are seeking democracy to exist in Indian schools, they aren't getting much opportunity to experience it.

What we are doing in this situation is 'attempting to change the teachers through re-training process whereby they are ready to introduce democracy in the classroom. Now here there is a difference when we say 'democracy in schools' and 'democracy in the classroom', the later is direct form of democracy to be implemented by teachers. Both teachers and students are seeking democracy but the school managements are in a real fix to change the school education scenario. According to Jerry Mintz, (Mintz, 2006) Director, Alternate Education Resource Organization, democracy in classrooms can work and be real. It doesn't matter much if the scope is limited. May be this is a better approach to the whole problem, later naturally extending it to the whole school.

On democratization process of schools, we need to relook at our methodologies which means that when the 'power / authority in school' is not distributed across all stake holders i.e. parents, teachers and students, (which is true of Indian schools), a new idea such as democracy in schooling process would be very hard, here the schools are Principal or director driven, but parents, students and teachers in these schools are open to trying new ideas in the way education is delivered to children in schools. I think this is the scenario in all the developing countries.

Asia

In the present context, we are attempting to sensitize schools, parents, children, teachers and the policy makers, but the democratization process at the Indian schools could not take off. What we can do now, we need to take progressive steps such as holding conferences regularly giving open invitation to all public and private schools, and spreading awareness through media, (media is quite child friendly here). It will help creating democratic culture in our schools. Now at least the schools here know that there is something called democratic schooling.

Democracy in school brings along a sense of responsibility among children which means self-discipline. Individual student can't go away with freedom, they have to take responsibility, and then only it would bring joy. Schools need to be democratized where children have the right to decide over matters that concern them in learning and education. The world needs democratic schools where children no longer suppress themselves but instead feel free to experience life the way they wish, and develop their natural potentials they are endowed with. Democratic schools offer a lot of opportunity for creativity and innovation in the school that the children enjoy. Schools and also families need to be democratized where the children have the rights to decide over matters that concern them in learning and education.

We need to look at the role of democratic schools in developing future societies. What competencies these schools shall be offering? What ideology shall they be developing? We also need to understand the schools broadly to deal with community issues and essentially play the role of a dynamic integrator of societies of the world. Democratic schools are an earnest effort towards democratizing communities and societies around us. Schools are essentially instrumental in building societies integrating cultural expectations.

Interventions in order to eradicate victimization of school children

It is also very necessary to understand as to why victimization in school children is not a concern of social policies of the State and Central Governments when such a large number of children (98% as revealed in qualitative analysis) are exposed to victimization of one or another kind in schools. Victimization of any kind of school children is a crime; it needs to be curbed by strict laws. The national and the state bodies of the human rights commission need to intervene.

Worst schools are those that abuse children and adolescents physically, mentally, emotionally, sexually and existentially. There are 58 worst things that happened to male and female children and adolescents in their school times. There are 105 mental health symptoms the students experienced as a result of worst experience in school. The worst experiences of children happen in the school context and environment, which needs an overhaul change. Our major intervention should be to increase awareness among teachers, principals and policy planners about the magnitude and effects of victimization on children in the school.

The teachers in schools disturbed and crushed the natural personality of the children so badly that the children lost their self-esteem and self-trust in school so much so that even they grew up, they could not face the real life situations in bold manner. The students got the education at the cost of losing their precious self (Kalia, 2003, 2006).

The schools are applying content-based, syllabus-pressurized approach in educating children; they have not given a choice to students to ask what they would like to learn. In the present structure of the schools; the children have no influence or say on matters what concern them.

Considering the complexity of above issues that impact school children, the following interventions have been suggested to the Government of Maharashtra (Kalia, 2002) in order to eradicate victimization of school children for ensuring their mental health:

- A school counselor, a special educator and a visiting psychiatrist to be appointed at every school;
- Child Rights Act should include 'victimization of children of any kind in school' as a cognizable crime;
- Civic authorities in each district must ensure and execute mental health programme in schools;
- Education inspectors in every State must conduct annual audit of mental, emotional and behavioral health of children in every school;
- Education inspectors in every State to be trained in mental, emotional and behavioral health of children;
- Mumbai Police Act should include 'victimization of children of any kind in school' as a reportable crime;
- Orientation to teachers on mental, emotional and behavioral health of children in every school;
- Peer to Peer counseling to be introduced in every school;
- Police stations in every State must investigate any such crime on victimization of children of any kind in school;

- Parent Teacher Association (PTA) members to be trained on mental, emotional and behavioral health of children in every school;
- Refresher courses to be introduced to update school counselors from time to time; and
- School mental health programme to be integrated in every school to ensure mental health of children, teachers, parents and others.

All these above programmes must aim at ensuring creating positive societies through building positive schools by interventions together with universities, media, school, civic, and state authorities. The school education department of every State must take lead in the school reform programmes.

SOME CRUCIAL QUESTIONS ON "*VICTIMIZATION OF SCHOOL CHILDREN*"

1. Why "victimization of children is prevalent particularly in schools and it has remained unquestioned, since 15 years?

Authorities at all levels have shut their ears and eyes, probably not aware of the magnitude of the child's pain. The Principals are not aware of the *victimization of children by the teachers going on in the classroom. The teachers are not aware of the mental health implications of maltreatment of children. Teachers don't know how to treat children with different levels of emotional, learning and behavioural difficulties. Teachers need educational updates.*

2. What can be done when a student becomes a victim to maltreatment in schools?

When a student becomes a victim to maltreatment in schools:

- He / she can go to a school counselor,
- Child abuse of any kind in school is a cognizable crime; it can be reported to police;
- Education inspectors must contacted;
- Orientation to teachers on mental, emotional and behavioral health of children in every school can help;

- Peer to Peer counseling to be introduced in every school;
- Police stations can investigate any such crime on victimization of children of any kind in school;
- Refresher courses to be introduced to update school counselors from time to time; and
- School mental health programme to be integrated in every school to ensure mental health of children, teachers, parents and others.

3. What kind of opportunities, should be provided to students in order to improve their creativity in schools as most of the schools try to kill the creativity in them?

Children are searching for a baseline meaning for their life. They need an open environment in which they can express and experiment with their original and novel ideas. At present most schools and teachers are unable to tap and develop the creativity in children, which is in abundance in them. Informal and formal structures of the school do impact on the child's learning, creativity and the way they absorb values, which they will unconsciously use when they grow into adults.

Schools need to be democratized where children have the right to decide over matters that concern them in learning and education. The world needs democratic schools where children no longer suppress themselves but instead feel free to experience life the way they wish, and develop their natural potentials they are endowed with. Democratic schools offer a lot of opportunity for creativity and innovation in the school that the children enjoy. Schools and also families need to be democratized where the children have the rights to decide over matters that concern them in learning and education.

4. What could victimized students do to overcome such experience?

When a child experiences the following in school: Problem	He/she may use following Psychosocial strategies to help him/her self/Intervention

• **Embarrassed**	• Talk to someone about it and explore the validity of the cause of embarrassment. Not let it grow further as it can result in avoidance behaviour. • Do not underestimate your distress. • May sometimes choose to avoid people who embarrass. • May prefer to keep quite and not speak again depending upon your situation. • Keep quiet for sometime and reflect upon the situation. • Don't pay much attention if it's just without any reason. • Sometimes just laugh it away.
• **Slapped and Pinched**	• Ideally, a non-violent approach handled at the child's level is more advisable. If it is a constant feature, it should be reported to the authorities. Once in a while, it is ok to give it back to the perpetrator, provided it does not become a habit. • He/she should report to the class teacher or any other teacher. • Ignore such people. • May slap and pinch back if friends do it regularly. • Make a complaint to higher authorities in school.
• **Beaten**	• The child needs to keep it very clearly in his head that he does not need to take this from anyone, teacher or a senior. Report to authorities immediately. • He/she should report to the class teacher or any other teacher. • May beat him back if regularly done by friends.

• **Sexual experience**	• If it is a voluntary one, the child just needs to be careful about the precautions. If involuntary, the child must talk to a teacher / councelor / parent about it as this has to be dealt with sensitively and the trauma removed from the system. A counselor's help may be useful here. • He/she reports the incident to his/ her parents and/or teachers. • Get help immediately from a trusted parent - you cannot handle it alone. • May slap if irritating in front of others. • Tell to your closest friend.
• **Pulled my hair or ear**	• If a classmate is doing this, the child just needs to convey that he cannot be taken for granted or bullied. For this, an occasional display of power may be useful. • Should deal with the situation himself/herself. • May choose to scream back.
• **Yelled at**	• If done by a teacher, the child needs to keep it in his mind very clearly that the teacher has no business doing that. However, the child needs to remember his limits at the same time and not lose respect for the teacher. If done by a peer, just turn a deaf ear. • Should deal with the situation himself/herself. • Leave the place. • One may choose to yell back.

• **Fight with peers**	• This is a part of the growth experience and makes children sturdier. However, the child either needs to fight back (if it is not a regular feature) or protect himself from it by taking someone's help i.e. teacher. • He/she should resist from fight and instead report to teachers. • One may choose not talking to them. • Find out reasons of the fight.

5. Should the parents and teachers come together in this matter? If so, then how should the parents involve themselves to sort out the issue?

Parent Teacher Association (PTA) members need to be trained on mental, emotional and behavioral health of children in every school. At the Dept. of Psychology, S.N.D.T. Women's University, we have conducted courses to train PTA members to ensure and create awareness on mental, emotional and behavioral health of children in schools. There are also parent-directed schools in the world. Parents and teachers coming together is a wonderful democratic way to improve schools.

What are the repercussions of such maltreatment on students?

Kalia (2007 in his recently released book, "Victimization of School Children" reported that there are 58 worst things that happened to male and female children and adolescents in their school times. There are 105 mental health symptoms the students experienced as a result of worst experience in school.

The following are a few of the reaction of the victimized children. When asked,

"How do the children feel after such maltreatment or one worst school experience?

* I got bad grades in school......
* I got very angry for no reason......
* I got very nervous about things......
* I hated going to school......
* I lost my appetite......
* I stopped eating......

* I thought I was not as good a kid as I used to be......
* I was more tired than I used to be ......
* I was not as happy as I used to be ......
* It was harder to make myself do things ......

Sex Education

In this research, it is found that a significant portion of the students experienced one time some one talked about sex, they did not like it. Is it due to lack of impart of "sex education in schools", what is present debate about the imparting of sex education in schools and colleges?"

Sex education in schools is an essential programme to be integrated. The another I feel that it will be a long time before this issue of *sex education* becomes comfortable for school authorities, particularly the teachers and principals. We have to break the attitude and sensitize the principals and managements to the issue of sex education in schools. Since it is a taboo in India a vast majority of the schools are not open to it. Maybe if we called it gender education and sensitization, it will have more acceptability. Schools are extremely reluctant to any new change or educational initiatives. Our major intervention should be to increase awareness among teachers, principals and policy planners about the effects of gender / sex / child abuse in the school.

Impact on Economy of the Country

Do these things have an impact on the growth on economy, if so, then how would it have a negative impact?

We need to look at the role of schools in developing future societies. What competencies these schools shall be offering? What ideology shall they be developing? We also need to understand the schools broadly to deal with community issues and essentially play the role of a dynamic integrator of societies of the world. Schools are an earnest effort towards democratizing communities and societies around us. Schools are essentially instrumental in building societies integrating cultural expectations. At present, largely, the schools are painting dark future of India by victimizing children and killing creativity in them. We can promote bright economy of India, if we promote creativity in children. Ninety eight percent of children in Indian (Mumbai) schools feel victimized by one way or another. We must stop it at the earliest, and allow children to raise their voice by democratizing schools.

Is mental health of children a State responsibility?

The idea of celebrating world mental health day on 10th October is to create 'mental health care as a value' in our schools. The mental health component in our society has not been woven. Whose responsibility is it? The NGO's, the educational and health institutions and the State must come together. But looking at the voluminous magnitude of the learning, emotional, behavioural and other mental health problems of the children in the country, the major share of the responsibility has to be managed by the State. In this regard, the States has the following tasks to perform:

(a) To allocate the mental health budget separately;

(b) To make appointment of counsellor compulsory in all the schools of the state;

(c) To organize refresher courses for the mental health professionals in order to update them on newer advances in the mental health field;

(d) To orient the school principals over mental health issues of the children as majority of the schools have no counselor on their roll;

(e) The State education officers are not aware of the mental health significance of the children; they need to be sensitized through orientation courses;

(f) To organize annual meet on the world mental health day for the mental health community; and

(g) As we seriously lack indigenous research data on the learning, emotional, behavioral and other mental health problems of the children, there is a need for a mental health institution at the State level that will exclusively address the research, education and advocacy aspects of the mental health of our children.

(h) The National and the State Human Rights Commissions need to take up these tasks with the State authorities towards better mental health of the children in the country.

What are the other ways that children are prone to "Victimization", other than in schools?

Other than in schools, children are prone to "Victimization", in families by parents and relatives, neighborhoods, during travel etc. Physical punishment in families is very much there. Child abuse is rampant in our societies, and mostly it happens by the people around us.

CONCLUSION

Indian schools have a long way to go as far as bringing about a radical change as needed by all those stake holders of school education. The child in school is to be heard for his / her choices and concerns, some schools are trying their best efforts as the globalizing and competitive society is impelling them to constantly change their curriculum and the methodology they adopt for its delivery to the students and also listening and responding to the concerns of parents. The teachers' sensitivity towards children remains an area of concern for which school teachers need regular cognitive and behavioural re-training towards holistic well-being of children.

REFERENCES

Hyman, I. and Shook, P. (2000) *Student Alienation Syndome: theory assessment and application.* Paper presented at the 108 National Convention of the American Psychological Association, August 6, 2000, Washington, D.C.

Kaila H.L. (2002). School Mental Health in Mumbai City: Review and Alternatives, *New Quest*, 149, 38-43.

Kalia, H.L. (2003). School Mental Health in Mumbai City: Review and Alternatives, *Journal of Psychological Researches,* Vol. 37, 31-35.

Kaila, H.L. (2006). *Counselling in Schools.* New Delhi : Icon Publications Pvt. Ltd.

Kaila, H.L. (2007). *Victimization of School Children*: New Delhi: Icon Publications.

Mintz, J. (2006) A Peronal Communication with Founder of AERO, USA.

Note: this paper is a part of a larger research study conducted at the S.N.D.T. Women's University, Churchgate, Mumbai - 400020, India.

8

Developmental Dyslexia: Current Scenario

—Azizuddin Khan

It is considered that the emergence of speech marks the greatest intellectual advancement of human beings. Reading and learning are two basic skills that determine success and development of children's career in school and in the outside world. Reading is a complex skill that majority of us have learnt quite easily. It involves decoding and comprehension. However, nearly 20% children face severe difficulties to learn written language. But not all reading problems are termed as dyslexia. According to Rayner and Pollatsek (1989) children with reading difficulties may be classified in three groups: Poor readers (PR): Score between 1 and 2 years below their expected reading level and have normal IQ; Dyslexic readers (DR): Score 2 or more years below their expected reading level with normal IQ; Backward readers (BR): Score 3 or more years below their expected reading level and have IQ equal to 80 or less. However, Vernon (1962) suggested three types of backward readers. The first type of backward readers is as a result of environmental factors such as lack of opportunity to read at home, inefficient teaching, lack of opportunity to read in general. The second type of backward readers are those who are not able to master reading and writing skill due to emotional maladjustment, and finally third type of backward readers are due to some organic or constitutional factor.

The word dyslexia refers to difficulty with words. The term dyslexia comes from the Greek words 'dys' meaning 'impaired', and 'lexis' meaning 'word' and is used to describe disorders of language concerning reading and spelling. Initially, researchers termed it as "word and letter blindness". However, the word dyslexia was used for the first time by a German ophthalmologist R. Berlin in 1896 to describe reading difficulties caused by cerebral disease or injury. The origin of dyslexia in the scientific literature came as language problem due to acquired aphasia. However, credit goes to Morgan (1896) for describing developmental dyslexia in medical literature. These patients were suffering from reading disability as well. Dyslexia is not a qualitative disease rather it is considered as a syndrome. Some researchers do not consider dyslexia as a defect but as a style of thinking which hampers development of skill with words specially printed one. Probably that is the reason, most of the dyslexic children show few or all the ability mentioned below. They are able to have good command over certain kind of cognitive abilities such as holistic thinking, clear visualization, intelligence which does not involve words, and linear thinking.

Types of Dyslexia

Researchers have categorized dyslexia as ***acquired*** and ***developmental dyslexia***. **Acquired dyslexia** is defined as reading disability as a result of injury or disease. There are basically three types of acquired dyslexia: "Surface dyslexia, "Phonological dyslexia, and "Deep dyslexia". Surface dyslexia is characterized by a specific disability in which individual can read known word but they have problem with reading irregular words (such as mouse/mice).Irregular words are those in which one or more letters do not represent their most common sounds. It is believed that surface dyslexics are not able to employ the lexical procedure for reading. Phonological dyslexic can read and write regular as well as irregular words. However, they have problems with nonword (such as \l "bous" bous, bzitz etc.) and translating grapheme–phoneme correspondence. Phonological dyslexia is consequence of a deficit in the conversion between sounds (phonemes) and letters (graphemes). Dyslexic children would be impaired in their abilities to segment and discriminate the sequence of sounds in a spoken language, that is, in their "phonological awareness" (Wise et al, 1999). Finally, Surface dyslexia is a type of acquired dyslexia in which a normal healthy adult develops reading disability as a result of head injury, stroke, disease, or operation in the left hemisphere.

Developmental dyslexia is a language pathology that hinders reading and writing acquisition of around 6-10 % of the children all over the world. Developmental dyslexia is not the result of any injury or disease. Dyslexia is a deficit in learning and developing automatized skills for conversion between letters (graphemes) and sounds (phonemes) (Bradley and Bryant, 1983; Brady and Shankweiler, 1991; Ramus 2003). It is a difficulty in learning to read fluently and causes severe handicap in many children affecting their school achievement, social adjustment and future career choices. Reading is based on a complex set of skills and cognitive processes, some of which have been identified, such as phonological processing, but the underlying reasons for these deficits are not yet well understood.

Symptoms of Developmental Dyslexia

The following symptoms have been identified.

- Dyslexic children often show lack of ability to notice sounds in words, sound order, rhymes, or syllable sequences, which is a primary skill that one needs to master reading and writing.
- Word reversal
  - Children with this kind of problem confuses 'b' with 'd', "won" for "now"
- Difficulty in Spelling
  - Right as 'rite'
- Difficulty with number and letter sequences, either read or written
- Children with developmental dyslexia have poor comprehension and consequently they have problems in retaining in their memory whatever they read
- Delayed Speech
- They have a hard time in completing their sentences. They generally stop in between the sentence.
- Children have difficulty in expressing their thought in words.

- Difficulty with directions (right and left, up and down, early and late, yesterday and tomorrow, months and days)
- They also show inability to distinguish between right and left direction.
- Difficulty with handwriting
- Difficulty in mathematics-sequencing of numbers and directional steps, or the language of math
- Difficulty staying organized

Theories of Developmental Dyslexia

Though a lot of work has been done to understand the causes of dyslexia for the last hundred years, there is still controversy regarding the exact precursor of the disorder? Some are more popular than others. However, currently, the scene of developmental dyslexia is dominated by at least four theories of dyslexia. Other theories also have been propounded by researchers. However, they are either in infancy or outdated in the light of current research findings.

Phonological Processing Deficit

The most widely accepted theory suggests that dyslexics have a phonological processing deficit causing them to have problems in learning to read and write (Vellutino et al. 2004). Phonological processing refers to "the use of phonological information in processing oral and written language (Wagner and Torgesen, 1987). Dyslexics have impairment in the representation, storage, and retrieval of speech sounds. Learning to read alphabetic system requires learning the grapheme- phoneme correspondence. Therefore, phonological theory of dyslexia assumes that there is a direct relationship between cognitive deficit and behavioral problems. However, it is also being observed that the origin of the disorder is a congenital dysfunction of the left-hemisphere peri-sylvian brain areas which is responsible for the representation, storage, and retrieval of speech sounds. Recent studies have shown that dyslexic population performs below average level on tasks requiring phonological awareness. It has also been observed that dyslexics show poor verbal short term memory and slow automatic naming. Phonological processing consists of phonological awareness, phonological recoding in lexical access, and phonetic recoding in working memory (Wagner and Torgesen, 1987).

Phonological awareness can be defined as "conscious access to the phonemic levels of the speech stream and some ability to cognitively manipulate representation at this level" (Stanovich, 1986). Phonemes are smallest units of speech (Liberman et al, 1985). Skill reading is contingent upon conscious awareness of the sound structure of an alphabetic system of language. It involves alliteration, counting, deleting, and substituting phonemes within words or syllables. Researchers have clearly established that dyslexic children show poor awareness of syllable-rhyme and alliteration. Similarly dyslexic children have hard time in deciding whether two words rhyme or identifying the non-rhyming words of short item sequence (Wimmer, 1993).

Phonological recording in lexical access refers to "recording written symbols into some kind of sound based representation, and finally using this sound based representation to access the lexicon (Wagner and Torgesen, 1985). To estimate phonological recording, tests of rapid naming, naming pictures of familiar objects or deciding whether a letter string is part of real or pseudoword. It is considered as one of the most important tool for early stages of reading acquisition.

Phonetic recording in working memory refers to "recoding written symbols into a sound based representational system that enables them to be maintained efficiently in working memory during ongoing processing (Wagner and Torgesen, 1985). It is assumed that efficient phonetic recording is prerequisite for learning to read alphabet. Researchers propounded that child starts learning to read by using cognitive resources for the blending of phonemes to generate words. Alan Baddeley (2003) propounded the idea that working memory is instrumental in blending phonemes. Working memory refers to the storage and manipulation structures involved. It has two components, phonological input store and rehearsal processes. Poor readers and dyslexic showed poor performance involving material that can be coded with verbal form, but there was no group difference when nonverbal material was used (Liberman, Mann, Shankweiler, and Werfelman, 1982;). Since verbal material can give rise to the activation of phonological codes, it is possible that verbal memory difficulty may emnates from inefficient use of phonological codes. Poor readers show phonological deficit (Liberman, and Shankweiler, 1985; Moddy, Studdert-Kennedy, and Brady, 1997). Phonological loop evolved to facilitate the acquisition of language (Baddeley, Gathercole, and Papagno; 1998). The segmentation of text into grapheme is considered one of the indicators of acquisition of reading ability. Grapheme is smallest part of the speech language and involves phonemes. It's capacity is a good predictor and indicator of the ability of children and adults to learn new language (Baddeley, 2003). Dyslexics have problem in extracting phonemes from the text.

The acquisition of the phonological system of one's native language proceeds via consolidation of short term acoustic and ensuing phonological representations into the long term memory codes (Näätänen and Winkler 1999). Sensory memory can be understood to consist of three phases (Näätänen, 1990). The incoming information from the environment is first encoded into a neuro-physiological mechanism of short term memory for very short period of time that last about 200 – 300 ms. If the information is attended it goes to second phase of sensory memory and last about 10 to 20s. Information at this phase is available for the conscious perception and for selective attention. It processes information in top-down fashion. It also provides basis for sound perception as an auditory event. Lastly, the long term sensory memory resides in the brain for longer period and some time whole life. Consequently, auditory sensory memory becomes crucial in the development of working memory for speech, which is involved in language learning.

Auditory Temporal Processing Deficit

The rapid auditory processing theory of dyslexia propounds that phonological deficit is secondary to more basic auditory processing deficit. Dyslexic children fail to perceive short and rapidly varying sounds (Tallal, 1980). Thus, the auditory deficit is considered as the primary cause of difficulty in learning to read. Temporal processing refers to the rate of information processing for encoding brief and rapidly changing or rapidly occurring successive events (Tallal, 1980). Researchers have shown that dyslexic children show poor performance on tone discrimination, temporal order judgment, backward masking etc. They have problem in distinguishing /ba/ versus /da/. Adlard and Hazan, (1998) reported that dyslexic children also show poor categorical perception of certain contrast. Hence, according to the auditory processing deficit, auditory deficit impairs phonological deficit, consequently children fail to learn language. Recently, few researchers opined that temporal processing deficit is not limited to the auditory system. However, deficit is also observed in visual and tactile modality.

Magnocellular Theory

The visual theory is one of the oldest theories of dyslexia. Basically first observation of dyslexic individual was made by ophthalmologists and physicians. Initially, they used the term world blindness to describe dyslexic symptoms. For them, dyslexia was a visual perception deficit. According to this, visual impairment is the cause of difficulties in the processing of letters and words on a page of text. It is observed that dyslexic population have abnormal magnocellular layers of the lateral geniculate nucleus (Linvingstone et al., 1991). In the visual system, there are two pathways: magnocellular and parvocellular. This theory postulated that there is a disruption in magnocellular pathway and consequently dyslexics fail to process information efficiently. It has been found that dyslexic population show, longer visible persistence at low frequencies and less sensitivity to gratings, at low spatial frequencies, low contrast, low luminances and high temporal frequencies. There are two channels in the visual system, transient and sustain system. The transient system is sensitive to low spatial and high frequencies, low contrast, and low luminances, while sustained channel is less active to medium and high spatial frequencies, low tempral frequencies, edium and high contrast. Large magnocells are responsible for transient visual processing that consist of magnocellular between retina and cortex. As far as sustained processing is concerned, it is contingent upon the sensitivity of the smaller parvocells of the retino-cortical parvocellular pathways (Merigan and Maunsell, 1993). Therefore, Lovegrove suggested that visual deficit in developmental dyslexia is the result of failure of the transient system on sustained inhibition. This theory was widely accepted until 1960s after that it fall from favor. Recently, researchers started looking ways at unifying the above mentioned theories into one grand theory. For this, they propounded that magnocellular dysfunction is not restricted to visual pathways, but that plays its role in all modalities such as auditory, tactile, visual, and motor.

Motor Control/Cerebral Theory

Cerebral theory postulates that there is mild impairment in the dyslexics' cerebellum. In human, it is a very densely packed and folded subcortical structure at the back of the brain. It is also called 'hind brain'. It account about 10-15% of brain weight and 40% of brain surface area. Impairment in different parts of the cerebellum may lead to different motor disturbances such as posture and balance, limb rigidity and decomposition of movement. It plays a crucial role in motor control and automisation of over- learned tasks, consequently in speech articulation. Dysfunction in articulation leads to deficient phonological representation. Evidence for cerebellum deficit in dyslexic population comes from poor performance in motor balance, time estimation, and non-motor cerebellar task. Recently, researchers have shown that damage to cerebellum can also result into attention and working memory impairment. However, researchers also raised question about the validity of the theory. For them, if there are problems in the cerebellum, why it is reflected in only reading domain?

Genetic Theory

Reading disability may occur due to social, educational or other causes. However, it has been observed that dyslexia runs in families. It shows that reading disability is not purely due to environmental factors. It is also found that the incidence of dyslexia is morefrequent in males than females. Therefore, researchers began to see the role of genetic makeup in dyslexic. Gayan et al., 1995 showed that there was association between chromosome 6 and reading disabilities. Another study (Schulte-Korne et al., 1998) confirmed the role of the chromosome 15 region in spelling ability. Behavioural genetic studies have shown that 50% reading ability is heritable other 50% is attributed to environmental factors and interaction of heredity and environment. Though researchers have started investigating the role of genes in dyslexia, it is still too early to conclude on the basis of a few studies.

Other Theories

Intersensory deficit theory propounded that dyslexics have difficulty in integrating the information of two or more sensory systems. However, this theory was criticized for lack of evidence. Some researchers are of the opinion that dyslexic population show erratic eye movement while reading. This situation results into reading disability. According to Stein and Fowler dyslexics have problem in eye convergence and binocular control. These above mentioned causation of dyslexia are no more tenable in the light of more recent theories.

Neurobiological Hypothesis of Dyslexia

Magnetic Resonance Imaging studies have shown that dyslexics' population have reverse asymmetry of tempo-parietal language region than normal population (Robichon et al., 2000). There was an atypical asymmetry of the planum temprale. MRI studies have also show altered plannar asymmetry in dyslexia. The planum temprale is situated on the supratemporal surfacejust behind the first Heschl's gyrus. The left planum is part of Wernicke's speech comprehension area. Some studies also show anomalies in the size of corpus callosum in dyslexic brain. The function of corpus callosum is to communicate and integrate information between left and right hemisphere. Galaburda propounded the idea that commissural connections between the hemispheres are inversely related to cerebral asymmetries. Hence, symmetric brains generally have stronger interhemisphereic connection which is refelected in larer size of the corpus callosum. However, no consistent structural correlates have been established with developmental dyslexia.

Recently, there is heightened interest in functional measures of cerebral blood flow and metabolism such as Positron

Emmission Tomography (PET) and functional Magentic Resonance Imaging (fMRI) in studying dyslexic population. Dyslexics have shown reduced blood flow in the left temporal-parietal regions. This indicate that dyslexics children have a left temporo-parietal dysfunction and it is associated with phonological demands of the rhyming task.

Event Related Potential Studies

Event related potential (ERP) is a non invasive technique which provides index of neural activity in response to some endogenous and /or endogenous stimulus. Recently, there is a surge of studies dealing with auditory ERPs.

P1, a positive going component of the ERP that is maximal over the occipital lobe and peaks between 100 and 150ms after stimulus onset. Specifically, the P1 is the result of neural activity in the extrastriate area of the visual cortex. As more attention is allocated to visual stimulus, more extrastriate neuron are recruited to process the stimulus and P1 amplitude increases, thereby giving a direct measure of attention allocation.

Mismatch negativity is a component of event related potential elicited by infrequent stimulus in a series of homogenous stimuli (Näätänen, 1992). It is considered to be a change detection response. The MMN occurs at about 100 – 300 ms post stimulus onset. It is not the infrequent stimuli per se which elicit MMN but the identification of change produces MMN. The MMN can be elicited by any change in a series of homogenous stimuli such as, frequency, intensity, duration and amplitude. It is attention independent mechanism (Alho, Woods, Algazi, and Näätänen, , 1992) The MMN phenomena indicate the existence of echoic memory in auditory cortex. Thus, whenever, deviant stimulus occurs in a series of standard stimulus, brain mechanism tries to match the current template with the coming information. Since deviant stimuli do match with existing one, it produces different wave form. The MMN shows polarity reversal below sylvian fissure. MMN component elicited by passive speech perception is attenuated in dyslexic children (speech condition but not with tone stimuli).It means dyslexics have speech deficit at sensory level. Impaired ability to discriminate speech in children with developmental language related disorder and learning problem (Korpilathi and Lang., 1994) and impaired tone frequency discrimination in dyslexic adults (Baldeweg et al. 1999) was associated with diminish magnitude of MMN.

LDN is negative going component that appears at around 400-500 ms after the stimulus onset which has been termed 'late discriminative negativity' (Cheor et al., 2001). This negativity was first reported in children by Korpilathi et al. (1994). The functional role of LDN is yet to be established. However, it is elicited under the same condition as the MMN. Therefore, it is believed that it reflects certain aspects of auditory change processing (Ceponiene et. al., 1998).

N250 is elicited by frequent repetitive stimuli (Näätänen and Picton, 1986) and was reported mostly in children (Ceponiene et al, 1998) shown in adults also. Karhu et. al, 1997) but with smaller amplitude (Ponton et al, 2000) and longer latency (Ponton et al, 2000). N250 changes as a function of stimulus content. In language impaired children, N2 is smaller and longer in latency than healthy children.

Conclusion

There are various competing theories of developmental dyslexia. But, the phonological processing theory is a strong contender. Almost all the theories accept that phonological impairment is the primary candidate in the disability of learning to read and write. Dyslexia is lifelong disability. However, its impact can be minimized through intervention. Intensive training in phonological awareness and the awareness of speech sounds is one of the tools which minimizes the intensity and severity of dyslexic symptoms. I would like to end the article with a positive note. Recent studies show that brain plasticity is active even at adulthood. Therefore, it is possible to change the way the brain works making a brain area more active through remedial training. Thus, one can strengthen connections in parts of the brain that enhance their ability to read.

REFERENCES

Adlard, A., and Hazan, V. (1998). Speech perception in children with specific reading difficulties (dyslexia). *Quarterly Journal of Experimental Psychology*, 51, 153-177.

Alho, K., Woods, D. L., Algazi, A., Knight, R. T., and Naatanen, R. (1994). Lesion of frontal cortex diminish the auditory mismatch negativity. *Electroencepholography and Clinical Neurophysiology*, 91, 353-362.

Baddeley, A.D., Gathercole, S., and Papagno, C. (1998). The phonological loop as a language learning device. *Psychological Review*, 105, 158-173.

Baddeley, A.D. (2003) Working memory and language: An overview. *Journal of Communication Disorders*, 36, 189-208.

Baldeweg, T., Richardson, A., Watkins, S., Foale, C., Gruzelier, J. (1999). Impaired auditory frequency discrimination in dyslexia detected with mismatch evoked potential. *Annals of Neurology*, 45, 495-503.

Brady, S. A., and Shankweiler, D. (1991). *Phonological processes in literacy*. Hillsdale, N J: Lawrence Erlbaum.

Bradley, L., and Bryant, P.E. (1983). Categorization sounds and learning to read-a causal connection. *Nature*, 301 (5899), 419-421.

Ceponiene R, Cheour M, Näätänen R. (1998). Interstimulus interval and auditory event related potentials in children: Evidence for multiple generators. *Electroencephalography and Clinical Neurophysiolcgy: Evoked Potentials*. 108:345-354.

Ceponiene R, Cheour M, Näätänen R. (1998). Interstimulus interval and auditory event-related potentials in children: Evidence for multiple generators. *Electroencephalography and Clinical Neurophysiology: Evoked Potentials*. 108:345–354.

Cheour, M., Korpilathi, P., Martyona, O., and Lang, A. H. (2001). Mismatch negativity and late discriminative negativity in investigating speech perception and learning in children and infants. *Audiology and Neurology*, 6, 2-11.

Gayan, J., Olson, R.K., Cardon, L.R., Smith, S.D., Fulker, D.W., Kimberling, W.J., Pennington, B.F., DeFries, J.C. (1995). Quantative traits locus for different measures of reading disability. *Behavior Genetics*, 25, 266.

Karhu J, Herrgård E, Pääkkönen A, Luoma L, Airaksinen E, Partanen J.(1997). Dual cerebral processing of elementary auditory input in children. *Neuroreport*. 8:1327–1330.

Korpilathi, P., and Lang, H. A. (1994). Auditory ERP components and mismatch negativity in dysphasic children. *Electroencephalography and Clinical Neurophysiology*, 91, 256-264.

Liberman, I.Y., Mann, V.A., Shankweiler, D., and Werfelman, M. (1982). Children's memory for recurring linguistic and nonlinguistic material in relation to reading ability. *Cortex, 18*, 367-75.

Lieberman, I. Y., and Shankweiler, D. (1985). Phonology and problems of learning to read the write. *Remedial and Special Education*, 6, 8-17.

Livingstone, M.S., Rosen, G.D., Drislane, F.W., and Galaburda, A.M.(1991). Physiological and anatomical evidence for a magnocelluar defect in developmental dyslexia. *Processding of the National Academy of Science,* USA, 88, 7943-7947.

Merigan, W.H., and Maunsell, J.H.R.(1993). How parallel are the primate visual pathways? *Annual Review of Neurosciene*, 16, 369-402.

Mody, M., Studdert-Kennedy , M., and Brady, S. (1997). Speech perception deficits in poor readers: Auditory processing or phonological coding? *Journal of Experimental Child Psychology, 64,* 199-231.

Morgan, W.P. (1896). A case of congenital word-blindness, *British Medical Journal,* 7 November, p.1378.

Naatanen, R., and Picton , T.W. (1986). N2 and automatic vs. controlled processes. In: McCallum, WC, Zappoli, R., Den-oth, F. (Eds.), *Cerebral Psychophysiology: Studies in Event-Related Potentials* (EEG Suppl 38). Elsevier Science Publishers, Amsterdam.

Naatanen, R., (1990). The role of attention in auditory information processing as revealed by event-related potentials and other brain measures of cognitive function. *Behavioral Brain Sciences* 13, 201–288.

Nataanen, R. (1992). *Attention and brain function*. Hillsdale, NJ: Erlbaum.

Näätänen R, Winkler I. (1999). The concept of auditory stimulus representation in cognitive neuroscience. *Psychological Bulletin*. 125:826–859, 1999.

Ponton, C. W., Don, M., Eggermont, J. J., Kwong, B., and Waring, M. D. (2000). Maturation of human central auditory system activity: evidence from multi-channel evoked potentials. *Clinical Neurophysiology*, 111:220–36.

Ramus, F. (2003). Developmental dyslexia; specific phonological deficit or general sensorimotor dysfunction? *Current Opinion in Neurobiology*, 13, 212-218.

Rayner, K., and Pollatsek, A. (1989). The psychology of reading. Englewood Cliffs, NJ: Prentice Hall.

Robichon, F., Levrier. O., Farnarier, P., and Habib, M. (2000). Developmental Dyslexia: Atypical cortical asymmetries and functional significance. *European Journal of Psychology,* 7, 35-46.

Schulte-Korne, G., Grimm, T., Nothen, M.M., Muller-Myhsok, B., Cichon, S., Vogt, I.R., Propping, P., and Remschmidt, H. (1998). Evidence for linkages of spelling disability to chromosome 15. *American Journal of Human Genetics*, 63, 279-282.

Stanovich, K. E. (1986). The right and wrong places to look for the cognitive locus of reading disability. *Annals of Dyslexia*. 38, 154-177.

Tallal, P. (1980). Auditory temporal perception, phonics, and reading disabilities in children. *Brain and Language*, 9. 182-198.

Vellutino, F. R., Fletcher, J. M., Snowling, M. J., and Scanlon, D. M. (2004). Specific reading disability (dyslexia): What have we learned in the past four decades? *Journal of Child Psychology and Psychiatry, 45,* 2-40.

Wagner, R. K. and Torgesen, J. K. (1987). The nature of phonological processing and its causal role in the acquisition of reading skills. *Psychological Bulletin*, 101, 192-212.

Wimmer, H. (1993). Characteristics of developmental dyslexia in regular writing system. *Applied Psycholinguistics*, 14, 1-33.

Wise, B., Ring, J., and Olson, R. (1999). Training phonological awareness with and without explicit attention to articulation. *Journal of Experimental Child Psychology, 72*, 271-304.

9

Psychosocial Trauma in Disasters: Child Development and Clinical Implications

—Sujata Satapathy

The International Federation of the Red Cross and Red Crescent Societies in the World Disaster Report, 2001 states that, on average, 242 million people were affected by natural disasters or armed conflict, each year, between 1991 to 2000. Of this number, at least 76.5 million were children under the age of 15 and the vast majority i.e. 75 million lived in developing countries. The data of human and economic loss due to disasters in this current decade is much more alarming than this particularly in Asian region.

Children differ from adults in physical, emotional and cognitive capacities, physiologic status, disease susceptibility and disease expression, and the types of supplies and equipment required to care for them. Therefore, their vulnerability and diverse needs in a disaster situation require knowledge of child health and child development as well as an understanding that the child exists in the context of the family. Disasters disrupt the sense of well-being by destroying normal predictable and consistent life routines of children thus, deeply hamper the process of healthy psychological and personality development. Since damage at this stage often cannot be overcome later and children constitute one of the largest segments of the vulnerable populations their vulnerability needs to be addressed adequately and appropriately.

EFFECTS OF DISASTERS ON CHILDREN

Children are affected by any disaster just the way adult are, although their reactions might differ from those of the adults.

The impact of any type of disaster on children depends largely on their developmental age, the nature of loss they experienced, the amount of exposure to trauma, sufferings/devastation they witnessed, social support dynamics prevail during that phase of disaster, and the nature of post-disaster care specially designed to meet their multifarious needs. Let us look at specific effects of disasters on children in terms of physical, psychological, social and educational repercussions.

Physical Effects Include

- Deaths of near and dear ones and witnessing a large number of deaths of known/unknown persons could be extremely traumatic
- Injury and physical disability, physical illness: infections, dehydration, etc. (Children differ from adults in physical, emotional and cognitive capacities, physiologic status, disease susceptibility and disease expression, and the types of supplies and equipment required to care for them, therefore, are at higher risks to suffer from any outbreak of diseases.
- Inadequacy in meeting the basic needs
- Loss of personal belongings, which is very crucial as the possessiveness and attachment with the belongings are very strong.
- Unsafe physical environment/loss of familiar environment

Psychological Effects Include

- Shock
- Continuing fear, insecurity and anxiety
- Loss of protected family environment
- Sadness and depression (often difficult to recognise)
- Anger and irritability
- Behavioural problems like aggression, lying, stealing
- Performance deterioration
- Difficulty in relationship/friendship

- Loneliness
- Increased risk of substance abuse
- Subsequent personality disorders

Social effects include

- Family disorganization
- Change of life style
- Change in social roles
- Unaccompanied children: starvation, child trafficking, sexual abuse/witnessing rape and other forms of violence, child labour/exploitation
- Juvenile delinquency
- Begging

Educational effects include

- Death of teachers
- Loss of familiar school infrastructure
- Loss of personal educational materials
- Lack of proper educational environment
- Gap in the continuation of learning
- Lack of concentration/poor performance
- Classroom disruptions
- School dropouts

The plethora of research studies on disaster affected children across different countries indicates significant increases in psychological problems following natural disasters such as lightning strikes (Dollinger, O'Donell, and Stanely, 1984), tornados (Bloch, Silber, and Perry, 1956), floods (Burke, Borus, Burns, Millstein, and Beasley, 1982; Earls, Smith, Reich, and Jung, 1988; Gleser, Green, and Winget, 1981; Newman, 1976), earthquakes (Galante and Foa, 1986), bushfire (McFarlane, 1987), and hurricanes (La Greca, Silverman, Vernberg, and Prinstein, 1996; Shaw, Applegate, Tanner, Perez, Rothe, Campo-Bowen, and Lahey, 1995; Vernberg, La Greca, Silverman, and

Prinstein, 1996). However, there is limited controlled epidemiological data available on psychological morbidity of children following exposure to major disasters (Pefferbaum, 1997; Shannon, Lonigan, Finch, Taylor, and Sallie, 1994; Vogel and Vernberg, 1993).

However, there is little global data on the breakdown of affected populations by age, though media reports shows that children form one of the largest segments of populations affected by the recent few horrifying natural and man-made disasters. Research studies and good practices on how to address children's capacities and vulnerabilities in times of disaster are very few in number when compared to the number of children affected. Many examples of disaster reports (Gujarat earthquake and Bangladesh flood, SPHERE Project, etc) hardly mention on these issues of children in their reports, although the social dimension of vulnerability assessment has been emphasizing on the vulnerability of children along with women. Disaster literature confines them to three areas: (i) they are part of studies on women, (ii) they are treated as the cohorts of psychiatric or psychological studies, and (iii) they become "icons" of suffering and sign of perilous plight (Marten, 2001). In the eventuality of the recent tsunami, many media reports stated about the danger of sexual abuse and exploitation of children in many affected countries. Any disaster planning and measure need to look at children as a separate category of victims in any disaster as they represent more than 50% of the populations of many countries in developing world, thus represent a sizeable proportion of individuals affected by all types of disasters.

Factors Affecting the Nature and Magnitude of Effects

The nature and magnitude of mental health and psychosocial effects of any disaster on children depend largely on the following factors:

their developmental age, type of disasters (disasters caused by manmade hazards affect children's psyche in a much deeper way, e.g. communal riots and terrorism) the nature of loss they experienced, the amount of exposure to trauma, sufferings/ devastation they witnessed, social support dynamics prevail during that phase of disaster, and the nature of post-disaster care specially designed to meet their multifarious needs.

However, irrespective of the type and severity of any natural and manmade disaster, or the equation between a child and a disaster, what is more important is that we should understand *how children who have experienced disaster would be processing the information and what sort of reactions they show as a result of such experiences.* Since children have limited capacities to process information their sense of what happened is often not realistic and they are not able to comprehend the totality of the situation. Often it is observed that the affected adults as well as the disaster workers overlook the need to respond and explain things to children but it is a well-known fact that children are the most badly affected population in any disaster and need extra care and comfort. If the management fails to address their fears and insecurities the internal turmoil and pain can leave them sad, confused and frightened and this will remain with them for a long time to come. Therefore, it is imperative to understand how children at various ages would be viewing their losses and trauma.

Age-specific psychological reactions of children to a disaster

These age-specific reactions are common and normal responses to an event that is beyond their coping abilities. In the training of trainers module on disaster case (NIMHANS, 2004) have listed a variety of age specific reactions and these are listed in Table 1 below:

TABLE 1: Age specific ractions of children to disaster

Pre-scholars (1-5 years)

- Templer tantrums and Crying
- Clinging and demanding
- Scary nightmares
- helplessness
- Regresstive behaviour (thumb sucking)

School age (5-11 years)

- Physical complaints-headache, stomach aches
- Aggression
- Fear of darkness/sleeping alone/separation from parents
- Lack of self competency
- Understand loss and become very anxious
- Regression to behaviours like thumb sucking etc.
- Nightmares and inability to sleep
- Fear of recurrence
- Difficulty in following routines
- Does not mingle with friends
- Behavioural problems
- Emotional problems like apathy, anxious, withdrawn, depressed
- Disinterest or difficulties in school work–disturbs others, worrying, being tense, undisciplined, refusal to go to school, poor concentration
- Feel guilty and responsible for the loss

Adolescents (13-18 years)

- Seeks isolation, becomes less communicative
- Sleeplessness or increased sleep
- Feel different or alienated because of their experiences
- Irritability
- Increased risk taking behaviours
- Increased substance abuse
- Avoidance of trauma related thoughts, feelings and activities
- Aggression—fights, destructive, arguments
- Feelings of hopelessness, feeling neglect and isolation
- Disobediaence, specially towards authority and parents
- Try to get involve in activities to get a sence of control like recscuing and organising the camps

- Angry, frustrated and may feel very helpless
- Depression due to loss
- Guilt for not being able to do enought or for having survived
- Inability to concentrate
- Behavioural problems like–aggression, lying stealing
- Dropping out of shcool or work
- Aches and pains due to stress

Source: National Institute of Mental Health and Neuro Sciences (NIMHANS) Training of trainers Module on disaster psychosocial care -2004

A number of psychological symptoms have been observed in children following disasters, including fears, sleep problems, depression, separation anxiety, somatic complaints, and conduct problems. The concept of post-traumatic stress disorder (PTSD) has been applied to children, studies have found symptoms of PTSD in children following natural disasters (Lonigan, Shannon, Finch, Daugherty, andTaylor, 1991; Pefferbaum, 1997; Vogel and Vernberg, 1993). For example, studies have shown a high rate of PTSD symptoms in school-age children following exposure to a severe hurricane (La Greca, Silverman, Vernberg, and Prinstein, 1996; Vernberg, La Greca, Silverman, and Prinstein, 1996). There is also evidence of PTSD among children exposed to other types of severe trauma such as sniper attack (Pynoos, Frederick, Nader, Arroyo, Steinberg, Eth, Nunez, and Fairbanks, 1987)), kidnapping (Terr, 1983), witnessing violence (Kinzie, Sack, Angell, Manson, and Rath, 1986; Saigh, 1989), and sexual abuse (Kiser, Ackerman, Brown, Edwards, McColgan, Pugh, and Pruitt, 1988). Available studies of children suggest that symptoms of PTSD are related to degree of exposure to life threat (Pynoos et al., 1987) and levels of parental distress (McFarlane, 1987), and may persist for long periods after the disaster (Galante and Foa, 1986; Kinzie et al., 1986; Terr, 1983). Thus, while studies have shown that symptoms of PTSD may occur in school-age children following exposure to natural disasters and other major stress involving life threat, little is known about PTSD in younger, pre-school aged children, and how PTSD may affect their overall development.

CLASSIFICATION OF VICTIMS

Children in disasters are often dislocated from their homes, subject to situations which may be difficult and different from their familiar, comfortable and accustomed lives. This along with the death of family members can be considered as the primary source of stress and insecurity in children. However, witnessing hundreds of deaths and injured can result in unhappiness, sadness, fear and worried. Again their and their family members struggle for food, shelter, and other amenities can add to their fear and insecurity and continue to threat their sense of well-being. Witnessing different forms of violence, social unrest and child abuse can also raise their level of vulnerability to the maximum and can have lifetime irreversible impact on their personality.

These factors which decide the magnitude and severity of psychological trauma in the disaster affected children could also be expressed by the equation between the child and the disaster, i.e. whether a child is a direct and/or peripheral, relational, or vicarious victim (Parson, 1994). This is very important for a clinical child psychologist to understand the difference in the type of victims to design right kind of psychosocial intervention.

Direct Victim or Peripheral / Immediate Victim:

(i) Victims who are injured or helplessly pinned down in a building and were rescued by first responder team members.

(ii) Victims who are in a building/disaster affected place and were rescued at a later time by firefighters, police, or emergency workers.

(iii) Victims who have actually witnessed impact of the disaster, but escaped luckily just before it happened.

Relational Victims:

(i) Children who have lost a parent or close family member in the disaster.

(ii) Children whose friend or friends and/or teacher perished due to the disaster.

(iii) Children who lost their valuables in the disaster.

Vicarious Victims

(i) Children who are deeply affected by the deaths and destruction witnessed on television and other news stories and print images of the disaster.

Victims with Special Needs

Keeping all the above-mentioned three types of child victims in view, the following groups of children could be considered to have special and/or pre-existing vulnerability in a disaster scenario:

- Neonates and infants
- Children with disabilities
- Children whose parents have remarried
- Unaccompanied minors, especially girls
- `Children who need critical medical care facilities
- Children with HIV-AIDS

While these factors definitely increase the vulnerability of all children coming in the age range of 1-18 years, we must look at the special vulnerability of some children within this bigger group in a disaster scenario. Their needs get compounded by the pre-disaster living conditions of some children and the new demands of post-disaster living conditions. These unexpected living conditions many a times go beyond their normal coping strategies and their ability to adjust with the new situation.

PSYCHOSOCIAL INTERVENTION

Planning of psychosocial intervention largely depends on the factors affecting the nature and magnitude of impacts along with the classification of victims. Designing a composite intervention package with a particular child focused approach which includes the family as a unit of intervention, is more effective.

Type of psychosocial intervention

The package of psychosocial intervention could include:

- Relevant play therapy methods to facilitate ventilation and expression of emotions of the children,
- Psycho-education for the family members,
- Treatment of family psychopathology if any,
- Timely and appropriate psychiatric drugs if the victim has clinical symptoms of mental disorders,
- Programme on social out reach or relaxation techniques,
- Peer and extended social support network,
- Psychotherapy and cognitive behaviour therapy (CBT).

The clinical child psychologist could select one or combine few methods as a composite package depending on the situation and type of victim and factors such as developmental age, sex etc. However, it has been seen that combining few selected methods yield better results across disasters. Nevertheless, it is important to remember that special care is needed to design psychosocial intervention for the children affected in man made disasters such as communal riots, bomb blasts and fire disasters as the physical impairment due to the burn and violence remain with the child life long thus could leave irreparable damage for the child's overall development.

Duration and Method of Application/Administration

While some of interventions can be planned at a group/ community/school level such as some play therapy methods (such as drawing, painting, clay modeling, etc), social programmes (such as drama/play), and peer counseling, others can be planned at an individual/ family level as home-based interventions. Duration of the intervention should vary depending on the severity of the problems the victim is facing and type of intervention selected. However, ideally the duration of such group interventions should be a week and more frequently repeated to know the effectiveness, and the duration of home-based intervention should be a minimum of 10days (at least one hour everyday). Time devoted to treat family psychopathology should not be considered as a part of the duration mentioned.

Guiding Principles for the Application of Psychosocial Interventions:

(i) These interventions should be planned along with the relief and rehabilitation, therefore should have an approach to address a spectrum of care services. The clinical child psychologist should be trained in basic psychosocial care in disasters and work along with other community level trained psychosocial care givers. As mental health professionals, believing in the principle that "everyone can facilitate the process of psychosocial recovery" therefore, should not consider that the application of intervention is only to be done by the clinical child psychologists not by the other care givers.

(ii) Each intervention (individual or composite) should have pre and post assessment by using culturally appropriate psychological/clinical diagnosis tools.

(iii) Immediate, mid-term and long-term interventions should be planned

(iv) All interventions should be socially and culturally sensitive. Stigma, and myths should be handled carefully.

(v) Language barriers can be overcome by including local trained care givers such as teachers. Any sort of "labeling" should be totally prohibited by any of the care givers in the group.

(vi) The psychologist/clinical child psychologist/therapist or care givers should take all required materials for applying any intervention.

(vii) The psychologist/therapist should also recognize the functionality of existing social and healthcare systems for preventive, curative and promotive mental health care prevailing in that country. Psychiatric referral should be done on the basis of that.

(viii) Follow up support should also be planned by the same group of care givers

(ix) Reporting and documenting all such evidence-based locally effective psychosocial intervention should be done and disseminated through different channels for larger application.

ROLE OF DIFFERENT CAREGIVERS

As adults in a caregiver's role we must understand the process and procedures of facilitating children's fast recovery from the trauma. It will enable the children to withstand the negative effects of the catastrophic event in a more appropriate way. Here the adult caregivers can be divided into 4 prime categories viz. parents/relatives, school teachers, and caregivers from outside, especially pediatricians. These caregivers must understand the emotional/behavioural reactions the child, then try to reduce the impact and then offer support and security to the child. They are also responsible to develop healthy coping mechanisms in the child. It is explained with exampels in Table-2 below.

TABLE 2: Steps to understand and support the child

Try and Understand the children	*Reduce the impact of the disaster on them*	*Give them care and support*
Observe their behaviour	Listen actively and allow ventilation	Use play to offer support and help
Accept their behaviour and what they say completely	Give them love and assurance and try to meet their basic needs	Talk with the children and find out what they need
Continuously monitor what they say to you and how they behave	Model positive living and good coping skills	Try and return them to their normal life routines

Moreover, taking care of children's physical and other needs will solve the problem to a larger extent. In addition to this psychosocial support directed towards the adults within the closet family circles and communities is highly favourable for their recovery. However, the role and responsibilities of each category of caregivers vary from the other. The diagram given below (Figure 1) will explain the roles of different caregivers.

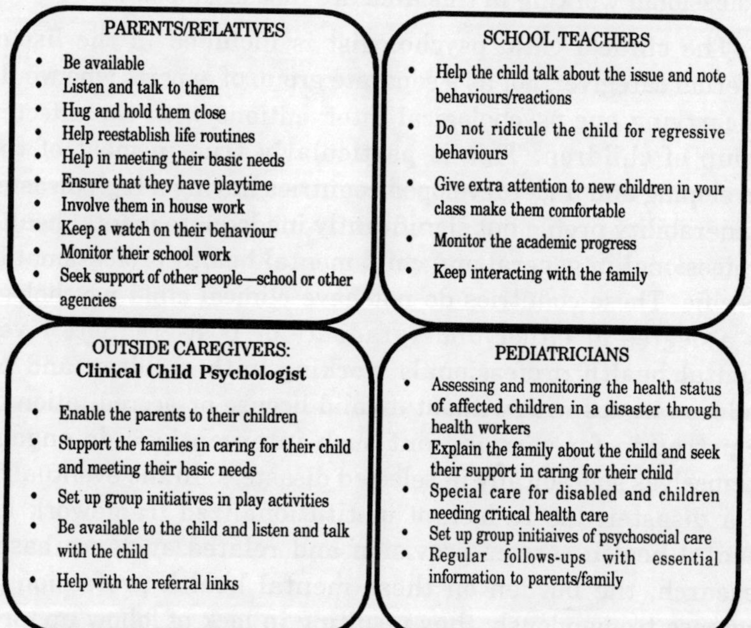

Fig. 1: Caregiver Model

Nevertheless, the caregivers have also a different set of roles and responsibility towards the children community in a disaster affected area. As the young people represent a significant portion of the population, they are affected by the decisions and actions taken today. They will also be important actors in the local community for many years to come. Therefore, investments made in developing their knowledge, skills, and social responsibility are the best investments the adults can make towards a better future.

Issues and Challenges for Clinical Child Psychology in Disasters

Clinical Child Psychology as a discipline within Psychology has been emerging slowly in Asian countries however, the role and application of clinical child psychology in disaster affected areas are limited to very few group interventions. Some of important issues and challenges in this area and mental health professional working in this area are discussed below:

The clinical child psychologist is included in the list of external caregiver, not as a separate group of experts who would be carrying our psychological interventions with the affected group of children. This is particularly true in most of the developing and underdeveloped countries having a high disaster vulnerability profile but significantly inadequate mental health professional in general and child mental health professional in specific. These countries do not have clinical child psychology as a degree at either undergraduate or post-graduate level. Mental health professionals working with children and on children issues with/without a valid license or accreditation or registration for carrying out such interventions do engage themselves sporadically in selected disasters. In the eventuality of a disaster due to lack of institutionalized framework for mental health service provision and related evidence based research, the burden on these mental health professionals increase tremendously thus resulting in lack of follow up, pre-post intervention, and interest.

The magnitude of child mental health problems remains invisible to policy makers in the absence of child mental policies to guide the process of service development. The belief systems about mental illness also prompt help seeking in alternative health systems, thereby reducing the evidence for the burden associated with health seeking (Omigbodun, 2008).

The recent tsunami affected countries confronted with the challenge to provide mental healthcare to children and adolescents who experienced loss, displacement and disruption of daily lives. The need to enhance the capacities for appropriate needs assessment in disaster affected area, systematic diagnosis on children's psychopathology, psychological triage, appropriate psychosocial intervention, follow up, post intervention assessment and reporting and other adequate advocacy tools, are some of the key aspects of clinical child psychology area.

Inadequate sharing and dissemination of information on findings of specific interventions among inter and intra country level organizations/institutions results in duplication of efforts and unplanned expenditure.

Project and supply driven ad-hoc approaches in the area of disaster psychosocial care and mental health services in disasters often limit the scope of child/family centric psychosocial intervention. Even small scale and frequently occurring disasters are often overlooked by the mental health professionals.

Children's mental health needs in disasters are varied, complex and intimately connected with their needs for security, food, shelter, education and family connection. This requires holistic, rights-based approaches that can access resources to address basic needs, advocate for security and protection, and recognize and address the needs of the more vulnerable children. Drawing on clinical experience and research in humanitarian settings, it calls for greater attention to the child's perspective, their individuality and the cultural, social and political context in which they live (Lynne, 2008). Those concerned with the psychopathology of children in crises should widen their frame of reference beyond narrowly defined traumatic reactions to include other mental health and psychosocial issues, including the current problems of daily life and the needs of children with pre-existing psychiatric disorders.

While available research has made important contributions to understanding risk factors for negative mental health consequences of disasters on psychological trauma of children and adolescents, the focus on trauma alone has resulted in inadequate attention to factors associated with resilient mental health outcomes (Bentacourt and Khan, 2008). Therefore, the professional working in this area should also focus on the role of a number of protective processes contribute to resilient mental health outcomes in disaster affected children and should utilize those protective factors as a part of composite package of psychosocial intervention designed for the children.

Last but not the least, the mental health professionals including the clinical child psychologists working or interested to work in this area should be adequately trained on the holistic view of disaster psychosocial support and mental health services by a designated institute.

CONCLUSION

The word disaster either natural or man-made reminds us the most horrific images of human sufferings in multifarious ways. Disasters disrupt the sense of well-being by destroying normal predictable and consistent life routines of children thus, deeply hamper the process of healthy psychological and personality development. Mental health is an important component of the well being of children exposed to disasters and critical to successful rehabilitation and their all round development. Although the psychosocial responses of children to a disaster vary on the basis of many factors, there is common pattern of age specific reactions of children and adolescents after a disaster. Socio-cultural and socio-economic variations are also there to make a difference in coping and early recovery. Clinical child psychology has not yet been evolved and emerged as a specialized field while considering intervention programmes for disaster affected children particularly in developing countries. This is more prevalent in Asian countries because of the educational and professional degrees and other system of recognition to this field provided in these countries. As caregivers, lot of issues and challenges are there for the mental health professionals presently working or intended to work in this field in future. Capacity building in disaster psychosocial support and mental health services of these professionals plays a major role in coordinated and collaborated approach to provide care services to disaster affected children. Nevertheless, a paradigm shift is being taking place in these countries in terms of legal framework and policy of government towards providing child sensitive disaster management frameworks.

REFERENCES

Betancourt, T.S. and Khan, K.T. (2008). The mental health of children affected by armed conflict: Protective processes and pathways to resilience, *International Review of Psychiatry*, 20, pp. 317-328.

Bloch, D.A., Silber, E., and Perry, S.E. (1956). Some factors in the emotional reaction of children to disaster. *American Journal of Psychiatry*, 113, 416-422.

Burke, J.D., Borus, J.F., Burns, B.J., Millstein, K.H., and Beasley, M.C. (1982). Changes in children's behavior after a natural disaster. *American Journal of Psychiatry*, 139, 1010-1014.

Dollinger, S., J., O'Donell, J.P., and Stanley, A.A. (1984). Lightning-strike disaster: Effects on children's fears and worries. *Journal of Consulting and Clinical Psychology*, 52, 1028-1038.

Earls, F., Smith, E., Reich, W., and Jung, K.G. (1988). Investigating psychopathological consequences of disaster in children: A pilot study incorporating a structured diagnostic interview. *Journal of the American Academy of Child and Adolescent Psychiatry*, 27, 90-95.

Galante, R. and Foa, D. (1986). An epidemiological study of psychic trauma and treatment effectiveness for children after a natural disasters, *Journal of the American Academy of Child Psychiatry*, 25, 357-363.

Gleser, G.C., Green, B.L., and Winget, C. (1981). *Prolonged psychosocial effects of disaster: A study of Buffalo Creek*. New York: Academic Press.

International Frederation of Red Cross & Red Cresecent Society (2002) *In World Disaster Planning Reports.* Quick Silver, Dr. Sterling V.A. 20/66 U.S.A.: Kumarian Press.

Kinzie, J. D., Sack, W.H., Angell, R.H., Manson, S., and Rath, B. (1986). The Psychiatric Effects of Massive Trauma on Cambodian children:I, *Journal of the Ameriacn Academy of Child and Adolescent Psychiatry*, 25, 370-376.

Kiser, L.J., Ackerman, B.J., Brown, E., Edwards, N.B., McColgan, E., Pugh, R., and Pruitt, D.B. (1988). Post-traumatic stress disorder in young children: A reaction to purported sexual abuse. *Journal of the American Academy of Child and Adolescent Psychiatry*, 27, 645-649.

La Greca, A., Silverman, W., Vernberg, E., and Prinstein, M. (1996). Posttraumatic stress symptoms in children after Hurricane Andrew: A prospective study. *Journal of Consulting and Clinical Psychology*, 64, 712-723.

Lonigan, C., Shannon, M., Finch, A., Daugherty, T., and Taylor, C. (1991). Children's reactions to a natural disaster: Symptom severity and degree of exposure. *Advances in Behavior Research and Therapy*, 13, 135-154.

Lynne Jones (2008). Responding to the needs of children in crisis, International Review of Psychiatry, 20, 291-303.

Marten, M. (2001) Creating Children Friendly environment in the aftermath of natural disasters. In *Save the children document as child focused disaster planning.* Land and EC1MYAR, U.K.

McFarlane, A. C. (1987). Posttraumatic phenomena in a longitudinal study of children following a natural disaster. *Journal of the American Academy of Child and Adolescent Psychiatry*, 26, 764-769.

Newman, C.J. (1976). Children of disaster: Clinical observations at Buffalo Creek. *American Journal of Psychiatry*, 133, 206-312.

Omigbodun, O. (2008). Developing child mental health services in resource-poor countries, *International Review of Psychiatry*, 20 (3), 225-235.

Parson, E. R. (1994). Post-Traumatic Stress Disorder: Its biopsychobehavioral aspects and management. In B. Wolman and G. Stricker (Eds). *Anxiety and Related Disorders: A Handbook* (p. 226-285). New York: Wiley.

Pfefferbaum, B. (1997). Posttraumatic stress disorder in children: A review of the past 10 years. *Journal of the American Academy of Child and Adolescent Psychiatry*, 36, 1503-1511.

Pynoos, R.S., Frederick, C., Nader, K., Arroyo, W., Steinberg, A., Eth, S., Nunez, F., and Fairbanks, L. (1987). Life threat and posttraumatic stress in school-age children. *Archive General Psychiatry*, 44, 1057-1063.

Saigh, P.A. (1989). The validity of the DSM-III Posttraumatic Stress Disorder classification as applied to children. *Journal of Abnormal Psychology*, 98, 189-192.

Shannon, M.P., Lonigan, C.J., Finch, A.J., Jr., Taylor, C.M. and Sallie, F.R. (1994). Children exposed to disaster: I. Epidemiology of posttraumatic symptoms and diagnostic profiles. *Journal of the American Academy of Child and Adolescent Psychiatry*, 33, 80-93.

Shaw, J., Applegate, B., Tanner, S., Perez, D., Rothe, E., Campo-Bowen, A., and Lahey, B. (1995). Psychological effects of Hurricane Andrew on an elementary school population. *Journal of the American Academy of Child and Adolescent Psychiatry*, 34, 1185-1192.

Terr, L. (1983). Chowchilla Revisited: The effects of psychic trauma four years after a bus kidnapping. *American Journal of Psychiatry*, 140, 1542-1550.

Vernberg, E., La Greca, A., Silverman, W., and Prinstein, M. (1996). Prediction of posttraumatic stress symptoms in children after Hurricane Andrew. *Journal of Abnormal Psychology*, 105, 237-248.

Vogel, J., and Vernberg, E. (1993). Children's psychological responses to disasters. *Journal of Clinical Child Psychology*, 22, 464-484.

Zeanah, C.H. and Burke, G.S. (1984). A young child who witnessed her mother's murder: Therapeutic and legal considerations. *American Journal of Psychotherapy*, 38, 132-145.

10

Perception of Work, Stress and Coping Among Street Children

—Veena Tucker and Poonam Phogat

"Street children" are those who work and live on the street day and night. Many of them do not have contact with their families and almost all of them use many kinds of drugs. The Street children sleep, play, eat, dress and treat themselves when they are sick in the streets. Many of them practice illegal activities such as stealing, gambling etc. (Ferrari, 2003). The needs of street children differ from other community children, as in addition to the usual socio-economic and health problems, they also have to deal with lack of emotional support, insecurity, exploitation and working in unhygienic conditions. Such unhealthy and hazardous environment adversely affects their physical and mental health. Street children are exploited. If they are not handled with care, they can drift into anti-social activities, such as pick pocketing, stealing, smuggling, drug-peddling, gambling etc. Street children come into the world of adults unprepared, with an unrealistic view of life. The community in which the child grows up is a significant influence on his or her development as emphasized in the ecological model of human development. Socialization involves bi-directional interactions between the child and significant others like family, peer, school and community (Berns, 2004). Psychosocial stress may adversely influence individual's psychological growth. Stressful life events are determined by psychological characteristics of the individual and the situations in the environment. For many street children negative psychological characteristics may lead to psychopathology and improper psychological growth in the absence of supportive psychosocial mediators and ineffective coping defenses.

Deprivations in the lives of street children

Various stress models describe how street children face deprivations, which are further compounded by poverty and economic constraints. Some of these deprivations are: diminished social support for children within the family and community; decreased opportunities for socialization; lack of opportunities to consolidate one's self-worth in broader societal sphere; experience of marginalization and uncertainty of future and poorly planned urban environment.

Ennett, Bailey and Federman (1999) found that the youth without a social network were significantly more likely to report illicit drug use, multiple sex partners and survival sex than youth with a supportive social network indicating that network characteristics were associated in both positive and negative directions with risky behaviors.

Various life stressors that street children face in different countries have been examined (Greenblatt and Robertson,1993; Janus, McCormack, Burgess and Hartman, 1987 and Rothman and Davis,1985). The most common stressor found in the lives of street children were the lack of proper homes and education, unemployment among parents, violence and hunger. Home rearing patterns can influence children to runaway from home. Highly positive relationship was found between home rearing patterns and the children found on the street. There was equally positive but low association between the level of family income and children running away from home (Matchinda, 1991).

Street children cope with their problems either by cognitive restructuring of their circumstances, adopting practical solutions to their problems and by maladaptive approach of avoidance. Street children live with few protective or mediating supports, and many risk factors, facing psychosocial trauma which generates profound problems in personality development. Street children describe a broad spectrum of home and work experiences that had led to their living on the streets. They made significant use of various resources found within their social network of peers local communities and NGOs (Baker, Panter and Todd, 1997; Hagan and McCarthy, 1997; Whitebeck, Hoyt, et. al. 1999)

Further it is found that among these children, the typical adaptation techniques such as time orientation, self concept, success-failure orientation, reinforcement system, sense of control over environment and coping strategies generally become adversely affected by the conditions of poverty. More professional intervention strategies would help these children learn positive coping skills.

Poverty and Street Children: Poverty exerts an impact by increasing a child's vulnerability to cumulative risk of health hazards. The health hazards on the child also impede the development of cognition and learning. Street children have low levels of education and come from families with five or more siblings. Parents of street children commonly had low education and were mainly found in unskilled occupations, were in contract polygamous marriages, which are also often characterized by marital disruption. Street children also left home because of parental/familial reasons. (Adernito, 2002; Clatts and Davis; 1999; Mustafa and Sharma, 1996; Sampa, 1998 and Segal and Ashtekar, 1994).

Perception of work: Poverty forces all the street children to work and earn. It becomes an activity that is a must for daily survival. Many of these children were forced earlier to work by their families because of poverty. The concept of work is a social and cultural construction. The expression "child worker" puts together two categories of a different type: the first belonging to a generational and cultural and the second to an economical and social one. There are four main components of work: game, means of subsistence, relationing identity. Work also has a double function of subsisting and socialization (Invernizzi, 2001).

The ideal picture of work and childhood do influence the way the child builds his perception and definition of subsistence activities (Myers, 1992). Also, the studies concerned with the children's point of view are also of the fact that the ideal work as a waged and steady worker is out of reach (Tellez and Abramo, 1985). They do not fully understand the ideal model of work and/or rather tend to redefine it from their own experience. They sometimes tend to valorize the work they are doing for some reason still to be determined. The link between a child and his survival activity comprises three dimensions.

The material or socio-economic one deals with material subsistence. The socio-cultural one refers to the child's links with other individuals (customer, employer, other children, policeman etc). At last the identity dimension regards the link built by the child with himself through his work. Through his work the child is looking for a positive personal recognition and self-valuation. Working gives the child a feeling of belonging since it enables him to be recognized as an active member of a family group or any other group. (Tellez and Abramo, 1985)

Health of Street Children

There is an adverse effect of child labour on the health of the child. Hazardous working conditions and impoverished unhealthy environment and starvation are associated with ill heath among street children. Health problems of street children ranged from common health problems like fever, cold eye/ear infections occurring very often. The serious health problems were stomachache, general weakness, animal bites, TB, and Sexually Transmitted Diseases (Baker, Panter and Todd, 1997; Butterflies, 1997; Tucker et.al, 2002 and UNICEF, 2004)

Coping in Street Children

Street children being 'at risk' face more challenges in their lives. Lack of vocational skills and low social competence make them face hazards and harassment from employers, police and public. WHO (1999) studied of the lives of street children relating to programmes on substance abuse, in seven developing countries and one developed country. Children reported that 'taking to the street is a way of searching for identity, earning a living out of it, and contributing to the family's income'. Further "most children felt that 'with positive support of the street educators and other elders in the family/community coping with the present stressful situation would become less problematic'. Some of the coping strategies and skills found in street children were prosocial example supporting each other emotionally and materially, playing sports, dancing, performing music, joining a gang for support and protection, being able to fight etc, attending groups, drop-in shelter, clinics run for street children. While others demonstrate skills and strategies utilized within anti-social activities such as drug use, cheating, begging, and commercial/survival sex etc. However, the skills themselves and the planning capacities used in the antisocial activities may be transformed to pro-social activities with proper-interventions and skill training.

The objective of the present study was to explore the lives of street children referring to their perception of work. Further, various problems and fears faced by the street children were also assessed. How these children coped with these stresses was also analyzed. The present study used the participatory methods for exploring the lives of the street children. Thus, the purpose of this action research was to take into account the multi-dimensional view of street children where their work was related to their family, education, health and overall psychosocial development.

Objectives

The objective of the present study was to study the perception of work, stress and coping among street children. This action research focused on understanding and analyzing their feelings, thoughts about living and working on the streets, their problems, fears and anxieties and how they cope with this.

Research Design and Method

As per the objectives of this action research the lives of the street children were investigated with the participatory methods.

The various phases in the Participatory Action Research were as follows:

1. Understand and analyze the street children through participatory methods initiated by listening and auto diagnosis.
2. Identification and prioritization of problems- the concept of stress as viewed by the street educators and psychological theories has to be dropped to facilitate learning from the experiences of the street children. Their feeling, memories and coping mechanisms have reflected what is social reality for them. Their illusions and reality may be adaptive from the adult's viewpoint. However, probing into their reality without any

assumptions and theories has lead to better understanding. Thus concrete action for helping the street children emerged from this process of understanding of the lives of street children through auto-diagnosis and other PRA methods.

3. In the final phase, street children reflected and analyzed their lives. This would help them in planning, taking action and developing new skills or building on their existing skills and knowledge and increasing their confidence. This process of empowerment may lead to potential change with the help of facilitator.

As the present study is a PAR paradigm, the variables and hypotheses were not explicitly stated.

Participants- The study being a participatory action research (PAR), with both cross-sectional and longitudinal approach. For understanding and analyzing the lives and social reality of street children, a few children were interacted for a longer period of time. The total sample constituted of thirty (n=30) male street children working in and around New Delhi Railway Station. These children were in the age range of 8-18yrs with mean age of 13.10 years and SD of 2.04 years, working as shoe-shine boys, rag-pickers, tea stall workers, porters etc. earning on an average Rs.25-40 per day. The sample was purposive and incidental. The sample was constituted of young children (8-12yrs, n_1= 11, Mean-l0 yrs 9months, SD-1.1) with short duration on the street (0-3yrs) and older children (13-18yrs, n_2= 19, Mean-14 yrs 3months, SD- 1.23) with long duration on the street (above 3yrs), who were studied through PRA. Most of the children studied were assisted by the NGOs.

Procedure: Participatory methods like PRA methods of daily activity, problem ranking, focus group discussion, in-depth interviews, case studies, and observation were used. These PRA methods can only be used once the facilitator listens and builds a trust among street children. Use of participatory methods along with case studies elicited qualitative information that helped in understanding and analyzing street children's lives in their social context. Children's emotions, experiences, decisions and needs/wishes were revealed through interaction with them and these collectively described every street child as a unique individual.

The study began with the selection of site and the NGOs working with street children in those areas. It was found that the NGO Salaam Balak Trust has a drop-in shelter for children at the New Delhi Railway Station. The NGOs were the primary source for contacting the street children for the present study. The investigator started visiting these contact places for familiarization and rapport formation with the street children. In the initial phase of the research observation method was used for studying the lives of street children. Investigator was trained to observe the children regarding their interpersonal interaction, their communication, daily activities etc. Detailed day-to-day dairy was maintained wherein the information was recorded. After the investigator felt that the street children had accepted her, the next phase of research was started. In this phase, the various methods as mentioned in the design were used for various objectives.

Results: The results the study for the various objectives are described below:-

Demographic Profile of Street Children

The age of the sample i.e. the street children ranged from 8-18 years. Majority (61%) of them were school dropouts who had not gone beyond the primary level. Majority of the children were Hindu (60%) and a few Muslims (40%) and most of them belonged to neighboring states like Uttar Pradesh (UP), Bihar etc. The average family size was five members. Besides the demographic and socio-economic information of the family (e.g. profession and financial status of the parents / family, structure of family number of siblings, education facilities), child's relation with the family members (e.g. parental behaviour, sibling relations), child's relation with peers and reasons for leaving home were also assessed through the detailed interviews with the street children.

Analysis of this information pertained to finding the causes for leaving home. Various reasons for leaving home were elicited by the street children. Maltreatment, physical abuse/neglect /

rejection by the extended family or step-parent were found to be the most pervasive reason followed by poverty. However most street children faced multiple stresses that compelled them to runaway or leave homes. For example, physical abuse / rejection often combined with poverty and as well as facing the trauma of death of a parent, forced work, ill treatment by step parent etc. In most street children cases the causes of leaving is complex stressful situation marked by poverty, large family and trauma of some kind (losing a family member). Specifically in young children the cause of leaving is ill treatment and neglect by parents / stepparent / family members which is rebelled against by the child. Many of these children were the eldest or youngest or belonged to a family of many daughters with only son.

TABLE 1: Reasons for leaving and frequency of a sample of N= 30, street children

S.No.	*Reasons for leaving*	*Frequency (Percentage)*
1.	Physical Abuse	13 (45.23%)
2.	Poverty	9 (28.57%)
3.	Illness/injury/death of parent	4(11.90%)
4.	Ill-treatment by step-parent	3 (9.23%)
5.	Forced work	7(23.80%)
6.	Family conflicts	2 (4.76%)
7.	Peer pressure/family influence (for e.g. brothers, father etc)	1 (2.38%)
8.	Discontinuation of education	2 (4.76%)
9.	Lost from home	1(2.38%)
10.	Others (for e.g. no interest in studies, fight at school, delinquent etc)	4 (9.23%)

Assessment of Wishes /Desires of Street Children

The Table 2 shows the various wishes/ desires elicited by the street children. The results indicate that most of the children i.e. 76.67% wished for happiness and protected with their family and loved ones. They also wished for the welfare of their siblings. 60% of the children wished for basic needs like clothes, food and shelter to be met.

TABLE 2: Wishes/needs of street children and related frequencies, N=30.

S.No.	*Wishes / Needs*	*Frequency*	*Percentage*
1.	Basic security and fulfilling basic needs	18	60%
2.	Buying things to fulfill desire	4	13.33%
3.	Emotional needs (Being with family)	23	76.67%
4.	Education/Vocational Needs	13	43.33%
5.	Health Related Well Being Needs	8	26.67%
6.	Higher Aspirations /Better jobs and money needs	13	43.33%
7.	Self improvement and overcoming helplessness	3	10.0%
8.	Other Needs (for community, country, religion etc)	2	6.67%

*Total 82 wishes elicited from a sample children where each child stated more than 2 wishes

Also the next preferred needs found in the wishes of the children were related to education and vocational needs and aspirations of a better jobs and money with both desired by 43% of children. Next 27% of children wanted better quality of life and wellbeing. They also wished that they be healthy and not get sick. The three kinds of wishes that were least desired were different things (like toys, cycle, bat etc.) to fulfill childhood desires of play, improvement in self and personality and some general wishes like progress of country or peace.

Assessment of fears of street children

The fears elicited were either threat because of the particular harsh life situations of these children or to some of their desires and problems arising due to stresses and homelessness. As shown in the results, the most frequent fear, 93.33% was of police harassment and social discrimination by other people. The next frequent fear was the various abstract fears (73.33%) like that of spirits ('Bhoot' and 'Chudael'), nightmares, death, God and natural calamities like earthquake and fire. The third most frequent fears were situational, which reflected the harsh life conditions (40%) in which these children live. The fears were those of accidents and being run over by various vehicles like car, trains etc and also traveling alone in night. Health related to getting AIDS, cancer or addicted to substances. Next, were the peer related fears (20%) like those of fights between them and also being bullied by older children. Lastly were the fears of losing self-control and committing wrong (6.67%) whereas family related fears were least frequent 3.33%) fear.

TABLE 3: Types of fears and their frequencies elicited from the street children (N=30)

S.No	*FEAR CATEGORY**	*Frequency*	*Percentage*
1.	Abstract / Unnatural fears	22	73.33%
2.	Situational fears (Being alone in night, accident by vehicles etc)	12	40%
3.	Fear of harassment (Police, social discrimination etc.)	28	93.33%
4.	Health related fears (AIDS, Cancer, Addiction etc)	7	23.33%
5.	Peer related fears (Fights, bullying by older boys etc)	6	20%
6.	Family related fears (concerning mother's health etc)	1	3.33%
7.	Fear of losing self control (e.g. Doing wrong)	2	6.67%

Assessment of Future Aspirations / Planning

The responses to future plans were categorized into different groups as shown in Table 4. Most of the children (36.67%) reported that they don't know what they will do in future, or had no aspiration at all. They also said that they would continue in the same manner.

Next were those children who said that they would start doing an unskilled job (20%) like a domestic servant, pan/tea stall owner, fruit seller, 'chowkidar' or a waiter. About 16.67% of children said that they would get into a semi skilled job with training like driver, mechanic, shoemaker, tailoring or candle making. Another 16.67 % of the children said that they would like to become an army man / policeman. Lastly there were about 13.33% who aspired to become cricketer or dancer or teacher.

TABLE 4: Future aspirations of street children (N=30)

S.No	*Future Aspirations**	*Frequency*	*Percentage*
1.	Uncertain / No Planning (Don't know/ No Aspiration / Continue like this)	11	36.67%
2.	Unskilled Work (Domestic servant, pan / tea, stall owner, fruit / peanut vendor, waiter)	6	20%
3.	Skilled Work (Driver, mechanic, shoemaker, tailor, candle making)	5	16.67%
4.	Fauji /Policeman	5	16.67%
5.	Miscellaneous (Cricketer, Teacher, Dancer etc.)	4	13.33%

*Total 31 future aspirations elicited from a sample of 30 street children.

Purposes of Saving

All the children were also asked what do they do with the money they earn and that which is saved. Most of the children said that they tried to collect / save some money and send it home. Some said that they used the money for their own purposes. There were others who said that they would use it to go on a tour and visit other places or would use it to start their own shop.

Problem Analysis

Problem Analysis was used to understand the street children's problems and the stress that they experienced as a consequence. These children using cards indicated problems scored out in the severity rating on a 5-point scale. These problems were perceived on the various indices elicited from the children that included disability, frequency, pain and overall severity. The problem analysis (Table 5) showed that the problems experienced by the street children varied from food and emotional insecurity to work related problems, police interference and physical and sexual abuse.

TABLE 5: Problem analysis by facilitator and street children.

S.No.	Problems	Frequency		Disability at work		Pain		Overall Severity	
		F	SC	F	SC	F	SC	F	SC
1.	Food Insecurity	1	2	2	1	3	1	3	1
2.	Emotional Insecurity	4	4	3	3	2	3	3	4
3.	Physical Abuse	5	5	2	4	5	3	3	4
4.	Sexual Abuse	3	-	3	-	3	-	3	-
5.	Drug Addiction	4	5	2	3	5	2	4	3
6.	Police Interference	4	5	5	5	4	5	4	5
7.	Social Discrimination	5	4	2	5	3	3	2	3
8.	Depression (well-being)	3	3	2	4	3	4	2	4
9.	General Sickness	4	3	3	5	4	3	3	4
10.	Work relate stress (older boys)	4	4	3	4	3	4	3	3

* 5-point rating scale [less (1)- more (5)]; n=30, age= 8-18yr and F= facilitator and SC= street children; Work= rag picker, bottles seller, tea-stall workers.

The problems that were perceived to be the most frequent by the facilitator were police interference, social discrimination, drug addiction, work related stress and physical and sexual abuse. The problems perceived to be least frequent was food security only. Police interference, social discrimination and physical abuse were found to be most disabling at work in comparison of facilitator and children's ratings, street children viewed social discrimination whereas facilitator didn't view discrimination as causing high disability.

On the pain index, police interference, depression and work related stresses were rated high by the street children, and food insecurity and drug addiction caused least pain to them. On the other hand physical abuse, drug addiction and police interference were rated high on pain by the facilitator. When all the problems were judged on the index of overall severity police interference, physical abuse, emotional insecurity and depression were found to be highly rated by the street children whereas food insecurity and drug addiction were rated low. The facilitator rated drug addiction and police interference, high on the overall severity whereas problem of social discrimination and depression were rated low. These problems are linked to the work they do.

Assessment of Coping Strategies and Resources:

The coping strategies and resources of street children were inferred from the detailed interviews, case studies and observation. The results are described below.

Coping Strategies: A variety of strategies and activities for coping with street life emerged from the stories included:

- Support from peers, both emotionally and materially. They also join gang for support and protection. It was widely evident in their interviews, e.g. taking help from mend when sick, helping another child in trouble with employer.
- Fighting and being aggressive as shown in behaviour as well as language. It is also a survival strategy. They fight for money also, using it as a means of coping both in happy as well as sad states. It also elicits the theme of searching for one's identity.
- Knowing how to effectively lie and manipulate the authorities and to get away with it. It was seen in the many ways children being registered at almost all NGO's and taking their benefits and facilities and not being attached to a single NGO. The children also lie to police, act novice when caught or lie about their state. They also keep in mind the weekdays on which police conducts raids on stations and they avoid roaming on those days.
- Engaging in high risk behaviors like fighting, jumping off and onto trains, playing games of dare and chance where physical harm may result. They also use substances like tobacco, gutka, bidi solution on which a major part of their earnings are spent.
- An ability to elicit alms by begging as it requires stamina, intelligence and imagination. Children easily resort to begging as shown in story where for a desire such as an ice cream, they would consider begging.

- Becoming "numb" psychologically, so that they felt nothing. Being in a harsh life and reality, they keep themselves in a shell or behind a wall and do not come up with emotions / feelings. They also try to suppress their experiences of maltreatment.
- Fantasy is one of the most commonly used coping mechanisms. It was evident in the interview where when asked what they would do on their birthday, all children fantasized elaborately how they would go about celebrating their birthday.
- Learning, educational aspirations and acquiring vocational skill.

Some of the coping strategies shown in the children being assisted by NGOs. These included:

- Playing sports-cricket being one of the most liked games in the country; children spent most of their idle time in cricket. There are also matches from different groups of children.
- Dancing, performing music and plays with NGO. This serves three purposes –one as a coping strategy, second reaching to community and thirdly to the donors for the projects for street children.

Some of these strategies are skills - prosocial, while others demonstrate skills and strategies utilized within antisocial activities. However, the skills themselves and the planning capacities used in the antisocial activities may be transferable to prosocial ends, if such ends are perceived as valid and rewarding alternatives.

Some negative aspects of the children indicated by statements were:

- Low self-esteem - "was thrown out of play because of dirty clothes" or "was thrown out of job".
- Escapism -"will run away from job, if there is a fight with employer. Showing no alternative thinking or problem solving.
- Stealing to have ice cream. Easy acceptance of the desire to commit crime.

Resources: The resources were also identified from the stories and detailed interviews. These resources were categorized in three, namely, self-resources, economic resources and social resources. Self-resources were those qualities that the children possessed and acquired on the street.

Personality characteristics and adaptive coping style that are capacity to work and earn a living; capacity to relate to others; sensitivity to perceive their own as well as others emotions; insight into their lives and situation, not being happy with their lives and in particular drug use, and wanting change in their lives; tolerance of pain; awareness of being discriminated; close attachment to parents, particularly mothers as in stories where the children wanted to spend their earnings with parents, celebrating birthday with parents or mother taking care when the child is sick; sense of responsibility as an earning member of family; and saving capacity.

Economic resources were the money they earn through working and the availability of cooperative banks for saving their money. Social resources include peer support and gang membership; family contact and support; NGO support (participation in projects; support and care from facilitator; shelter homes; centers for education and vocational training; 'Time out' programs e.g. outings and camps in Delhi as well as outside Delhi and providing bank and money saving facility.) and other community support such as police becoming more sensitive to children, donating items like clothes, shoes etc and some even taking charge of education of some children. Police support to street children is available minimally; visiting doctors, teachers, social work trainees and help from religious places of worship church (night shelter), temples, Gurudwara etc shelter, education, food etc.

The presence of street children in urban areas is not a new phenomenon. They have been a part of the urban scene mainly due to unabated migration from the villages to cities in search of a livelihood. Acute poverty of their families has denied them a proper shelter, forcing them to squat on public land on pavements, below flyovers, at or near railway stations, bus stations and other public places. Street children are, thus, a living and sordid symbol of urban malaise, their growing numbers giving the problem a high degree of visibility in cities where squatter settlements as well as the numbers of such children are mushrooming. The lives of street children have been explored from their perspective in the present study.

The causes of street children phenomenon have been found to be associated with various psychosocial variables. The main reasons for leaving home or running away from home were found to be poverty, physical abuse or neglect by family, illness/injury/death of parent and forced work besides other reasons of peer influence and delinquent tendencies etc. The factors were not exclusive of each other and in most cases there was a combination of factors like poverty, death of parent, along with forced work or ill treatment by step-parent, or poverty, discontinuation of education and forced work etc. (Whitebeck, Hoyt, et.al. 1999). Sometimes physical abuse at home and undesirable peer influence were the reasons for child running away from home. Similar findings have been reported from some of the studies on street children. Aptekar (1988) found that physical violence and abuse at home by parents was the primary reason for running away from home. Also many studies have shown that street children have high experiences of maltreatment, sexual abuse, and discrimination and faced traumatic events (Lalor, 1999; Manihara, 1997; Panter-Brick et al, 1996; Sampa, 1998 and Suda, 1997).

Most of the children belonged to lower socioeconomic class, which are poor, large families with extreme parental rejection, neglect and maltreatment of the child. These families showed strained parental relations and parents were not nurturing, unconcerned and distant from the child. The families were very poor, resulting in neglect or discontinuation of education of the child. Many children were forced to work and share the financial responsibility towards family. Hence, most street children faced extreme deprivations, neglect, and maltreatment for a long period of time. These children lacked family and peer support. (Gelles, 1998; Kotch, Muller and Blakely, 1999; Sampa, 1998).

Perception of Work: Interacting with the street children and the observation of their daily activities showed the way children perceived their work. Children were also asked about their future plans/aspirations. Most of the children had no future aspirations regarding the type of work they would like to do and many wished of getting an unskilled job like being a domestic servant/worker; owning a tea/pan shop, fruit seller, 'chowkidar' or waiter. Some of the children desired to become an army men/ policeman etc. and rest of them (13%) desired to become cricketer, teacher, dancer etc. The aspiration to become a policeman was present in the children as they see that police has a lot of power over others. The children also faced harassment and discrimination from the police; hence they wanted to attain a status of authority where others would not be able to harm them.

These children were aware of the harsh working conditions of their work. Their work was not ideal work as a waged and steady work was out of reach. It has been reported by Tellez and Abramo (1985) that working children do not fully understand the ideal model of work and/or rather tend to redefine it from their own experiences. They sometimes valorize the work they are doing for some reason still to be determined. It could be to increase their self-esteem and have a more substantial identity. Children were also asked about the way they spent/used and saved money. Work for street children is survival and subsistence of many of their families. The amount of earned money and subsequent savings are small. Street children are young and not supposed to work. Their circumstances forced them to work. Invernizzi (2001) described the socialization of working children through four activities namely work as survival, playing, relationship and building one's identity. Family background of the street children reflected that the street children have not been exposed to the ideal middle class protected family and School environment. Majority of these children have experienced the consequences of poverty both at home and on the street. The street child is exposed to work as a necessity for subsistence, which is combined with socialization. Street children working as rag picker, shoe shiners, in tea stall and even as beggars, have not learned the work skills, social competencies, value of work and money management. Many a times these children play a role of victim to gain sympathy of adults to make more money, for example, while begging, rag picking or working at tea stalls. Though the children did not show clear definition/meaning of work, for them working meant long hours involving efforts and subsequent malnutrition and health problems. Activities of many street/ working children contribute to material survival of the family and have the same function as that of a waged worker. Moreover older children may see work in terms of competence as seen in their future plans and desire to learn a vocational skill. These children had a desire to learn a vocation with the help of NGO and then start their own work in future like candle making, tailoring, driving vehicle etc. Street children wished for a 'happy future' along with their family and also desired for the well being of their sibling. Some of these were supporting their families financially and showed concern for the well-being of their siblings. Children even faced parental neglect and rejection showed strength and positive attitude of responsibility and this may be resilient factor for their survival and adjustment on the street without a family.

Through work, the child is trying to survive and looking for a positive personal recognition and self-evaluation, especially where this working child is also supporting family members. Wherever the work involves competencies as seen in the skilled work the child is motivated to excel and it would improve the self-valuation and identity of the street child. It is reflected in their desires for a better job and money and self-improvement. They wished for general well-being and better health. Many of them were aware of their unhygienic working conditions and desired for better life.

Problem Analysis: Problems were also rated on the indices of frequency, disability, and pain. It was found that police harassment was perceived to be most frequent, painful and disabling both by the street children and facilitator. Physical abuse was perceived to be most frequent , disabling , but not painful as compared to the facilitator who perceived it to be more painful Emotional insecurity was perceived to be more frequent , however moderately painful by street children but the facilitator did not consider it painful. Similarly depression was found to be moderate in frequency, high in disability and high on pain and overall severity by the street children. On the other hand facilitator perceived it to be moderate on frequency, low in disability at work and moderate. The facilitator did not consider it to be severe. Hence the street children perceived emotional insecurity and depression as more painful and severe as compared to the facilitator, as the facilitator lacked an internal frame of reference. It must also be remembered that not all young children who have experienced familial maltreatment and societal discrimination end up in trouble. Many survive and do well, their stories are very important for in them, we may be able to see resilience to work in the face of adversity, and be able to identify effective strategies for better assisting those who appear to be as vulnerable but not as resilient. Case studies of street children in the present study show that despite adversities in life, they enjoyed gaining pleasure from traditional Indian games like 'gulli-danda', choker, and cricket etc. It was also reflected in the wishes that children elicited, where 76.66% wished for "being with family and loved ones" and having a happy family in future.

Perception of work is also related to other problems faced by the street children. Problem analysis comparisons of street children and facilitator showed that as compared to facilitator who also judged the problems of street children, police harassment and drug addiction were perceived to be more severe whereas social discrimination and depression as less severe. Hence both facilitator and street children perceived police interference and social discrimination as major obstacles in street child's life. D'lima and Oosalia (1992) and Paniker and Nangia (1992) reported that street children were arrested because the police considered them vagrants or suspected they might have committed crimes. Even the NGOs Salaam Baalak Trust having the support of Delhi Police have not been able to solve the problem of police interference and insensitivity towards these children. It was also reflected in the fears of children where police harassment was perceived to be the major threat.

Coping Strategies: Coping strategies of the street children relating to their problems of basic needs fulfillment, work situations, peer relations have been explored through qualitative methods like case studies, daily activities and observation. Forming close peer bonds, seeking support from peers, joining street gangs helped the child adjust to the harsh environment and may be compensated for the lack of home and family. Using drop-in shelter, seeking support of sympathetic facilitators and counselors could built up the resilience of the deprived child and promote well-being. Emotional coping strategies of being aggressive, tendency to show high risk behavior of using drugs, gambling, watching porn movies, stealing, begging and other anti-social activities were the survival strategies. These coping styles were seen in the children who were influenced by the street 'gangs'. Lacking self-confidence and social skills, these children fail to engage in satisfying peer relationships and drift into increasingly deviant peer groups which provide them some kind of corrective environmental experience that might buffer earlier neglect from the parents. Street children want to be accepted and seek identity. As Jackson and McBride (1985) reported that gang members identify themselves with names, clothes, tattoos, slang, sign language etc, in the present study also there were evidences of such gangs functioning. Younger children are compelled to join a 'gang' to save themselves from being exploited and bullied by older boys.

Street children's erratic working hours and work (rag picking, sweeping in trains, working in tea-stalls etc) make them prone to intense physical strain and harassment. They try to cope by using drugs like chewing tobacco ('gutka') drinking 'whitener' solution, ganja etc. Case studies showed that children reported "smoking makes them alert", "drinking solution make them forget their fatigue and get refreshed". They missed their homes and families, remembering those with whom they were attached to like their mothers, sisters. These thoughts were depressing and made them cry and withdrawn.

Police harassment and abuse by older street boys was painful. However, they tried to forget these incidences and moved from one place to another. Peer support was found to be very essential, which gives a street child support and protection. Sharing and talking with each other they are able to survive in the harsh conditions. Those children assisted by the *NGOs* started sharing their problems with the facilitator. A child's own attitude toward him and positive psychosocial characteristics were related to self-related resources resulting in resilience. Some of these are sense of responsibility toward the family, warm feelings towards some family members like mother, hope for future, saving money, learning vocational skills etc. It is emphasized in the ecological model (Berns, 2004) that competence and skills of the street child in coping with the stress would affect his/her adjustment and may pose high risk for drug use and impede the psycho-social development.

Many researches explaining the street child phenomenon in detail highlighting the possible causes and the negative outcomes of street life. However little empirical work has been dome on the social networks of street children which helps them to survive the harsh realities of street (Kipke, Montgomery, Siman and Unger, 1997). These street children often congregate in groups which are differentiated by degrees of involvement in deviant activities and amplify the pressure on child to use alcohol and drugs or to engage in unprotected sex (Ennett, Bailey and Federman, 1999; Kipke et.al, 1997). It's however important to acknowledge that peers on the street often play dual roles in the life of a homeless adolescent. They are sources of nurturance and support as well as of risk. These "street families" provide both physical and emotional association as well as protection from the many dangers of street life (Hagan and McCarthy, 1997; Whitebeck and Hoyt, et at., 1999).

Addressing the problem of street children would emphasize the development of close, guardian-like relationship between resource persons (of govt. and non-govt. Organizations) and the homeless youth (Cauce et al, 1994). Such trusting relationships with adults on the street appear to serve a protective function and afford to potential to break the cycle of victimization and re-victimization. It is critical to recognize, that children and adolescent homelessness represents a failure of our society on multiple levels: social, political and economic. These structures of the society should address this issue and embark upon a change, however to have a desired attack on the problem, we need to learn to intervene effectively. Programmes that focus on acquiring effective social skills, making positive attachments and access to health, welfare, educational, vocational and recreational services have potential to ameliorate some stress that street children may experience.

REFERENCES

Aderinto, A.A. (2002) *Social correlates and coping measures of street children: A comparative study of street and non-street children in south-western Nigeria.Child Abuse and Neglect* 24: 199-213.

Aptekar, L. (1988). *Street Children of Cale.* Durham,NC: Duke University Press

Baker, R., Panter-B, C. and Todd, A. (1997). Homeless street boys in Nepal: Their demography and life- style. *Journal of Comparative Family Studies.* University of Calgary, Alberta, Canada.

Berns, M. (2004). *Child Family. School. Community: Socialization and support.* Wadsworth: Learning, USA.

Butterflies. (1997). *History of Butterflies programmes of street working children.* Report by Butterflies, NGO, New Delhi.

Clatts, M.C. and Davis, W.R. (1999). A demographic and behavioural profile of homeless youth in New York City: Implications for AIDS outreach prevention. *Medline Anthropological Qbarlerly* 13, 365-74.

Cauce, A.M., Morgan, C.J., Lohr,Y., Wagner, V., Moore, E., Wurzbacher, K., Weeden, K., Tomlin, S., and Blamchard, T. (1994). Effectiveness of intensive case management for homeless adolescents : Results of a 3-moth follow-up. *Journal of Emotional and behavioral Disorders*, 2, 219-227.

D'Lima, H. and Oosalia, R. (1992). *Street children of Bombay: A situational analysis.* Noida: National Labour Institute.

Dohrenwend, B.S. (1978). Social stress and community psychology. *American Journal of Community Psychology,* 6, 1-14.

Ennett, S.T., Bailey, S. L. and Fedennan, E. B (1999). Social network characteristics associated with risky behaviors among runaways and homeless youth. *Journal of Health and Social Behavior,* 40, 63-78.

Ferrari, A. (2003). Rehabilitation of street children in Africa: An experience in Nairobi, Kenya. In J. Gerald Young et al. (Eds.), *Brain, Culture and Development* (pp. 160-167). New Delhi: Macmillan India Ltd.

Gelles, R J. (1998). The youngest victims: Violence toward children. In R Bergen and Kennedy (Eds.), *Issues in intimate violence* (pp.5-24). Thousands Oaks, CA: Sage.

Greenblatt, M., and Robertson,M. (1993). Life-styles, adaptive strategies, and sexual behaviors of homeless adolescents. *Hospital and Community Psychiatry,* 44, 1177-1180.

Hagan,J., and McCarthy, B. (1997). Mean streets: Youth crime and homelessness. New York: Cambridge University Press.

Invernizzi, A. (2001). The work of children is not only work. In Manfted, L, Overwien.B, and Recknage, A (Eds.) *Working children's protagonism: Social movements and empowerment in Latin America, Africa and India.* (c) London: IKO.

Jackson, RK. and McBride, W.D. (1985). *Understanding Street gangs.* Sacramento: Custom.

Janus, M., McCormack, A., Burgess,A., and Hartman,C.(1987). *Adolescent runaways: Causes and consequences.* Lexington, MA: Lexington.

Kipke, M.D., Montgomery, S.B., Simon, T.R. and Unger, J.B. (1997). Homeless youth: Drug use patterns and HIV risk profiles according to peer group affiliation. *AIDS and behaviour,* 1, 247-259.

Kotch, J.B., Muller, Gi.O.and Blakely, C. H. (1999). Understanding the origins and incidence of spousal violence in North America. In T. P.Gullotta and S. J. McElhaney (Eds.), *Violence in homes and communities* (pp.1-38). Thousands Oaks CA: Sage.

Lalor, K. J. (1999). Street children: A comparative perspective. *Child Abuse and Neglect,* 23, 759-770.

Manihara, S. (1997) Street children: An International problem. In R. Barna (Ed.), My Home is today. *Child in News,* 1, 120-140.

Matchinda, P. (1991). *Child Abuse and Neglect.* Mar 23: 245-255.

Mustafa, M. and Sharma, M. (1996). *Child labour in India: A bitter truth,* New Delhi: Deep and Deep.

Myres, R. (1992). *The twelve who survive: Strengthening programmes of early childhood development in the third World.* London: Routldge.

Panicker, R and Nangia, P. (1992). *Working and street children Delhi,* Nodia: National Labour Institute

Panter-Brick, C., Todd, A. and Baker, R.(1996). Growth status of homeless Nepali boys: Do they differ from rural and controls? *Social Sciences and Medicine,* 42, Pergamon Press, Oxford, UK.

Rothman, J., and Davis, T (1985). *Status offenders in Los Angeles Country: Focus on runaway and homeless youth.* School of social welfare, Los Angeles, CA: University of California.

Salaam Baalak Trust (1998). *SBT-Annual Report*. NGO, New Delhi.

Sampa, A. (1998). *Journal of Psychology in Africa, South of Sahara, the Caribbean and Afro Latin America,* 2, 1-23.

Segal, U. A. and Ashtekar, A. (1994). Child *Abuse and Neglect,* 18, 957-967.

Suda, C. (1997). *Child Abuse Review,* Vol. 6, 199-217.

Tellez,V.S and Abramo, H. (1985) "Experiencia urbana trabajoe identidad. Apuntes a una investigation sobre menores proletario en Sao Paulo", in Carrion, D Vainstoc, A (eds.) La ciudad y los ninos. Quito.

Tucker, V., Tucker, S., Phogat P., and Pandey A. (2002). Effectiveness of participatory techniques with street children for planning intervention programmes. In V.Veeraraghavan., S. Singh and K. Khandelwal (Eds.), *The Child in the New Millennium* (pp. 136-141), New Delhi: Mosiac Books.

UNICEF (2004). *The State of the World's Children,* 2004, New York: UNICEF.

Whitebeck, L.B., Hoyt, D.R., and Yoder, K.A., CAuce, A.M., and Pradise, M. (1999) *Deviant Behavior and victimization among homeless and runaway adolescents.* Technical Report. Ames, IA : University of Iowa.

World Health Organization (1999). *Report of the Consultation on Child labour prevention*, Geneva: WHO.

11

Perceptual and Attitudinal Influences in HIV Risk

—Sandeep Singh and Sunil Saini

HIV/AIDS is growing rapidly in developing countries like India and Africa. Of the world's total cases, it is estimated that, by 2000, 75% were in developing countries; and by 2010, as many as 90% of cases will be in developing countries (Stine, 1995). The situation become more deleterious for country like India, where even basic infrastructure e.g. in health care sector have not been developed adequately. Recent estimates of National AIDS Control Society (NACO) indicate that death toll due to HIV/AIDS, particularly among youth is increasing day by day in India. Youth population being highest in India, is most vulnerable to world's most severe epidemic HIV/AIDS.

The rates of infection are increasing day by day due to lack of knowledge, risk perception and unhealthy attitude towards alcohol abuse, drug abuse, and sexual contacts. Since the onset of first HIV infection in early 80's, drug abuse and sexual route have been the most frequent cause of HIV infection. Most research to date on HIV infection has been in clinical and medicine. There is lack of studies on perceptual and attitudinal domain of HIV risk in India as well as in global research. Research has also shown that people in India have very biased perception and attitude towards sexual issues, for example, Chowdhury and Gill (1993) reported that of their sample (716 students of 12 Grade), 18.5% agreed that only prostitutes get AIDS, 11.8% agreed that only homosexuals get AIDS, 35.6% agreed that anybody can get AIDS, 67% reported that they were not the type of person to contract AIDS, 36% of the students believed that they could do little to protect themselves against

AIDS, and 17% of the boys and 9.17% of the girls would actually risk AIDS rather than miss the chance of having sex with an attractive stranger. It means that perceptual and attitudinal influences may be very significant in HIV risk. The present research examines how perceptual influence like risk perception in HIV infection and attitudinal influences like attitude toward alcohol, drug and sex affect HIV risk vulnerability. The findings will be very informative for parents, teachers, policy makers, and professionals working in the area of HIV education.

Risk perception has been identified as the most important risk factor in health behaviour particularly in case of HIV risk (Prohaska, 'Albrecht, Levy, Sugrue, and Kim, 1990; Singh and Saini, 2007). "Optimistic" bias is a central theoretical issue for adolescent research on perception of risk. Optimistic bias theory, a fundamental part of the cognitive approach in social psychology, says that many people think along the lines of "AIDS/STDs/pregnancy/cancer etc. can't happen to me" with a consequence that many systematically underestimate their risk in comparison to the real risk. The bias toward underestimation of risk may include the difficulty in realizing that an illness that may affect you in later years needs to be actively prevented today, and therefore it is treated as a very distant possibility. Adolescents tend to undervalue their own risk, certainly when they compare themselves with adults, but even in comparison to their own peers (Macintyre, Rutenberg, Brown, and Karim, 2004).

HIV risk perception has been found to be associated with number of risky factors e.g., number of sexual partner, knowledge of sexual partner's past sexual behaviour, fear of AIDS, shame associated with having AIDS, community perception of AIDS risk, knowing someone with AIDS, discussing AIDS at home, closeness of parent-child relationships, religious affiliation, and peer pressure (Macintyre et al., 2004; Prohaska et al., 1990; Singh and Saini, 2007) which further put vulnerable to HIV risk. Tikoo, Bollman, and Bergen (1995) also noted that there is paucity of information regarding the spread and progression of HIV, level of knowledge, attitudes, and behaviors in Indian population. People will only carry out appropriate preventative behaviours if they accurately perceive the behaviours they engage in to be risky. The most difficult question is how to evaluate HIV risk perception; we did not find any valid scale for this purpose. The scale used to assess HIV risk perception has been developed by the authors in their previous study (Singh and Saini, 2007) in which it had shown significant relationship with peer pressure and attitude towards alcohol and drug abuse.

Attitude toward alcohol use and drug abuse has consistently being found to be associated with HIV infection. Research has shown that attitudinal bias towards alcohol and drug abuse is highly related with HIV risk perception (Auerbach, Wypijewska, and Brodie, 1994; Singh and Saini, 2007). When there is a positive attitude towards alcohol and drug use, vulnerability towards HIV infection increases and younger age is most vulnerable to this. Leigh and Stall (1993) have found that both casual and chronic drug users are more likely to engage in high risk behaviour, such as unprotected sex that further increases the HIV risk.

Attitude towards sex also plays a very significant role in HIV risk. It is generally seen that youths involved in sexual relationships thinks that HIV infection can not happen to them and do not involve in preventive practices. They have unhealthy attitude towards sex, for example, advocacy for sex before marriage, pornography, number of sex partners, free sex with romantic partners, sex is not sin, etc., which in turn have strong relationship with HIV risk. Research has shown that heterosexual relationships are largest infection category for women and second largest for men (Centre for Disease Control and Prevention, 2005, 2007). Furthermore, individuals tend to believe that it is highly unlikely that their partner engages in behaviours that would put them at risk for HIV infection (O'Donnell, San Doval, Vornfrett, and Dejong, 1994). Therefore, attitudinal influences towards sexual behaviour are very important to examine for the better understanding of risky sexual behaviour in HIV risk.

Objectives:

1. To study the relationship between HIV risk perception and attitude towards alcohol and drug abuse.

2. To study the relationship between HIV risk perception and attitude towards sexuality.
3. To study the gender differences in HIV risk perception, attitude towards alcohol and drug abuse and sexuality.

Hypotheses

4. There will be a significant relationship between HIV risk perception and attitude towards alcohol and drug abuse.
5. There will be a significant relationship between HIV risk perception and attitude towards sexuality.
6. There will be significant gender differences in HIV risk perception, attitude towards alcohol and drug abuse and sexuality.

METHOD

Sample:

The sample of 180 (100 girls and 80 boys) was taken from 10+2 level and undergraduate students from schools and colleges of district Hisar. All the students were in the age range of 16-19 years and were from same socio-economic background.

Measures

HIV risk perception (Singh and Saini, 2007): It is a 25-items questionnaire developed by Singh and Saini to assess HIV risk perception among adolescents. It is a 5-point Lickert scale with 1 (strongly disagree) to 5 (strongly agree). Higher the score, higher will be the risk perception of an individual towards HIV infection. Cronbach's alpha was reported to be .87.

Alcohol and drug attitude scale (Saini and Singh, 2007): It is a 31-items questionnaire developed by Saini and Singh to assess attitude towards alcohol and drug abuse. It is a 5-point Lickert scale with 1 (strongly disagree) to 5 (strongly agree). Higher the score, higher will be the risk perception of an individual towards HIV infection. Cronbach's alpha was reported to be .82.

Attitude towards sexuality (Abraham, 1997): It is a 31-items questionnaire developed by Saini and Singh to assess attitude towards alcohol and drug abuse. It is a 5-point Lickert scale with 1 (strongly disagree) to 5 (strongly agree). In the present research we are using two out of five subscales of the scale i.e. attitude towards sexuality. Higher the score, higher will be the risk perception of an individual towards HIV infection.

Statistical analysis: Product moment correlation coefficient and t-test was used to analyse the data.

Procedure:

Participants were given proper instructions to fill the questionnaire and were told about the purpose of the study. Scoring was done according to the instructions provided for the each questionnaire and results were analysed by using SPSS package.

Results and discussion

The findings indicated that HIV risk perception was highly correlated with attitude towards alcohol and drug abuse and attitude towards sex and the results are shown in Table 1. The findings suggested that HIV risk perception has highly significant relation with attitude towards alcohol use and drug use (.467**) and sexuality (.448**) that means perceptual and attitudinal influences have a strong relation with HIV risk among adolescents which were our first and second hypotheses and hence proved (Table 1). When we look over the reasons behind these strong relations this might be due to that industrialization, rapid urbanization, dual earner family, emergence of nuclear families in India, people do not have proper time for themselves as well as for their children resulting in poor parent-child relationship, which in turn, leads to perception of risk relating to HIV infection, harmful effects of drinking and drug abuse and early and non-protective sexual relationships. Previous researches have also supported the present findings (Macintyre et al., 2004).

TABLE 1: Correlation Matrix

Variables	*HIV risk perception*	*Alcohol and drug attitude*	*Sexuality attitude*
HIV risk perception	—	467**	.448**
Alcohol and drug attitude	—	—	.399**
Sexuality attitude	—	—	—

Attitude towards alcohol and drug was found to highly related with sexuality attitude (.399**) which was also consistent with the previous findings (Weinhardt and Carey, 2000; MacDonald, Zanna, Fong, 1996; Testa, 2002) suggesting that alcohol and drug abuse related with unhealthy sexual relationship which further put an individual vulnerable to HIV risk. Unprotected sexual behaviour is the most frequent cause of HIV infection around the world. When it is combined with alcohol and drug use that further increases the vulnerability of HIV infection.

One of our hypothesis assumed gender differences in HIV risk perception, alcohol and drug abuse and sexual attitude, the obtained results indicated that there was significant gender difference on HIV risk perception ($t=3.88$, $p < .01$), attitude towards alcohol, drug ($t=3.45$, $p < .01$) and sex ($t=5.67$, $p < .01$), and the results were in expected direction and are shown in Table 2. The findings revealed that mean score on all the three variables was high in boys as compared to girls indicating that boys have more HIV risk perception and attitude towards alcohol, drug and sex.

TABLE 2: Gender differences in HIV risk perception, attitude towards alcohol, drug and sex

Variables	*Male*		*Female*		
	Mean	*SD*	*Mean*	*SD*	*t-value*
HIV risk perception	77.562	11.35	72.15	7.09	3.88*
Alcohol and drug attitude	92.73	12.32	86.67	11.12	3.45**
Sexuality attitude	94.15	8.81	85.33	11.46	5.67**

These findings are consistent with previous research also noted similar gender differences on risk perception (Barden-

O'Fallon et al., 2004; Maswanya et al., 1999) suggesting that boys have more risky perception, attitude towards alcohol and drug abuse and sexuality as compared to girls. The high significant gender differences on HIV risk perception, attitude towards alcohol and drug and sexual behaviour may also be due to that girls might have inhibited their responses as Indian cultures do not allow girls to talk on these issues.

To conclude, the results of the current study demonstrate that adolescents often have inaccurate perception towards HIV infection, and attitude towards alcohol and drug abuse and sexual behaviour. The current study was conducted on college and university students, more researches on diverse populations are needed to generalize the results.

One limitation of the study that data were collected only from urban areas, rural area students should also have been included in the study as students from rural area are most likely to have inaccurate perception towards HIV infection and attitude towards issues like HIV infection, alcohol and drug use and sexual behaviour.

Despite limitation, the study also has implications for intervention targeting adolescent boys and girls in colleges and university who have most risky perception and attitude towards alcohol, drug and sexual behaviour as indicated in the current study. The findings further suggest that wide spread HIV infection might be due to that individual does not perceive the partner's sexual behaviour as risky, indicating his/her inaccurate perception. Research has also shown that many people in committed relationships do not feel that they are at risk for HIV infection (Exner, Seal, and Ernhardt, 1997), so they tend not to engage in HIV prevention practices with their primary partners (Bowen, Williams, McCoy, and McCoy, 2001; Misovich, Fisher, and Fisher, 1997). Therefore, everyone should have this perception that anybody may have HIV infection and should take all possible preventive measures. The most important implication of the current research is that targeting risky perception and attitude towards alcohol, drugs and sexual behaviour, effective intervention can be provided to youths at school and college level to help reduce the further spread of HIV infection in India.

REFERENCES

Auerbach, G.D., Wypijewska, C., and Brodie, K.H. (1994). AIDS and behaviour: An integrated approach. Washington, DC: National Academy Press.

Barden-O'Fallon, J.L., deGraft-Johnson, J., Thomas, B., Sulzbach, S., Benson, A., and Tsui, A.O. (2004). Factors associated with HIV/AIDS knowledge and risk perception in rural Malawi. *AIDS and Behavior, 8*, 131-140.

Bowen, A. M., Williams, M., McCoy, H. V., and McCoy, C. B. (2001). Crack smokers' intention to use condoms with loved partners: Intervention development using the theory of reasoned action, condom beliefs, and processes of change. *AIDS Care*, 13, 579–594.

Centers for Disease Control and Prevention (2005). HIV/AIDS surveillance report: Cases of HIV infection and AIDS in the United States and dependent areas. Retrieved from http://www.cdc.gov/hiv/topics/surveillance/resources/ reports/2005report/default.htm.

Centers for Disease Control and Prevention (2007). CDC HIV/AIDS fact sheet: A glance at the HIV/AIDS epidemic. Retrieved from http://www.cdc.gov/hiv/resources/ factsheets/At-A-Glance.htm.

Chowdhury, S., and Gill, F. P. T. (1993). *A study of knowledge, beliefs, and attitudes regarding AIDS, STDs and human sexuality among senior secondary students in Delhi.* Unpublished manuscript.

Exner, T. M, Seal, D. W., and Ernhardt, A. A. (1997). A review of HIV interventions for at-risk women. *AIDS and Behaviour, 1,* 93–124.

Leigh, B., and Stall. R. (1993). Substance use and risk sexual behaviour for exposure to HIV: Issue in methodology, interpretation, and prevention. *American Psychologist, 48,* 1035-1043.

MacDonald, T.K., Zanna, M.P., and Fong, G.T. (1996). Why common sense goes out the window: Effects of alcohol on intentions to use condoms. *Personality and Social Psychology Bulletin, 22,* 763-75.

Macintyre, K., Rutenberg, N., Brown, L., and Karim, A. (2004). Understanding perceptions of HIV risk among adolescents in KwaZulu-Natal. *AIDS and Behaviour*, 8, 237–250.

Maswanya, E. S., Moji, K., Horiguchi, I., Nagata, K., Aoyagi, K., Honda, S., and Takemoto, T. (1999). Knowledge, risk perception of AIDS and reported sexual behaviour among students in secondary schools and colleges in Tanzania. *Health Education Research, 14,*185-196,

Misovich, S. L., Fisher, J. D., and Fisher, W. A. (1997). Close relationships and elevated HIV risk behavior: Evidence and possible underlying psychological processes. *Review of General Psychology, 1,* 72–107.

O'Donnell, L., San Doval, A., Vornfrett, R., and Dejong, W. (1994). Reducing AIDS and other STDs among inner-city Hispanics: The use of qualitative research in development of video-based patient education. *AIDS Education and Prevention, 6,* 140–153.

Prohaska, T. R., Albrecht, G., Levy, A., Sugrue, N., and Kim, J. H. (1990). Determinants of self-perceived risk for AIDS. *Journal of Health and Social Behavior, 31,* 384–394.

Singh, S., and Saini, S. (2007). HIV risk perception in relation to peer pressure and drug abuse behaviour. *Indian Journal of Sexually Transmitted Diseases,* Vol (28) 53-4.

Tikoo, M., Bollman, S. R., and Bergen, M. B. (1995). Knowledge level of youth in India regarding human sexuality and AIDS. *Journal of Sex and Marital Therapy, 21,* 246-252.

Testa, M. (2002). The impact of men's alcohol consumption on perpetration of sexual aggression. *Clinical Psychology Review, 22,* 1239-63.

Weinhardt, L.S., and Carey, M.P. (2000). Does alcohol lead to sexual risk behaviour? Findings from event-level research. *Annual Review of Sex Research, 11,* 125-57.

Acknowledgement: The grant for the current research was issued by University Grant Commission (2007-2010), New Delhi.

12

Perceived Stress Among Caregivers of Mentally Handicapped Children : Effects of Sex, Income and Severity of Handicappedness

—Joginder Kairo, Radhey Shyam and Priti Singh

Although mental retardation has now been recognized as distinct from mental illness DSM IV, (Carson, Butcher, Mineka and Hooley, 2008) yet it has got to be free from the stigma attached to it. The birth of an intellectually sub average or below average child has life long implications for the child, his parents, and his entire family. The parents have to face the stigma on the one hand and have to put extra effort on the care giving responsibilities on the other. They have to bear the extra financial burden on care giving beside they are required to adjust their working and social engagements. These add to their stress and strain and put extra demand for coping.

Parenting is a stressful job and some degree of parental stress is experienced by almost all parents, but parenting of child with disabilities require great amount of effort, time and skill therefore it may result into more stress. Studies (e.g. Abidin, 1995) have reported greater amount of parenting stress in parents of children with disabilities than normal children. Beckman (1991) compared parental. Stress of 27 mothers and fathers of children with disabilities with the parental stress of equal number of mothers and fathers of normal children. It was found that mothers generally reported more stress in parent domain than fathers but both parents experienced high level of stress in child domain. Parents of disabled children reported greater amount of parenting stress than parents of normal children in the child and parent domain of parenting stress inventory. Salovita Italina and Leinonen (2003) have emphasized the importance of intervening factors in explaining the stress. In mothers the single most important predictor of parenting stress was the negative definition of the situation while in fathers it was associated with the social acceptance of the child.

Every prospective parent has expectation about the child to be born. Birth of child results into major responsibility on the part of the parent and the family. When the parent and the family members discover that the child is not normal or having certain disabilities it is a kind of shock to them and may result into dismay and disbelief and some of them may not accept it. This may result into anxiety and depression in the parents and other family members (Singer, Song, Hill, and Jaffe, 1990; Blakeney, Moor, Broemling, Hunt, Herndon, and Robson, 1993). It is beyond doubt that birth of a child in the family puts certain responsibilities on the part of parents which may result into parenting stress but the birth of a mentally handicapped child or with other disabilities put greater demands in the form of caring on the parents. It may sometime lead to anxiety about the child's welfare and well-being. Some parents may react differently and may perceive the extra demands as burden on them and their family. To adjust with the extra demands in the form of care in some cases the mothers may have to leave the job which may add financial constrains on the family. Several studies have reported higher level of perceived burden in parents of children with disabilities in the form of care giving (Soyal, 2004) and family functioning (Luircher, Dede, Gitten, Fenhell, and Maria, 1999).

The stress, strain, anxiety, depression, and burden perceived by the parents of mentally handicapped child may vary alongwith variation in the level of mental retardation. It appears that these may increase with the severity of the retardation. But there are studies (e.g. Luircher, et al. 1999) reporting that though the caregivers burden was significantly more in case of the parents of disabled children yet caregivers burden was not simply related to the severity of the child's illness or disability rather it depend more on the parents coping skills and on the level of family functioning.

Thus it is beyond doubt that the presence of a mentally handicapped child in the family certainly add stress, anxiety, depression and the caregivers / parents may perceive increasing level of burden, which in turn may influence their attitude towards them and may also effect their relationship with each other and with the child. If we consider the WHO reports about the incidence of mental retardation we find that there about three percent children who are mentally retarded (Carson, Butcher, Mineka and Hooley, 2008). Moreover, even if we take the statistical probability than there are 2.5 % children with mental retardation in the general population. At present we in India have crossed one billion mark in term of population thus there are about 3 crore affected children and adding both parents there are about 9 crore people who are directly affected by this problem. Thus it is very important to understand the problems of the parents of mentally retarded which may not only help us in understanding their woes, rather children may help us in designing intervention programs for them. Thus the present study was aimed at understanding / assessing the stress as perceived by caregivers of parents of mentally handicapped children. It was also intended to assess the effect of sex of child, income of family and severity of handicapped ness on the perceived stress of the caregivers.

Method

Sample: the study was conducted on a sample of eighty caregivers of mentally handicapped children of both sexes [mean age 14.14 (SD=7.06) years] selected randomly out of those who visited department of Psychiatry Pt. B.D. Sharma PGIMS Rohtak. The caregivers were from both rural as well as urban areas of Haryana.

Tools:

1. Seguin Form Board (Goel, 1984) was used for measuring intelligence of the mentally handicapped subjects.

2. Family interview for stress and coping (Girimaji, Srinath, Seshadri, et.al, 1999). It has two sections. It is a semi structured interview schedule to study stress and coping in families of children with mental retardation. Section I measures perceived

stress (daily care, emotional, social and financial etc) and section II is for measuring mediators or coping strategies (awareness, attitude, expectations, rearing practices and social support). Section I was used in this study. It has eleven sub scales which include extra inputs of care, decreased leisure time, neglect of others, disturbed behaviour, personal distress, marital problems, other interpersonal problems, effects on sibs and other family members, altered social life, social embarrassment and financial implications. The caregivers were rated on a 5 point scale (no or minimal stress to very high level of stress). The absence of stress was rated as zero and a score of four was given for a very high level of stress.

Procedure:

All the mentally handicapped children were administered Seguin Form Board for assessing their intelligence level. After this the caregivers were interviewed for assessing their perceived stress in various areas (as described under tools). Scoring was done as per standard procedure for each test. Data were analysed by employing simple ANOVA in addition to measures of central tendency and variability with post hoc Duncan's test wherever required.

Results: and Discussion:

The objective of the study was to examine the effect of sex of the child, income of the family and level of mental retardation on the perceived stress of the caregivers of mentally retarded children. The data were analysed by simple ANOVA with Duncan's post hoc test wherever required and the results alongwith means and SD's are given in Table 1, 2, and 3.

TABLE-1: Means, S.D.'s of perceived of caregivers along with F values

	Sex	*Mean*	*SD*	*F*
Extra care	Male	2.76	.80	
	Female	2.62	.69	.47
Decreased leisure time	Male	2.37	.81	
	Female	2.11	.70	.16
Neglect of other	Male	2.25	.80	

	Female	1.89	.64	.12
Distressed behavior	Male	2.17	.80	
	Female	1.89	.64	.12
Personal distress	Male	2.04	.80	
	Female	1.71	.71	.11
Marital problems	Male	.06	.30	
	Female	.04	.19	.77
Interpersonal problems	Male	.28	.49	
	Female	.15	.36	.23
Effects on sibs and	Male	.46	.81	
other family members	Female	.37	.68	.62
Altered social life	Male	1.69	1.02	
	Female	1.78	.89	.69
Social embarrassment	Male	1.83	.64	
	Female	1.67	.68	.28
Financial problems	Male	1.39	.86	
	Female	1.33	.83	.78
Awareness	Male	2.50	.57	
	Female	2.26	.81	.13

As far as the sex of the child was concerned, it was found (Table-4) that it had no effect on the perceived stress of the caregivers in all the eleven areas. It indicates that diagnosis of mental retardation itself is important no matter whether it is male or female child. Though it appears a little bit contrary to the expectation in the sense that in our society the birth of a female child itself is considered stressful and several state governments (particularly in North India) are struggling to counter the problem of adverse sex ratio for female. But in case of child with disability sex of the child have had no effect.

TABLE-2: Means, S.D.'s of perceived stress of low, middle and high income group caregivers with F ratio's and Post hoc comparisions

	Group	*Mean*	*SD*	*F*
Extra care	Low	02.74	0.73	
	Middle	02.73	0.81	1.31
	High	02.50	0.67	

Decreased leisure time	Low	2.64a	.76	
	Middle	2.35a	.70	5.89**
	High	2.86b	.83	
Neglect of other	Low	2.47a	.61	
	Middle	2.23ab	.69	3.79*
	High	1.86b	.72	
Distressed behaviour	Low	2.21a	.63	
	Middle	2.03a	.77	4.57**
	High	1.54b	.80	
Personal distress	Low	2.21a	.63	
	Middle	2.03a	.77	4.57**
	High	1.54b	.80	
Marital problems	Low	.11	.46	
	Middle	.05	.22	.78
	High	.00	.00	
Interpersonal problems	Low	.46a	.61	
	Middle	.15b	.36	3.70*
	High	.18b	.39	
Effects on sibs and other family members	Low	.79a	.98	
	Middle	.28b	.68	3.01*
	High	.41ab	.67	
Altered social life	Low	2.11a	.81	
	Middle	1.80b	1.04	4.82**
	High	1.23b	.81	
Social embarrassment	Low	1.84	.69	
	Middle	1.83	.71	.71
	High	1.64	.49	
Financial problems	Low	1.74	.99	
	Middle	1.30	.72	2.58
	High	1.18	.85	
Awareness	Low	2.63a	.50	
	Middle	2.53a	.64	5.45**
	High	2.05b	.72	

*Significant at .05 level
**Significant at .01 level.
a, b, c subscripts indicate significant means differences similar/same subscript indicate absence of significant difference.

The income of every caregiver was recorded and three groups were formed on the basis of income. Those having monthly/ income Rs 5000 /- were taken in the first group. The subjects having monthly income more than Rs 5000 /- but less than 10,000 were taken in the second group and those above Rs 10,000 /- were taken in the third group. The means and standard deviations of perceived stress in various areas along with F values are given in Table-2 for all the eleven sub scales. The caregivers in the three income groups viz lower, middle and higher scored, respectively 2.64, 2.35 and 1.86 mean perceived stresses due to decrease in leisure time. The F value was 5.89, (df 2, 78 p<.01) and was significant at .01 level of confidence. Post hoc Duncan's test revealed that the caregivers of the higher income group scored less on perceived stress due to decreased leisure time than both the lower and middle income group caregivers which in themselves did not differ (Table-2).

The higher income group caregivers scored significantly less than both the lower and middle income groups' on disturbed behaviour, personal distress and awareness subscales of perceived stress. The lower and middle income groups didn't differ from each other (Table-2). Perceived stress due to neglect of others was found to be significantly different among the caregivers of three income groups (F=3.79, df 2, 78, p<.05). Post Duncan's comparison revealed that the lower income group perceived significantly more stress than the high income group. The lower and middle income group caregivers as well as the middle and high group did not differ (Table-2). In case of the perceived effect of mental retardation of the child on other family members and siblings the mean stress scores of the caregivers differed significantly (F=3.01, df 2, 78, p<.01). Post hoc Duncan's comparisons revealed that lower income group perceived significantly more stress due to effect on siblings and other family members than the middle income group. The higher income group caregivers did not differ from the lower as well as middle income group caregivers (Table-2). The perceived stress due to altered social life because of child having mental handicappedness among the three group was significantly different (F = 4.82, df = 2, 78 p<.01). Duncan's post hoc mean comparison revealed that the low income group caregiver perceived significantly more stress due effect on social life compared to both the middle as well as lower income group caregivers, which did not differ from each other. The findings can be interpreted in the light of the argument put forward that the persons in the lower and probably in the middle income group have less helping hand for caring the child whereas in the higher income group they may make some arrangement hence less perceived stress. Surprisingly, the caregivers in the higher income group scored less than lower and middle income groups on awareness component of the scale.

The study was also intended to assess the effect of level of mental retardation of the child on perceived stress of the caregivers. The means and S.D.'s along with F values and post hoc Duncan's comparison are given in Table-3. Level of mental retardation was found to have significant effect on all the sub scales of perceived stress of caregivers except financial, marital interpersonal problems and effect on siblings and other family members. It also had significant effect on level of awareness of the caregivers. Perceived stress in the areas of extra input of care was significantly different ($F = 11.57$, $df = 4, 76$ $p<.01$). Post hoc Duncan's mean comparison revealed that the caregivers of children suffering from severe and profound level of mental retardation perceived more stress than the caregivers of children of moderate, mild and borderline mental retardation. The level of mental retardation of the child also had significant ($F = 22.92$, $df = 4, 76$, $p<.01$) effect on perceived stress of caregivers in the area of decreased leisure time. The caregivers of children of severe and profound mentally retarded children experienced more stress than the caregivers of borderline, mild and moderately retarded children. Caregivers of moderately retarded children perceived more stress than caregivers of borderline cases. Similar was the case of perceived stress in the area of neglect of others (Table-3). The caregivers of severely and profoundly retarded children experienced more personal distress than the caregivers of moderate, mild and borderline level of mental retardation. Caregivers of moderate and mildly retarded children also experienced higher level of personal distress than the borderline children (Table-3). Severity of retardation was also found to have significant impact on distressed behaviour of the caregivers ($F = 15.15$ $df = 4, 76$ $p<.01$). The caregivers of severely retarded children displayed

TABLE-3: Means, S.D.'s of perceived stress of caregivers of children with different levels of Mental Retardation

	Level of MR	*Mean*	*SD*	*F*
Extra care	Profound	3.57a	.53	
	Severe	3.78a	.67	
	Moderate	2.63b	.58	
	Mild	2.43b	.51	
	Borderline	2.17b	.71	
Decreased leisure time	Profound	3.29a	.49	
	Severe	3.00a	.59	
	Moderate	2.17b	.48	22.92**
	Mild	1.93bc	.27	
	Borderline	1.16c	.70	
Neglect of other	Profound	2.86a	.69	
	Severe	2.89a	.47	
	Moderate	2.17b	.48	18.88*
	Mild	1.86bc	.66	
	Borderline	1.50c	.51	
Distressed behaviour	Profound	2.43ab	.53	
	Severe	2.83a	.71	
	Moderate	2.08bc	.41	15.15**
	Mild	1.71cd	.61	
	Borderline	1.44d	.77	
Personal distress	Profound	2.71a	.95	
	Severe	2.44a	.62	
	Moderate	1.88b	.43	10.07**
	Mild	1.86b	.66	
	Borderline	1.28c	.75	
Marital problems	Profound	000	000	
	Severe	.11	.47	
	Moderate	000	000	.51 NS
	Mild	.07	.26	
	Borderline	.05	.24	
Interpersonal problems	Profound	.29	.49	
	Severe	.39	.61	
	Moderate	.17	.38	**1.68 NS**

	Mild	.36	.49	
	Borderline	.05	.24	
Effects on sibs and other family members	Profound	.42	1.13	
	Severe	.67	.91	
	Moderate	.42	.65	1.33 NS
	Mild	.57	.85	
	Borderline	.11	.47	
Altered social life	Profound	2.71a	.95	
	Severe	2.22ab	1.00	
	Moderate	1.79b	.66	10.76**
	Mild	1.64b	.74	
	Borderline	.78c	.73	
Social embarrassment	Profound	2.43 a	.53	
	Severe	2.17 ab	.62	
	Moderate	1.75 bc	.53	7.44**
	Mild	1.38c	.63	
	Borderline	1.50c	.51	
Financial problems	Profound	1.43	1.13	
	Severe	1.78	.94	
	Moderate	1.25	.61	1.47 NS
	Mild	1.21	.89	
	Borderline	1.22	.81	
Awareness	Profound	3.00 a	000	
	Severe	2.89 a	.32	
	Moderate	2.62 a	.49	17.05**
	Mild	1.93 b	.47	
	Borderline	1.83 b	.71	

*Significant at .05 level.

**Significant at .01 level.

more distressed behaviour than the caregivers of moderate, mild and borderline children. The caregivers of mild and moderate, severe and profound children however did not differ in terms of distressed behaviour. Level of mental retardation of children also had significant effect on perceived stress of altered social life (F = 10.76 df = 4, 76, p<.01) and social embarrassment (F = 7.44, df = 4, 76, p<.01). Post hoc Duncan's mean comparison revealed that caregivers of profoundly retarded children experienced significantly more altered social life than caregivers of moderate, mild and borderline retarded children. However caregivers of severely retarded children did not differ in terms of perceived stress due to altered social life from those mild and moderate level. Caregivers of profoundly retarded children perceived more social embarrassment than the caregivers of moderate, mild and borderline level retarded children. The caregivers of severely retarded children perceived more social embarrassment than the caregivers of mild and borderline level mentally retarded children. Caregivers of severe, moderate, mild and borderline retarded children did not differ with each other in terms of social embarrassment. Level of awareness of caregivers of profound, severe and moderately retarded children displayed higher level awareness than mild and borderline children. Caregivers of profound, severe and moderately retarded children as well as mild and borderline retardation however displayed equal level of awareness about mental retardation.

Several studies (e.g. Beckman, 1991, Abidin, 1995, Majumdar, Pereira and Fernandes, 2005) have reported significantly greater stress in parents of mentally retarded and children with other disabilities. It is beyond doubt that these children put extra demands in terms of care and other responsibilities and consequently perceive greater stress. The present study however was aimed at assessing the effect of sex and level of mental retardation of the child and income of the caregivers on the perceived stress. It was found that sex of the child have had no effect on perceived stress in any of the area where as caregiver's income has significant effect on decreased leisure time, neglect of others, distressed behaviour, personal distress, interpersonal problems, effect on siblings and other family members social life. Similarly, level of mental retardation was also found to have significant effect on caregiver's stress in almost all the areas excepting, marital, interpersonal financial problems and effect on siblings and other family members. In almost all cases the caregivers of children having severe and profound level retardation perceived more stress than those of moderate, mild and borderline retardation. It may be because of the greater amount of efforts required for the care of these children as compared to the others.

On the basis of the findings of the study it can be concluded that the sex of the child having mental retardation does not matter on the other hand it is the retardation itself which matters. Income of the caregivers does have impact on the perceived stress of the caregivers. Similarly level of mental retardation has variable effect on perceived stress of the caregivers. Further studies however, are required to understand the role of these factors on larger samples selected on random basis.

REFERENCES

Abidin, R.R. EBD. (1995). *Parenting stress index* (3rd edition) New York: Psychological Assessment Resourses.

Beckman, P.J. (1991). Comparisons of mothers and fathers perceptions of the effect of young children with and without disabilities. *American Journal of Mental Retardation,* 95, 585-595.

Blakeney, P., Moore, P., Bromeling, L., Hunt, R., Herndon, D.N. and Robinson, M. (1993). Parental stress as a cause and effect of paediatric burn injury. *Journal of Burn Care and Rehabilitation,* 14, 58-64.

Carson, R.C., Butcher, J.N., Mineka, S. and Hooley, J.M. (2008). *Abnormal Psychology,* (13th edition), New Delhi: Pearson. Education.

Girimaji, S.C., Srinath, S., Seshadri, S. et. al. (1999). Family interview for stress and coping in mental retardation. *Indian Journal of Psychiatry*, 32, 50-55.

Goel, S.K. (1984). *Guidelines and norms for Seguin form board.* Agra : National Psychological Corporation.

Luircher, J.L., Dede, D.E., Gitten, J.C., Fennell, E., and Maria, B.L. (1999). Parental burden, coping and family functioning in primary caregivers of children with Jorbert Syndrome. *Journal of child Neurology*, 14, 642-648.

Majumdar, M., Pereira, Y.D.S. and Fernandes, J. (2005). Stress and anxiety in parents of mentally retarded children. *Indian Journal of Psychiatry*, 47, 144-147.

Saloviita, T., Italina, M., and Leinonen, E. (2003). Explaining the parental stress of fathers and mothers caring for a child with intellectual disability: A double ABCX Model, *Journal of Intellectual Disabilities Research,* 47, 300-312.

Singer, L.T., Song, L.Y., Hill, B.P., and Jaffe, A.C. (1990). Stress and depression in mothers of failure to thrive children. *Journal of Pediatric Psychology,* 15,711-720.

Soyal, K. (2004). The role of parental burden in child mental health service use: longitudinal study. *American Journal on Child Adolescent Psychiatry*, 1328-33.

SECTION–III : CHILDHOOD PROBLEMS/ DISORDERS AND ASSESSMENT/ DIAGNOSIS

13

Child Psychiatric Assessment

—Hitesh Khurana and Jyoti Kapoor

The psychiatric assessment is the process of collecting information usually from multiple sources about the behavior related problems that would lead to some diagnosis. A clinical psychiatrist often tries to categories the behavioural symptoms in one or other category as per existing diagnostic criteria. This helps him in identification of the problem in a widely acknowledged way and plan treatment on the basis of available guidelines. Diagnosing a disorder means having complete knowledge about it. When a patient comes to a clinician it is important for him to know (i) what disorder he is suffering from. (ii) what factors initiated the problem (iii) what factors are maintaining the problematic behavior (iv) what is the impact on patient's environment.

It is generally seen that any disorder of an individual has a biopsychosocial etiology and it not only affects the individual but to a variable level it has some effect on the patient's environment too. Hence to plan a comprehensive management of any behavioral problem a biopsychosocial approach in the assessment is necessary.

Is Child psychiatric assessment different from the adult assessment?

While conducting an interview with adolescents and older children, the assessment process may quite resemble the adult patient's assessment. But while assessing a younger child, he can't be equated to a miniature adult due to biological or developmental, psychological and social peculiarities. A young child cannot be interviewed in alone like adults. Most of the time children feel comfortable in presence of their parents. Due to the stranger anxiety it might be difficult for the psychiatrist to separate the child from his parents which is quite normal for preschool children. It is almost never that the child would walk to psychiatrist room by himself. Usually he is brought to clinical attention by some referral agency which may be school, parents, pediatrician or any law enforcing authority. The child is not likely to perceive himself as ill and consequently would fail to provide any historical details about the symptoms or reason of referral. His language felicity and may not be adequately communicate their feelings. A child in the examination room is very important source of information since he is the identified patient. A child psychiatrist Psychologist need to sensitive to such peculiarities. He might have to use play room techniques or even some other projective techniques to have in depth understanding about his relationship with important others in the environment and his own perception about the problem.

Adults differing widely in age may behave quite similarly however; such is not the case with children. Due to fast growth spurt and changes in their label of adaptability, behaviour of children at shorter interval may be quite different. Consequently any two children looking similar for age would differ markedly in their behavior. Compared with adults, fear of loneliness and animals is too frequent among children but such behaviour doesn't qualify for phobic disorder. Bed-wetting too similarly be very common at younger age but if persists even in the school age, then it needs proper attention. Therefore a child psychiatrist psychologist has to take into consideration the developmental stage of the child while assessing his behaviour. Any delay in development of behaviour or a behaviour of early childhood persisting till very late in childhood may require special assessment or referral.

A child psychiatrist psychologist generally needs to organize the information from different sources so that he can understand the child's problems in an objective manner. He may also have to collect information from different sources in order to identify the important psychological and environmental variables accounting for a particular behaviour unlike adults where at one or two key informants are generally sufficient to provide historical details about the symptoms. Different sources may provide conflicting information. The psychiatrist/ psychologist also needs to decide credibility of the information. A child with learning difficulties may be reported normal to his parent's but here the teacher's report needs to be given credibility. A child may report perceived threat and internalized feeling of anxiety. However they might not be able to give a proper account due to their limited but age appropriate vocabulary they may tend to somatise their problems. But the care giver can provide a better account of externalizing disorders and aggressive behaviour seen in the child and how it has affected their lives. Information about the siblings, family environment, and relationship problems can also be better provided by the family members

Most of the clinician tend to diagnose the child's problem as per standard diagnostic criteria being followed in the region. Since behaviour of the child under consideration is an outcome of biopsychosocial etiology. Therefore, at the end of assessment it is not necessary that the psychiatrist would reach some psychiatric disorder listed in the classification systems. Diagnosis means complete understanding of the behaviour from biopsychosocial aspects. Therefore the psychiatrist/psychologist may supplement the information he has collected with various standard interviews or rating scales and psychological investigation techniques etc. These tools can provide better information about the understanding about the behaviour and its management strategy which is the aim of any psychiatric assessment.

TABLE 1 : The Purpose of Assessment

To identify the behavioural syndrome
To identify the aetiological factors
To mange the behavioural syndrome/symptoms.

GETTING STARTED

Generally the assessment starts with a referral or request of assessment. In the ordinary situation it is always better to give an appointment for a detailed assessment, that would allow the clinican to take all aspects of the behaviour into consideration. At the time of request it is important for the clinician to see how the request is initiated. Was it just a telephonic call to seek appointment or visit to the emergency psychiatric room. At the time of request how was the complainant's attitude. An open mind to all these questions would help the clinician to decide how and when to conduct the assessment(Cox and Rutter,1985) The person requesting should be given some idea about how the process of evaluation and treatment would go. If any other informantion is also required, it may be asked for at the time of seeking appointment. If the informant expresses any worries, the clinician should be sensitive to adequately addressed these. Spending a little more time in the beginning avoids many problems in future. The child should also be adequately informed about appointment with the psychiatrist and what all would be talked about. He should be prepared to present his perceived part of problem. Many times children have apprehension about the painful procedures or treatment carried out on him as an essential part of visiting a doctor. The clinician should encourage the parents to allay the child's anxieties about being blamed or pained in the doctor's room.

Examining the Reason of Referral

Obviously the child is brought for help seeking due to some problematic behaviour which may have its roots in different parts of child's life. Generally any clinical interview starts with exploring the reason of referral. The care givers coming with the child may perceives the problems from their own point of view. They may have developed their own theories about the problematic behaviour and may even tend to blame the child too for such reasons the clinician here need to take a very neutral and nonjudgmental stand while collecting data about the problematic behaviour. Certain set pattern of enquiry would be helpful to him. He needs to know:

Who initiated the referral?

What was the reaction of others to the request for consultation?

Why referral at this particular **time**?

Since **when** the problematic behaviour has been noticed?

What are the likely factors that initiated and maintained this behaviour?

How the family members and others involved in taking care of child have been coping with the child?

Whose problem most likely it is? Is it the child's (biological/ psychological or the family's/school or peer group(social) or there are multiple sources.

The basic aim of collecting this information is to understand the child problem form the clinician's own theoretical background so as to plan an effective management. The complaints generally need to be organized in a chronology so as not to have any missing link. All precipitating factors aggravating and reveling factors must be specifically addressed. Any kind of behaviour would influence the behaviour of others. The problematic behaviour in this way may set up a vicious circle of behavioural symptoms in all with the child. Their reactions and coping therefore is important to be addressed. Not surprising that the child's behaviour itself may be the outcome of certain family pathology, where the other family members may project their own need of help seeking on the child. Therefore the child psychiatrist needs to understand the family dynamics surrounding the child's behaviour too. It has to be kept in the mind that child is brought to the clininical attention because of some problem. This problem may not essentially be that of the child, quite likely the child is acting in a particular manner because of some problems in his surroundings. Therefore the child's problem may just be the reflection of some problem in family etc. (Shepherd et al 1971) In this way the clinician collects a comprehensive detail about the recognised problematic behaviour about the child. Often this is the experience of the clinician that even the parents living with the child differ a lot in giving their own version of child's problem. It would clearly tell the psychiatrist that both are relating to child in different manners so their relationship with the child too needs to be explored besides examining the child. This all follows the simple axiom that every behaviour has some antecedent factors, nothing is happening by chance. Different problems by different sources of information must have different reasons too. Many times as in case of manchausen's by proxy, the anxious parents may project their own vulnerability and need of dependence on the child and bring him to care for fulfilling their own needs. Most of the time when child's physical symptoms are falling short of explanation such possibility should be suspected. Thus the problem of the child may be the problem of parents and care givers. Poor scholastic performance of child too needs assessment of teching environment. The problem may be in the school instead/in addition to child's learning disability (Rutter, 1975) The timing of the referral is also important to be taken care of. A childs problems may be persisting for long but referral may be recent on the request of teacher or some other reason. This would clearly reflect the ignorance of parents about child's behaviour or even their lack of concern for him. On the other hand the child might be having some separation anxiety related problem or learning disability, or mental retardation which gets manifest on giving him specific learning task. This kind of referral would also require examining the structure of instructions to the child at school. Therefore just one problem may open the Pandora box in front of the interviewer who has to to separate and arrange the events in such a way that it makes the meaningful understanding of child's behaviour. If the child has been examined or referred by some other clinician/teacher previously, it is always wiser to get details about the assessment and opinion from him. But caution is needed not to get biased by any other practioner; findings and method of treatment. Quite likely the child's having different problems when he was taken to some other clinician. Since the present would be responsible for treating the child he has to make his own judgement and formulation about the treatment plan. He may ask for any investigation too if he feel necessary. For this reason he must discuss the same with his care givers too. If the assessment is not complete in single visit which is generally the case, it should be also be discussed adequately with the parents and subsequent appointments should be planned.

The First Encounter

Different psychiatrist clinical psychologist may differ in their approach of assessing the child. After a brief session of introduction and rapport establishing, it is appropriate to address the problem directly. It requires some training to conduct interview. The psychiatrist must master his own anxieties too.Many times psychiatrist own apprehensions is assessment generates apprehensions in the complaints too and then the whole process of assessment goes erratic. Under such circumstances it is good to postpone the appointment preferably telephonically prior to the appointed time.

Most of the psychiatrists follow an unstructured free format of clinical interview. This method is highly flexible as it allows the psychiatrist to ask questions as per need of the context. It is easy to shift from one topic to other without fear of any disruption of continuity. The assessee also gets ample opportunity to answer the questions in detail.

It is customary to begin with exploring the reason of referral. Generally open ended questions provide better exploration than the specific for a detailed inquiry multiple sources of information such as parent's assessment; school report and classroom observation may all be required. It is unto the psychiatrist to decide whom to include in the interview at first instance. If the details are felt inadequate is should certainly be not a problem to ask for another appointment and calling the other important persons in the child's life.

Many psychiatrists would prefer to see the child along with his parents or care giver. There are no hard rules about the child's or parents presence in the interview room. Seeing the child and parents together has some advantages as it gives an opportunity to observe the pattern of interaction between parents and child. Under certain specific circumstances such as in cases of separation anxiety disorder the parents would also be at ease in telling the problem. But a child having conduct disorder or oppositional defiant disorder would make the situation difficult. Therefore many times psychiatrist would feel it worthwhile to spend some time with the parents separately. In the Indian context many parents would prefer to meet the psychiatrist alone at some time fearing that speaking about the problem in front of the child is just like putting blame on the child, or they may fear embarrassing behaviour of the child in their presence. If such is the case it is always better to see the parents first and allay their anxieties. The children generally feel secure in presence of some one familiar to them. Seeing children with their caregivers is therefore generally preferred.

Use of Toys

Despite any interview setting the psychiatrist should not assume the child's presence in the interview room to be an uneventful process. At times the child may make the conversation between parents and psychiatrist quite difficult. He may interfere with conversation or would make his presence all around in the room. A separate provision of play room is often helpful to overcme such situations.The room should have sufficient objects like toys such as dolls, blocks, cars, pillows, balls, sand pit, toy stove, dishes, toy guns, drawing material, etc. to engage the child. Play is the natural way in which child expresses himself. Presence of such objects make the child feels accepted and capable to tell about his anxieties, relations with others and his own ways to handle problems. Under such circumstances they communicate better through the language of play and projecting themselves on toys and pictures. Many times the interview room provides the child lifetime opportunity to behave as they wish. Such items should be culturally appropriate and just sufficient to engage the child rather than confusing or over stimulating him. Such environment is of great help in assessing the child's problems and exploring his creative potentials which often gets ignored while focusing on the problem in a non directive interview. It also helps in examining the child's motor skills, coordination, attention, aggressive tendencies. (Axline, 1989).

VISITING THE CHILD'S NATURAL ENVIRONMENT

It is always beneficial for the psychiatirst to observe the child where he has to spend most of the time. He may ask nurse or social worker to visit the child's family and school to know what and where the things are exactly wrong, child may have learning disabilities. But it may also be due to faulty environment at the school. Similarly a child may have temper tentrums that may arise from his his faulty behaviour being reinforced by the care givers. A child may be depressed due to the frequent quarrels between his parents and getting scape goated or he has to carry out certain other family roles not expected of him. Under such circumstances he may also show some signs of abuse.

Medical History

Medical illness during perinatal period to early childhood may have their own psychiatric sequelae. Birth anoxia is one of the most common cause of consequent mental retardation. Maternal infection especially during the first trimester and the drug treatment for them may also affect the child's physical and mental development. Infections like rubella,toxoplasmosis syphilis are known to cause congenital malformation and mental retardation. Lead toxicity and nutritional history suggesting poor zinc intake is likely to be associated with the symptoms of ADHD. A child with problems like impaired hearing and tongue tie may exhibit poor linguistic mile stones which can be corrected with appropriate treatment. A detailed list of child psychiatric symptoms associated can be seen in the table 1. The child may also show neurotic symptoms in response to any visible physical handicap whereas a child with good coping ability may also over compensate it.

Family History

Family history generally begins with asking about the people living with the child and making a three generation(at least) genogram. One important component of this history is to understand the genetics of the illness. Along with it is is also essential to understand the psychosocial environment around the child's problems. The psychiatrist may find marital problems between the parents of a younger sibling where both parents are working. Autistic children may have parents who are too occupied with their philosophic intrests. In indian set up sex of the child also matter how he /she is brought up at home the child who is feeling depressed. The child may also be scapegoated for their problems and be used as messenger for their interpersonal communication. The child may have been performing parental role for his younger siblings. In poverty struck families the child may also perform the role of bread winner quite ahead of his age.

Child rearing practices vary from culture to culture. The psychiatrist should be sensitive to this aspect and identify what is recognised as normal in that culture. The cultural aspects also have their importance on detemining the family's acceptability to the proposed treatment plan. At times even the idea of taking the child to psychiatrist may be unwelcome. Getting an idea about this aspect right in the beginning of interview would help the psychiatrist in educating the family and gaining acceptability.

TABLE 2: Assement of Child with Problem Behaviour

1. Biological and Developmental Aspects.
2. Parents and Parenting
3. Schooling
4. Siblings and Peer Relations
5. Cuture and Value System

INTERVIEWING THE CHILD

Most psychiatrists are able to generate a differential diagnosis about he the child's mental health problems by the end of interview with informants.. The purpose of examining the child two fold. First to confirm and refine the differential diagnosis, and secondly to plan the management strategy including the assessment for the need of any biological and other investigations.

Like in any pediatric patient the psychiatrist should generally ask about neutral question first.Doing so allays the anxiety of the child which also helps in establishing rapport with the child. It further helps in conducting the interview with the child. For a psychiatrist it is important to intact with the child in an age appropriate manner. The younger children should be relieved of any fear of injections and painful procedures. It is generally better to begin the interview with them in presence of parents. The patients with separation anxiety disorders would not leave themselves away from their parents. They may not find any interest in the toys in the room, whereas a child with pervasive developmental disorder would isolate himself from parents without any effort or provocation and would also not appear interested in what is happening around him. For younger children it is further useful to use projective techniques in the interview. A child engaging in the game of father doll and baby doll may communicate his perceptions, emotions and relationship quite easily which would not have been possible with the verbal part of language. His manner and level of engagement with the toys and play activities would also give sufficient idea about his concentration and activity level. Pencils and colours can also be used in similar manner. The child may be asked to draw with free mind to know his fantasies.It can be additionally supplemented with the asking him to draw something specific like a family scene or a scene of playground depending on the leads received from the history. Draw a person test can also provide an idea about child's intelligence.

Interview with the older children and adolescents generally doesn't require any special need and it can go as for an adult.(Angold and Costello, 2000) They generally have some idea about the reason of referral and they might even prefer to talk to the interviewer first when parents are away. It goes with all ages that people are often suggestible to anwer the interviewers questions. Therefore a caution must be observed to put open ended questions first. The best information is generally obtained through the questions that are worded simply. As the complexity of questions, its length or its languages increases the possibility of misunderstanding by the child and it would lead to misleading answer. The details provided by the child and also by the parents to such questions may awefully be vague and lacking in the required details. To avoid this kind of problems a preferable approach is the free format interviews to ask simply worded open eneded questions. Care should be taken that questions do not provide any lead to the respondant to give a specific answer (Ceci and Friedman 2000). Interiswing children aged below 8-9 years is marked by many problems. They may give good account of the event having taken place in their lives, but they may tend to forget details and may even mix up the details of events. They are generally incapable of providing details about how a particular behavior or event started. They may express their worries apprehensions sexual and physical abuse when they feel comfortable. It may surprise many parents that they passed the details told by the child for something usual. Under such circumstances the child may be the only source of information which need to be handled very carefully. Bructs et al, 1998). To elicit all such details the examiner need to ask careful and sensitive questions to the child's needs without questioning in any leading way. Environment may also be modulated to suit the child's need by including or excluding some informants during interview. Use of toys to act out stories and asking the child to complete it as in Mcarther Storey Stem Battery (Warren et al, 2000) may also be used. The Berkley's Puppet Interview in which the child is forced to tell which of the two puppets he likes and dislikes most in orders to elicit his social relationships feelings of hostility, depression and anxiety (Measelle et al 1998). These interviews can be video recorded and scored, these have been found inadequate to provide sufficient information to a psychiatrist oriented to standard diagnostic criteria like ICD-10 and DSM etc. here child psychiatrist must be aware of it that not all the behaviours recognized as problems necessarily fit in any diagnostic criteria.

The younger children may provide information on closed ended questions but it is likely to be erroneous (Orneistein et al 1992; Bruck et al, 1998). This kind of questioning may be used with caution where certain missing links in the information are to be completed. As such in child psychiatric interview it is best to start interview with open ended questions and avoid closed ended questions. Leading question that directly suggest the answer to the child (e.g. when you were beaten by your mom, you must have been hurt very badly, isn't it like that) leaves no place for the child to answer elaborately but say yes or no. Asking about the two things at the same time is equally bad for assessment e.g. when you went school and got your grade cards did you feel happy or sad, the child may answer but it may be confusing if the child has answers about going to school or receiving grade card. Similarly asking multiple choice questions whether you feel happy sad, angry or fearful is less likely to tap the exact emotional state. Generally it has been seen that in such situations the respondant may choose the last option provided. Quite likely that such multiple choice question asked doesn't contain the option the child want to anwer. Due to forgetting especially in little children the information provided can be quite misleading (Ornstein et al 1992).

PROBLEMS DURING INTERVIEW

Whenever there is suspicion of some misleading answers or defective interview, it is not the end. There is always a chance to verify and obtain correct information by increasing the redundancy and repetition of questions after some gap in the redundant questions the same situation is presented in two or more different form, such as a child may be asked did you felt very bad when your mother scolded you ..did you not bad at all when your mom scolded you. ..what bad feeling means to you etc. The repeated questions are the rephrased questions e.g. did you go to that place? where did you actually go ? Ok what were you telling about going somewhere? A respondent may back out on such questions but rates of such retractions is quite low(Bruck et al, 1998) To seek clarification the response may be elicited again. After asking few questions the child may be asked about the same theme e.g you were telling about problems in the school. Can you tell me once again about it.

TABLE 3: Types of Questions and Relevance in Unstructured Interview

1. Open ended Questions	Generally preferred mode of questioning especially in the beginning of interview, questions are basically non directive, encourage the respondent for free recall, opens options for wide range of possible answers. For example: what do you know about him? (the respondent can now tell about any aspect whether family, developmental, behavioural, academic known to him.)

2. Closed ended	like open ended questions but focuses the response to one more specific dimensions of behaviour. These questions are generally asked to elicit specific information. For example, what do you know about his performance at school? (as expected the respondent would now be telling about the academic achievements of the subject. He is however nowhere given any suggestion about the answer.
3. Leading Questions	These are very specific questions and generally give an idea to the respondent about the expected response. These questions do not ask for detailed answer. For example: Did he started schooling quite late ? (clearly the interviewer is assuming the respondent having knowledge about the behaviour in question and making the response also quite biased.)
4. Questions with Multiple Choices	These questions are like leading questions but accompanied with multiple responses from which the respondent may choose any. This is not generally the preferred mode of questioning as it may confuse the respondent in addition to eliciting misleading information. For example: Did you feel sad, angry or embrassed at that time ? (quite likely the respondent was surprised, but no such option is there. This may add to confusion of the respondent as to what to answer now.)
5. Double Questions	In this situation two unrelated questions are asked simultaneously. Such as –How have been your sleep and working? (now two different thing are asked from the respondent and he may tell about any one or both such questions often create confusion for the respondent and also for the interviewer as to what aspect has been informed by the respondent)

INTERVIEWING CHILDREN IN SPECIAL SITUATIONS

The Infant

Presentation of a child below one year age is though less frequent, but is becoming increasingly common. Generally the referral is initiated by a paediatrician or some social or legal agency. A pediatrician may seek psychiatrist opinion about the child's behavior for management of presenting symptoms whereas the legal or social agency would be interested in the child's well being for possibility of adoption or suspecting child abuse.

With infants too assessment begins with exploring and collecting details about the presenting complaints. Besides that, functions such as sleep pattern, feeding habits, sensitivity to change in the environment such as on bed wetting, change of care giver etc. also tell about the infant's feeling of relatedness and security. He needs to know about the planning of conception, antenatal care and parents' attitude towards the child. Any exposure to drugs /radiations during pregnancy especially during 1st trimester, pre maturity, complication at the time of delivery and the other illnesses, jaundice, trauma, loss of parents during early childhood leaves the child specifically vulnerable to develop behavioural problems later on. A detailed information about the development of the child is always required. The child's motor accomplishments – movements – their frequency and intensity, in all limbs or restricted area, jerkiness, maintain a posture, eye hand coordination, sensitivity to touch/pain, reflexes communication skill and vocabulary, social mile stones such as smiling on recognizing parents, stranger anxiety etc should be noted carefully for their age appropriateness. Most of the times to assess the child's social maturity standard scales are also required.

Evaluation of the infant's environment is also equally important. The psychiatrist must spend some time to know about the child's whereabouts, his family's culture and status, who others live with him and his primary care givers. The parent's expectations about the child tell about the exact kind of relationship between them. One or the other parents is likely to be indifferent to the child if they have any marital /financial dispute. In the suspected cases of child abuse also the family member(s) may underestimate the reason of referral. Therefore opportunity to examine the child with primary care givers must be availed. During interview how the child and care giver reciprocate with each other gives confirmatory information about the quality of relationship between the two. In a healthy relationship both the care givers are emotionally available to the child and regulate the affective experiences and the infant too feels comfortable and secure with them. The other parent child charecristics that merit exploration include: protection / vigilance vs security, comforting vs comfort seeking, teaching vs learning, discipline vs self control, routine vs predictability (Talmi and Harmon, 2005)

During assessment another difficulty a child psychiatrist likely to experiences is diagnosing the infant's behavioural problems. The adult categories of ICD-10 or DSM system may not be very appropriate for the children below three years as these are based on the adult population and older children. The developmental stage of the individual is not adequately considered in these classifications whereas infants differ markedly from the older children for their developmetal stage and maturity. A multi axial classification of mental Health and developmental disorders of Infancy and early childhood (Zero to Three, 1994) takes into consideration this problem in diagnosing the infantile behavioural syndromes.

Single Parent Child

Both parents play a crucial role in the upbringing of child. They have certain roles independent of each other such as mother is mainly responsible for nurturing the child.Whereas the father plays role in the cognitive development, bread winner and play mate for the child. Mother's presence induces a feeling of safety and security in the child.

With the changing scenario two kinds of situations can be assumed for a maternally deprived child. Early death of mother leading to permanent deprivation is a serious loss to the child.If the child is infant he may adjust easily to the new care taker. but older children would clearly manifest behavioural problems.

Mental subnormailty due to social reasons, habit disorders, bedwetting, depressive feelings are the common problems associated with such children. The psychiatrist needs to be sensitive to these issues as soon as he learns motherless status of child and focus specifically on this issue too.

Temporary separation due to the changing scenario where mothers have to leave home for work and the child has to live alone or with some care taker is less difficult situation. Usually the child may through tantrums when mother has to leave but again adjusts to the situation. In Indian situation where joint family trend is still prevalent such separation usually is less roublesome to the child. But in case of a child from nuclear family the psychiatrist again need to discuss the isuue specifically with the child.

A fatherless child may also develop problem quite similar to a motherless child, but these problems are usually less severe because of mother's presence at home. This situation is more prevalent in most of the cultures where fathers have to work away from home or leave the home when the child is sleeping and come back late at night. Such children may be more prone to acute and chronic physical illnesses.

Sibling Rivalry

This situation is so common in almost all setups that a clinician can afford to assume it existing before he begins the interview. It is a feeling of jealousy which one child feels due to the presence of other child in the family. It manifest in more severe forms in younger children but some symptoms may persist even with advancing age of child, genrally the younger child in the family is the victim of such behaviour. The psychiatrist again need to assess what starts such behaviour. What sort of violence such as fighting, slapping, snatching article etc are exhibited and how the parents are managing it. Many time just stopping the child from behaving in such way may actually provke the behaviour. Catching the children when they are good or even often acts as reward for the child and may make such behaviour go. (Suesser, 2008)

Precious Child

A child born long after wedding is often a source of anxieties for the parents. Such child might be over protected both physically and socially. The parents usually tend to behave in a neurotic manner. His minor demands which can wait may also be gratified immediately. The parents may develop conflicts among themselves and end up blaming each other for his problems and upbringing. Such a child because of overprotection would have poor frustration tolerance and coping skills. Thus temper tentrums oppositional behaviour are quite expected in the clinics while examining such child.The child because of poor social relations may indulge excessively in day dreaming and may learn to cope up with difficulty with fantasy. On growing up these children may prefer isolation and have social phobia like problems.

Adopted Child

Mostly a child adopted at young age doesn't show behavioural difficulties much different from the those living with their biological parents. Older children may show some difficulty in adjustment in the beginning. The younger parents are also likely to cope and help the child efficiently in comparison with the older adoptee parents. Due to any conflicts if at all the adoption status need to be revealed to the child, it hould be a gradual process and need to be done under professional guidance. Preferably adoption should not be revoked as it develop further more anxieties and insecurities in the child which are detrimental to his growth.

The Only Child

The only child in the family also menifests behavioural difficulties like that of a precious child. But now a days due to changing economic scenario such families are increasing in number. The child may feel lonely and develop many escape behaviours to avoid social isolation. The parents need to evaluated about their family planning. They might be inexperienced and feel just overwhelmed with the care of child,or alternatively they might be too occupied with their professional work that they have little time for themselves too and may avoid conception for fulfillment of their ambitions. Alternatively poverty struck families may also adopt single child norm, the child may feel insecure if parents are away for long time. The child may also feel lonely due to lack of companion to play and thus may show problems like uderstimulated child or retardate.In such cases a complete family assessment approach may be required instead of assessing the child alone.

The Abused Child

This is one of the most serious kind of problems seen in the child clinics. This is also known as battered child syndrome in medical literature (Kempe et al, 1962) Beside medical complications such cases have legal implications too. Such children may be refered through legal or school authorities for unexplained injuries. The parents may also present such children to outdoor for evaluation which often need to be differentiated from manchausen by proxy for diagnostic purpose (Baldwin, 1996). In child abuse cases the motive of abuse is always conscious whereas in manchausen by proxy the motive of inflicting injuries is unconscious but the mode is always conscious, for social and legal purpose manchausen by proxy too means child abuse. A close examination often revels multiple old and fresh injuries which are not usually explained by the the details provided by the parents. Suspicion of abuse is even strongly suspected when a non ambulatory child or a child who has not yet developed sufficient motor skills is presented with unexplained injuries or illness(Wadhera et al, 2008). Examination for sexual abuse is essential in all such cases. Complete medicolegal formalities should also be carried out once problem of abuse is detected. Such problems are more often seen with female and illegitimate children. The abuser in most of the cases is likely to be a person well known to the child and/or family who has some psychological or personality disorder (Harren, 2002). The child is generally malnourished, looks depressed and fearful and may not prefer to speak in front of parents or abusers. They may express the details of abuse quite well through their play in the clinic or by means of drawings. The details may reveal psychological abuse in the form of not allowing the child to play, not sending to school, asking for work quite inappropriate for age, physical abuse such as food deprivation, beating and sexual abuse etc. a thorough and careful assessment is required in such cares. The psychiatrist should handle it quite sensitivily with appropriate protection for the child. Before diagnosing child abuse it is essential that all other possibilities must be ruled out as the abuse case would involve some legal procedure too for which the examining Clinical child Psychologist psychiatrist should have a credible evidence (Warner and Hansen 1994).

The Delinquent Child

Delinquent behaviour is also on the rise among school goers and teenagers in our society. Bullying and sexual offences among the tenagers are now a happening of any common day. The term delinquency means acting out behaviour which might invite but not necessarily conviction under law (Cavadino and Allen 2000) Delinquent behaviour is oftent the result of poor frustration tolerance, impulsivity and lack of concern for others. Learning through witnessing violence in the media also make them prone to develop delinquent behavior. Psychosis or any other mental disorder underlying delinquent behaviour is rare. (Clare et al 2000). In such cases information needs to be gathered from multiple sources especially about the past similar behavior. The quality and severity of delinquent behaviour and risk invoved to the victim also need to evaluated. To predict the occurance of such behaviour in future and assesseing need to send to some reformatory institute, the childs attitude knowledge about the consequences of such behavior, his ability to empathise with the victim must be evaluated, (Sheldrick 1999). The information collected can also be supplemented with rating scales (Augimeri et al, 1998)

The Suicidal Child

It is too rare for a young child to attempt suicide, however among older children and adolescent the rates of suicide are day by day going high. In our country also the situation is similar, leading to setting up of helpline especially during examinations time and problem. Not all suicides can be avoided but a timely and effective intervention can avoid most of such incidences.

Therefore, in the metropolitan cities and places where helpline facilities are available any brief reference to suicidal ideas should also be taken seriously and all help should be provided to the person where he is. Any such reference is a strong indication for complete assessment.

Completed suicides are generally seen in male whereas attempted suicide are common among female. Each attempt indicate a possibility of occurring of such event in future too which at times is difficult to predict. After a brief assessment on referral call it is mendatory to carry out thorough psychiatric examination to assess the antecedednts and the possible future action by the person.

Among adolscents and older children suicidal attempts are not necessarily impulsive. Such attempts are strongly linked with the stressors like failures in exams, breakup in relations. Even marital conflict between parents can also lead to onset of such ideas. Any such presentation therefore again means a complete assessment of the context of the problem, i.e. assessment of the stressors and coping abilities, mood state of the child family support system, peer elations, persons own desires and ambitions and level of satisfaction with achievement. During interview a clear and detailed discussion for the assessment of suicidal risk is must. It is a very common myth that any such discussion means implanting this idea in patients mind. But a person who is distressed, talking of suicide to him gives him a chance to ventilate his feeling thereby reducing the probality of its occurance. On finding any evidence of underlying psychiatric disorder treatment should be provided immediately if the person is fit.

A child brought to the emergency room due to suicidal attempt should be provided full life support to take him out of danger. Once stable it is mandatory that he should not be discharged without a thorough psychiatric assessment with special emphasis on the assessment of occurrence of similar attempts in future. A person talking about his problem and asking for help may be less dangerous to him that a person who shows a sudden flight to health by immediate recovery from mental agony. Many times such flight indicate the persons strong determination to make a serious attempt in near future or may be even immediately.

Child with Imaginary companion

Such problem is quite common in the childhood when the parents come complaining that their child plays and speaks in alone as if he is interacting with someone. Nearly 25 – 45% of child psychiatric population may present with this problem of imagininary companions (Stephens, 2008) in most of the cases such imaginary friends are invisible but some may make use of dolls and toys to mimic their friends. The parents may be preoccupied with the myths like their child being socially inadequate or having lower IQ. The child having imaginary companion is a normal phenomenon in the child's development and the parents should be reassured of it. They should realize that the child is able to fulfill his emotional needs through his imagined companion which is normal for his age. The parents attitude must be examined in more details. They should be corrected if they ridicule or make fun the child or his imaginary friend. If the family members are taking some advantage of the child imagined friend to tame or discipline the child they must be discouraged from doing so. Most commonly it is seen in preschool children and they out grow this imaginary friendship by adolescence.

Research has shown that the children with imaginary friends tend to be emotionally well-adjusted;intellectually and creativily adequate, outgoing and social, not typically shy, isolated or withdrawn; advanced in understanding of social relationships; verbally skilled; able to take others' perspectives to create complex play themes; able to focus on an idea and maintain good attention span. They are more self-directed during unstructured time, preferring to play rather than watch television; and, able to enjoy fantasy play while also grasping the difference between "real and pretend" rather than playing.

The imaginary friend and the child should be a focus of concern when a child having an imaginary companion has no friends or interest in them, engages in violent behavior and blames it on the friend, appears fearful of the friend, shows signs of physical, sexual, or emotional abuse.

Mental Status Examination

This portion of assessment is the psychiatric equivalent of physical examination of a pediatric patient. This however doesn't over rule the need of physical examination.

Mostly the child's appearance and the pattern of dressing up, hygiene mainly reflects the child's bringing up pattern in his family. A child belonging to a well to do family, looking malnourished, poorly groomed is likely be an abused one in the omnipresence of unexplained scars, injuries would further confirm it. Certain physical stigmatama like mongoloid facies, cleft lip/palate, polydactyl would give an idea of further more congenital malformations than simply a suspicion of mental retardation. Presence of involuntary moments like tics,nail biting, thumb sucking would suggest presence of neurotic disorders. Autistic children and mentally retarded children may unusably persist with an activity and may even show self destructive behaviours, whereas the ADHD child would have difficulty in maintaining a particular posture and likely to be constantly on run in the interview room. He may make frequent interruption in the interview process also. It is also important to note how the child regulates his behaviour and how he responds to the instructions for the same.

ABILITY TO RELATE

The children are usually anxious in presence of strangers and new situation. It is to some extent quite normal for children, a child would show cooperation with the interviewer after some time is spent in rapport establishment and the interview may go smoothly with them. However they might feel a bit uncomfortable even when the parents leave them alone in the interview room. However an over anxious child or a child with separation anxiety disorder may show extreme clinging behaviour and crying. That would make it difficult for the parents to leave the child alone which would also corroborate with the history provided. Autistic children on the other hand may not appear interested in making any social contact with the interviewers. But their would be gross absence of the display of the social smiles and approach towards the interviewer despite sufficient warming up. They may avoid eye contact and any meaningful communication.

SPEECH AND LANGUAGE

Speech is the mechanical part of mechanism of sound production. It deals with the movements of vocal chords, force of speech production and coordination of other muscles to produce words, hence while examining speech the interviewer should evaluate volume, tone and articulatory processess essential for speech production. The child may stammer or he may have stuttering problems, he may mispronounce certain syllables due to articulatory difficulties like tongue tie etc.

Language is more complex process than speech it actually involves use of language in socially and grammatically correct manner to establish communication. Hence it is very important to consider the developmental age of the child while examining the language functions. The interviewer should make observations for both receptive as well as expressive part of language component. Besides this verbal and nonverbal language should also be assessed. It is again better to use the age appropriate methods for assessment here. The younger children would welcome having crayons or pencil and paper to express themselves. The younger children may prefer to the use of pictures to tell their thoughts. Showing them some diagrams or photographs especially of the children related themes make examination not just interesting for them but also more meaningful for the interviewer. The interviewer should be aware of level of expected vocabulary of the child. At the age of two the child is usually able to produce monosyllables to two three simple words. While at the end of toddler age the child should have sufficient vocabulary to combine the words into sentences. The examiner should specifically note for the use of subject, object and the verb in the sentences formed by the child. The written language also helps in knowing any dyslexic problem if the child has.

While assessing speech and language the interviewer should be specifically able to assess the following:

1. Is child able to produce audible sound.
2. Does the child has the child age appropriate vocabulary(Does he understand the meaning of words)?
3. Can he make out the meaning of words spoken to him.

4. Can the child write his thoughts in grammatically correct manner, the interviewer need to make a specific notice of any reversal or substitution of alphabets.
5. Can the child understand the meaning of arithmetic symbols and carry out instructions as expected.

To examine this aspect the following decision making tree is often helpful.

It may be noted here that presence of speech and language difficulties doesn't simply means problems in this age only. Many time it is just one of the symptoms of other clinical syndromes. Children with mental retardation, autism, hearing related problems too manifest problems in their speech and language functions.

Mood and Affect

Many times mood and affect terms are used interchangeably. But these carry different meaning. The mood is the pervasive and persistent state of once emotional feelings It can be best assessed historically by asking the parents about the child's general tendency to react towards different situations. Whereas the affect is a emotional state at a given particular time, which can be assessed during the interview by observing the child whether he is happy/sad or angry. Generally the children can't express their emotions especially the sad emotions effectively. This part of emotions is generally expressed in the form of anger or irritability and the child may appear withdrawn too. The interviewer should make an attempt to elicit the range and reactivity of affect. Care should be taken to elicit the irritable or the other negative emotions naturally and the child should not be provoked hard to express these feeling, it can hamper the flow of further examination processes of certain family. Pictures and toys the child likes and dislike are often helpful in the younger children. Like in the adult interview a specific notice should also be made about\the appropriateness, range and intensity of the affect elicited during interview.

Thinking

Play and pictures are the children's favourite methods of expressing their inner world. The child may be shy or reluctant to talk to a stranger or in a new situation. But it doesn't mean that the child has limited thinking ability or doesn't feel or reast to their environment as much as adults. The children often have a rich fantasy. They generally express their thoughts and fantasies through their age appropriate language would be difficult for an adult psychiatrist to elicit delusion and hallucination like phenomena. But when the child is given play material or asked to draw, they may express their fantasies and fears The coherence or any formal thought disorder,autism can also be easily elicited in the sequence of child's play and drawings. But all these need to be interpreted with reference to the developmental stage of the child and also if such is seen persistently in the child's behaviour. Any theme related to death in the child's play or drawing should provoke the psychiatrist for further questioning about homicidal or suicidal wishes too besides exploring the child for having witnessed any such scene of violence. The sensitive issues like sexual abuse can also be enacted by the child through play without any difficulty. The child at such observation can be asked quite comfortably about who are the people involved in this play. The children can be asked if they feel something special in them or their family and should be asked to play that in the observation room. Any perceptual psychopathology may also be easy to elicit in this way. However before concluding about any psychotic phenomenon in the child caution is generally required. It is rare for a prepubertal child to have any psychotic phenomenon. Hypnogogic and hypnopompic hallucinations are common in preschool children, but these do not carry any diagnostic value. Any sign of impaired reality testing should also be interpreted carefully as these may be normal for the developmental age of child, especially when there is no history of such episode in the past.

Cognitive Functions

Cognitive function assessment should be aimed to check the child's age appropriate general fund of knowledge. It is quite likely that some of these things like place of his residence, school names of teachers friends have already been asked in the beginning of interview in the rapport establishment phase.

Memory and reasoning conceptualization should be examined through child based themes and stories with which the child is familiar.

Idea of child's level of comprehension and intellectual abilities can be made by the time interview has progressed to this stage. However it is always better to make an objective assement about all this ability through proper questioning. For this reason it might be required to ask for certain specific tests to examine the child's vocabulary, decision making and intelligence which may be done by the person specially trained in these assessment. These tests are of special value when specific learning problems are suspected. In a busy setup a quick assessment of the child's intelligence can be made through 'draw a person test' and copying the figures. A child of 3, 4, 5 years of age can copy the shapes of circle, square, and triangle respectively.

Formulating the Diagnosis

The diagnosis is the complete knowledge about the persons illness, its precipitating and perpetuating factors. This is just one of the most important functions of the psychiatric examination. From the information collected the psychiatrist need to organise the information in a chronological manners to get the life sketch of the child's illness. It need to be translated into psychopathological or scientific terms so as to reach a diagnosis. A caution must be observed here that the diagnosis doesn't necessarily means the condition or the syndrome listed in the standard classifications. It may just tell us about the identified problematic behaviour which might need clinical attention. Many time the overanxious parents may bring the child for minor issues which do not fit into any classification and need to be counselled. Under all circumstances the formulation should be drafted with due care taking into account all cultural, social factors. The formulation should not be just the description of problem in a scientific language. It should clearly describe the context in which the problem is experienced. So that adequate and appropriate pharmacological, psychological, social and rehabilitative interventions can be planned.

USE OF STRUCTURED INTERVIEWS

In most of the clinical setup the psychiatrist prefer a free format or a semistructured interview pattern for children. This format has advantage as it gives the examiner and patient both adequate flexibility to shift between the topics. Some particular aspects require special attention to be explored in greater details. However there can be bias on the part of patient as well on the psychiatrist. Some features that are quite obvious may get full attention but other area may unknowingly be ignored. Therefore a psychiatrist too need a thorough training in administering such interviews.

Fixed format or structured diagnostic interviews on the other hand are becoming increasingly popular where there is ease in collecting data. Unlike the non directive interview where the interviewer observes the child's play and informants version of the problem, in structured interview the interviewer guides the child to collect information relevant to his problem. Such interviews generally do not need any interpretation of observation or clearing the meaning of the questions to the interviewer. As reliability and validity of these interviews are quite well established, these are generally preferred for collecting information along with the standard diagnostic criteria such as ICD-10 and DSM. Such interviews improve the clinical decision making by preventing the clinician from getting led away and preventing him from asking in an idiosyncratic way. Presence of one phenomenon may lead the clinician to assume the presence of other. In this way presence of suicidal attempt may lead the clinician to assume an underlying depressive episode, therfore even a mild sadness may get over rated and treated as symptom. The structured interviews prevent such confimatory bias (Bruck et al 1998). The representativeness heuristic may also bias a free format interview, when the clinician may assume the normal behavior also as representative or symptom of a particular disorder simply due to presence of one specific phenomenon (Dawes, 1988).

In the interviewer based interviews guide the interviewer to conduct the interview. These interviews generally have detailed glossary providing definition of each phenomenon to be looked for. The interviewer can observe till he feels the particular phenomenon is present or absent. Child and Adolescent Psychiatric Assessment (CAPA, Angold and Costello, 2000) , Child assessment Schedule (CAS, Hodges et al,1982)Kiddie Schedule for assessment of Affective Disorder and Schizophrenia (K-SADS, Ambrosni, 2000), Diagnostic Interview schedule for Children and Adolscents DICA, (Reich et al 2000) and Pictorial Instrument for Children and Adolescents–IIIR (PICA-IIIR; Ernst et al 2000) are few examples of such interviews. K-SADS and CAPA have detailed glossary of definition of different phenomena along with guidelines for coding.

In the respondent based interviews, the language of the questions is more structured and meant for the ease of interviewee. Hence the questions are logically sequenced and there is little scope in restructuring the question or changing the sequence. At times there might be a problem like the respondent would misinterpret the question but he is not provided any explanation for what is being asked. The pure verbal respondent based interviews are adult like interviews and they solely rely on questions whereas the pictorial interviews use illustrations like cartoons and pictures to ask the questions from the child. Diagnostic Interview Schedule for Children (DISC, Shaffer et al 2000) is among the most widely used verbal interview used all over the world. In such interviews the clinician has almost no role in making a clinical judgement. He may find it easy and time saving with the use of computer based version. Computer based version allows additional advantage of not skipping any question accidently. However wherever possible for clinical purpose the interviewer based interviews are preferred over the respondent based interviews.

USE OF SCALES

There are many rating scales and inventories and screening instruments available for use in child psychiatric assesment. It is not essential that these should be used in all cases. The scales, invetories or screening instruments can be used for just supplementing and quantifying the information collected about the child's behaviour. The scales offer a specific advantage, i.e. these help us quantifying the behavioural problem of the child which can be evaluated quantitatively so that progress in the child's behaviour can be easily monitored in the subsequent contacts. These scales also do not label the child as psychiatric case and therefore assessment is free from stigmatising the child.This information also relieved the already anxious parent's anxieties. Before using any such instrument the clinician need to know if (a) would this instrument tap the required information?, (b) Is this instrument comprehensive enough to provide complete required information, (c) who should respond to the questions?, (d) Is there any normative data for this instrument, (e) What is the age group this instrument is meant for, (f) Are the psychmetric indices reach the adequate level of reliability and validity. Using this criteria the psychiatrist may choose one or more instrument listed in the table below:

USE OF PSYCHOLOGICAL TESTING

Test is a specialized way to systematic understanding and quantifying behaviour. Keeping this definition in view all diagnostic interviews and use of rating scales would also qualify for the psychological test. However, in clinical sense the test and procedure are the methods to collect and quantify information in more objective or operationalised way i.e. these methods are based on observation and interpretation which can tell much more than the subjective and 'filtered account' of behaviour provided by the parents or care givers. A teacher may say that the child is not able to concentrate well. Whereas the parents may describe the behaviour normal and suspecting the method of instruction to the child. A clinician now needs to visit both home and school environment to confirm the information, whereas a psychologist can examine the situation in the laboratory condition through a scientifically validated procedure using reliable and established tests. Thus the psychological testing not only confirms the information elicited by the clinician but saves time also.

Some common conditions for which the psychologist is often asked for testing a child involve measuring cognitive ability of the child such as IQ testing, memory testing, language

TABLE 4: Some Common Rating Scales Frequently used for Children's Assessment

S No	*Scale / Instrument*	*Brief description*	*Mode of administration*	*Indications for use*
1	2	3	4	5
1.	Paediatric Symptom checklist(Jellinek, Murphy and Burns,1986)	35 items, designed to evaluate emotinal and behavioural factors of the child. Limited psychometric properties	To be administred on tha parents, doesn't require any specific training	Screening quetinnaire, Scores exceeding cut off need further evaluation of child
2.	The instructional environment Scale (Ysseeldyke and Christenson, 1987)	Developed to help the teaching professionals	Teachers and trainers in schools	Used to assess the instructional/training environment of the student

1	2	3	4	5
3.	Family Environment scale (Moos and Moos, 1994)	90 items divided in 10 scales, measures family relationship pattern , personal growth, good psychometric properties.	Physician/Psychiatrist rated	It should be used where a dysfunctional family environment is considered etiogenetic in determining childs problematic behaviour.
4.	Youth self report (Achenbach and Rescorla, 2001)	A broad based scale, 2 competence scales, 7 problem oriented scales	Self rated, the child can respond to the questions without anybody's help,useful for age 11-18.	A general scales can be used for a wide variety of behavioural problems.
5.	Check List for Autism in toddlers (Baron, Cohen and Gilberg, 1992)	Nine item questionnaire	To be rated by nurses or any medical professional only	Meant for children with autistic behaviour. A modified version of this (M-CHAT) by Robin's et al (2001)can also be used as screening device for autism.
6.	Social Communication questionnaire (Rutter, Bailey and Lord, 2003)	Formally also called autism screening questionnaire, has good agreement with Autism diagnostic interview-revised	To be completed by parents and/or care givers for children above 4 years age.	To be used for children suspected to have autism spectrum disorder.

1	2	3	4	5
7.	Childhood Autism rating Scale (Schopler et al, 1988)	Rates autistic behaviour in 15 dimensions on 7 point scale.	Administred to multiple care givers by little training to physicians ,psychologists and those working with children.	A good tool for comprehensive assessment of autistic behaviour.
8.	Revised children's manifest anxiety scale (Reynolds and Richmond, 1994)	Useful for age group 6-19 years. Provides total score as well as scores for physiologic anxiety, worry , oversensitive and difficulty in concentration.	Self administred tool, with good reliability, validity not well established.	Can be used in clinical settings , more data are required for its usefulness for research pupose.
9.	State Trait anxiety Inventory for children (Speilberger, 1973)	20 statements divided in two inventories. Designed for 9-12 years age group. Good reliability and validity indices.	Self report instrument which child can adminster himself.	Can be used assess the severity of anxiety proneness (trait) and transitory (state) anxiety. Norms for normal as well as children with emotional disturbance available. It can be used for younger children too.

1	2	3	4	5
10.	Children's Depression Inventory (Kovacs, 1992)	27 items. Good correlation with Beck's depression inventory, Caution should be used to use it on children alredy diagnosed depressed.	Self repot instrument, easy to understand. Useful for age 8-17 years.	It should be used preferably to measure severity of depressive symptoms rather than a diagnostic or supplemental information tool.
11.	Beck Depression inventory	Well established tool, can be used over wide age range.	Self administerd tool, tranlated into many languages	Many reserches reported adolescent finding it difficult to use despite its easy language. It can be used for screening as well as diagnostic purpose.
12.	Children's depression Rating scale (Poznanski and Mokros,1995)	6-12 years age group, good reliability and validity	Clinician's administered, Can be used on inpatients also	Useful to supplement information collected through sef report.
13.	Suicidal ideation questionaire (Raynolds, 1988)	Clinicialn administerd tool useful over age 6-13 years	Can tap information about the suicidal ideas and ideas of hopelessness and negative views of life.	It is recommendable to use clinical interview to judge the suicidal risk rather than administring this tool alone.
14.	ADHD rating scale (DuPaul et al, 1997)	18 item scale for age 5-17 years extensive normative data available	Parent or teacher rated scale.	Doesnot address or eliminate the possibility of oppsitional behaviours.

1	2	3	4	5
15.	Attention Deficit disorder comprehensive teacher rating scale (Ùltman et al, 1997)	Four subscales oppositional behaviour, attention, hypractivity and social problems, extensive normative data for children in 5- 12 year age, psychometric data limited.	Commonly administered by teachers.	Being used in schools for long time
16.	Children's action tendency scale (Deluty, 1979)	Forced choice type questions, suitable for 6-15 years age group, useful to rate aggressiveness, assertiveness and submissiveness. Good psychometric properties.	Self report instrument	Useful to assess conduct related problem in children
17.	Eyeberg Child behaviour Inventory (Eyeberg and Pincus,1999)	36 item inventory,provides assessment of intensity and number of problem behaviours.	Administered on parents for children 2-17 years age	A useful tool to know conduct problems at home, many physicians prefer to use it in conjunction with Sutter-Eyebrge student behaviour Inventory for children of same age range, thus providing behaviour profile in home and school environment.

1	2	3	4	5
18.	Scale for independent behaviour -revised (Bruininks et al, 1997)	14 subscales to assess adaptive behaviour good psychometric properties	Clinician adminstered instrument	Useful to assess the behaviour of mentally retarded children. This instrument can also measure frequency and severity of challenging and maladaptive behaviours.
19.	AAMD Adaptive behaviour scales (Nihara, Leland and Lambert, (1930)	Two parts: part I deals with adaptive behaviours on 10 domains, part two deals with maladaptive behaviours on 14 domains. Limited data on psychometric properties.	Informant administred tool, school version is also available.	Widely used despite limited psychometric data.Useful in clinics for following progress in the behaviour of mentally retarded children.
20.	Vineland II Adaptive Scales (Sparrow, Balla and Ciccheti, 2004)	Widely used instrument for mentally retarded children. Three versions available-survey version with 297 items, classroom edition 244 items and expanded form (577 items)	To be adminstred by teachers and child health workers. Depending on the situation specific version should be used.	It can be used to make comprehensive assessment of communication, daily living skills, socialization and motor skills. The manadaptive behaviour can be assessed through survey and expanded form version.

1	2	3	4	5
21.	Abbaranrt behaviour check list (Aman and Singh, 1986)	58 items, used for children 5 years and above age. community and residential versions are available good psychometric properties.	Informant Rated scale	This scale is specifically used to see the effect of pharmacological and other interventions on the behaviour of mentally challenged.
22.	Paediatric symptom check list (Jellineck, Murphy et al, 1988	35 items, Normative data available.	Parent /care giver administered	Useful for listing and measuring severity of the problematic behaviour.
23.	Rutters Children's behaviour questionnaire (Rutter, 1967)	26 items, scored on 4 point scale.	Teacher administered	Useful scale to identify oppositional and ADHD like behaviour.
24.	Conner's abbriviated parent or teacher quetionnaire (Talbot, Hales, Yudofsky, 1988)	10 items, rated on 4 point scale.	Parent or teacher rated	Best used as screening quetionnaire.
25.	Overt aggression scale modified (Coccaro et al, 1991)	25 item scale scored on 5 point likert scale, good psychometric properties.	Clinician rated, generally used in conjunction with semi structured interview.	Useful to measure the problematic behaviour like verbal and physical aggression against animate and inanimate objects, irritability-general and specific and suicidal tendencies.

development, neuropsychological testing to know brain – behaviour relationship and localize the dysfunction. The child may also be referred for knowing his special aptitude in certain skills. The schools may refer the child for achievement testing to know if the child's achievement in a particular area is upto what is expected from his intellectual ability. The clinician may refer for confirmation of diagnosis where different projective tests may be required to explore the child's relationships, conflicts and psychopathology.

Besides quantifying and providing the objective assessment of dysfunction these tests also provide some clue about why such a dysfunction is there. The Bender gestalt's visuomotor gestalt test, despite being simple to administer also provide clue for organic brain damage.

The psychological test do confirm and quantify the behavioural problems. Their usefulness in cognitive testing has been confirmed in many studies.But certain precautions are often needed to interpret their findings.The test used must be standard ones i.e. their reliability and validity must be established and norms should also be available for comparison and assessing severity. These tests need to be administered and interpreted by trained psychologists only.

The clinicians must keep all the possibilities open while using the test results. Most of the time there might be an anchoring effect i.e. the clinical impression is made generally on the basis of information which has come first. The information coming late during interview or tests often gets overlooked whereas this may provide some vital clue towards patients behaviour. Most of the time the test reports are interpreted for the frequency of the occurance of similar findings which are likely to get more credibility from the clinician. Such a bias also needs to be taken care of while interpreting the results. The tests often confirm the findings on one or few dimensions of the behaviour whereas the behavioural problems or the psychiatric disorders may not be so localized in the patients behaviours. Therefore the tests which are not comprehensive may confirm one hypothesis but can't reject the other possibilities. This possibility can also be minimized by the use of screening instruments. Therefore while referring the child for psychological testing the clinician should be fully aware of this possibility and therefore provide full information to the psychologist regarding the behaviour in question so that a sufficiently comprehensive test may be selected.

SUMMARY

In this chapter we have basically tried to bring out the fact that in clinical situation interviewing a child is much different than interviewing adult. The child have a different rate of development than adults. The clinician need to be adequately informed of the developmental level of the child before making any conclusion about his mental status. The usual method of adult interview may not be suitable for younger children. The non directive unstructured interviews are undoubtly popular among clinicians but wherever possible use of scientifically validated structured interviews should be preferred. Psychiatric rating scales do not provide any diagnostic information but these are useful in measuring severity of a particular dimension of behavior. Therefore these are useful in measuring progress of behavoural problem following an intervention.

REFERENCES

Achenbach TM Rescorla, LA (2001) Manual for AESBA school age forms and profile, Burlinton, vermont, University of Vermont, research center for children, youth and families.

Aman MG, Singh NN (1986) Abbaranrt behaviour check list Manual. East aurora, New York, Slosson educational publications Inc.

Ambrosini PJ (2000) Historical development and present status of the schedule for affective disorders for school aged children. Journal of the American academy of adoscent Psychiatry, 39, 49-58.

Angold a and Costello EJ (2000) The child and adolescent psychiatric assessment (CAPA) Journal of Child and adolescent psychiatry, 39, 39-48.

Augimeri LK, Webster CD, Keogh CJ, Levene KS (1998) early assessment risk list for boys,version 1, Consultation edition Earls court child and family centre, Ontario, Torronto.

Axline VM (1989) Plat Therapy, Longman Singapore Publishers, Singapore.

Baldwin, C. (1996). Munchausen Syndrome by Proxy: Problems of Definition Diagnosis and Treatment. Health and Social Care in the Community. 4, 3159–165.

Baron-Cohen S, Gilberg C(1992) Can autism be detected at 18 months? The needle, the haystack and CHAT. British Journal of Psychiatry 161, 839-843.

Beck A T, Steer RA (1993) Beck Depression inventory: Manual San Antonio, Psychological Corporation.

Bruck M, Ceci SJ, Hembrooke, H (1998) reliability and credibility of young children's reports:from research to policy and practice. American psychologist, 53, 136-151.

Bruinink RH, Woodcock RW, Weatherman RF, Hill BK (1997) Scale for independent behaviour –revised Itasca, Illinoise, The riverside publishing Company.

Cavadino P and allen R (2000) The children who kill :trends reasons and procedures in violent children and adolscents In : Asking the question Why (ed. G Bosewell) 1-18 Whurr, London.

Ceci SJ, Friedman RD (2000)The suggestibility of children: scientific research and legal implications. Cornell law review, 86.1010-182.

Child behaviour Checklist

Childhood psychopathology measurement schedule

Coccaro et al 1991) Overt aggression scale modified

Conner's abbriviated parent or teacher quetionnaire (Talbot, Hales,Yudofsky, 1988)

Cox A and Rutter M (1985) Diagnostic appraisal and Interviwing. In Child and adolescent psychiatry : Modern Approaches (eds M. Rutter and L herslov) pp. 233-248. Blackwell scientific publication, Oxford.

Dawes RM (1988) Rational choice in an uncertain world. Harcourt Brace, Jovanovich, New York.

Deluty RH (1979) Children's Action Tendency scale a self report measure of aggressiveness, assertiveness, and submissiveness in children. J consult Clin Psychol. 47, 1061-1071.

DuPaul GJ, Power TJ, Anastopoulos AD, Reid R, et al (1997) Teacher ratings of attention deficit hyperkinetic disorder symptoms:factor structure and normative data, Psychological assessment. 9,436-444.

Ernst M,Cookus BA,Moravec BC (2000) Pictoral instrument for children and adolescents (PICA-III-R). Journal of Academy of Child and adolescent psychiatry, 39,94-99.

Eyeberg S, Pincus D (1999) Eyeberg Child Behaviour Inventory and stutter –Eyeberg student behavior Inventory –Revised, Odessa, Florida, Psychological assessment Resources

Gilliam Je (2003) Gilliam's Asperger Disorder Scale Examiner's manual.austin, texas, Pro-Ed.

Harren E. (2002) Fragile : handle with care –protecting babies from harm, Child abuse Review, 11, 65-70.

Hodges K, McKnew D, Cytryn L, Stern L, Knline J (1982) The child assessment Schedule (CAS) Diagnostic interview : a report on reliability and validity. Journal of American Academy of Child Psychiatry, 21,468-473.

Jellinek MS, Murphy JM, Burns BJ (1986) Brief Psychological screening in out patient paediatric practicejournal of Pediatrics, 109, 371-378.

Kempe CM Silverman FN, Steele BF, Droegemuller W, Silver HK (1962) The battered child syndrome journal of American medical association.1818 17-24.

Kovacs M (1992) manual for the Children's Depression Inventory. North tondawanda, New York, Multi-Health systems, Inc.

Moos RH, Moos BH (1994) Family Environment scale. 3rd edition manual. palo Alto, California, Consulting Psychologists Press, Inc.

Nihara K, Leland H Lambert N (1993)AAMR Adaptive behaviour scales-residential and community, 2nd edition Austin texas, Pro –ed.

Ornstein PA, Gordon BN, and Larus DM. (1992) Children's memery for a personally experienced events: Implication for testimony, applied Cognitive Psychology, 6,49-60. Stewards MS and Stewards DS (1996) Interviewing young children about body touching and handling. Monographs of the society for research in child development, serial No. 248, 61.1-236.

Poznanski EO, Mokros HB (1995) Children's depression Rating scalerevised –administration booklet:a Preliminary Description Los angles, western psychological services.

Raynolds WM,(1988)Suicidal ideation questionnaire : Professional manual, Florida, Odessa, Psychological assessment resources.

Reynolds CR, Richmond BO (1994) Revised children's Manifest Anxiety Scale Manual los angles, Western Psychological services.

Riech W (2000) Diagnostic interview for Children and Adolscents, Journal of american academy of Child and Adolescent Psychiatry 39, 59-66.

Rutter M, Bailey A, Lord C(2003) Manual for Social Communication Questionnaire. Los angles, Western Psychological Press.

Rutter, M. (1975) *Helping troubled children*. Harmondsworth Penguine Books.

Rutters Children's behaviour questionnaire (Rutter, 1967)

Schopler E, Reicher RJ, Renner BR (1988) Manual for Childhood Autism rating Scale. Los angles, Western Psychological Press.

Shaffer D, Fisher P, Lucas CP, Dulcan MK, Schwab Stone ME (2000) NIMH Diagnostic Interview Schedule for Children version IV (NIMH DISC –IV) Journal of American academy of Child and Adolescent Psychiatry, 39, 28-38.

Sheldrick C(1999) Practitioner review: The assessment and management of risk in adolescents.Journal of Child Psychology and psychiatry, 40, 507-518.

Shephard M, Oppenheim B, and Mitchell, S (1971) *Childhood behavior and mental health*. London: University of London Press.

Sparrow SS, Balla DA, Ciccheti DV (2004) Vineland II Adaptive Behaviour Scales. Circle Pines minnesota, American Gguidance Services.

Speilberger CD(1973) Manual for State Trait anxiety Inventory for children Palo alto, Consulting Psychologists Press.

Stephen K (2008) Imaginary Friends: A Fun, Helpful, and Normal Part of Childhood.down loaded from www.ParentingExchange.com on 05th December, 2008.

Susser K. (2008) Sibling Rivalry and Conflict: Helping Your Children Get Along More Often downloaded from www.drsuesser.com on 27th nov 2008.

Ultman RK, sleator Ek, Spraugue RL (1997) ACTeRS : Teacher and parents forms manual. Champaign, illinoise, meri tech.inc.

Wadhera R, Gulati SP, Garg A, Ghai A(2008) Bronchial foreign body: an unusual case of child abuse, International journal of pediatric otorhinolaryngology, 72,1,133-135.

Warner, J.E. and Hansen, D.J. (1994), 'The Identification and Reporting of Physical Abuse by Physicians: A Review and Implications for Research', Vol.18, Child Abuse and Neglect, p.11

Warren SL, Emde RN,and Sroufe A(2000) internal representations predicting anxiety from child's play narratives.

Ysseeldyke JE Christenson SL (1987) The instructional environment Scale: A comprehensive Methodology for assessing an individual students instruction. Austin, Texas, pro-ed.

14

Psychological Tests Developed for Children in India : A Review of Recent Trends in Research, Practice and Application

—Maheshwar Satapathy

The most Characteristic feature of Indian life is the existence side by side of clearly marked groups-the one which has the benefit of literacy and formal education and the other which is deprived of it. Proportionately the illiterate group is very much larger (Bhatia, 1984). Dr. Bhatia was very right when he observed this before a half a century ago, though the situation has quite changed in India too, still most of the Indian people are not that educated to an extent of going through series of foreign tests and other tools. But, when we talk of psychological tests, do we really understand as to what these stand for? Even, if we claim to do so, let's have a look at this again. The term has been made more vivid in words of Wig et al. (1983) as they define it as the standardized tools to assess the behaviours of the individual or groups of persons. The tests used for adults vary from test used for children markedly because of drastic differences between children and adults. The mode of test administration, faculties tested, and the ways of assessing are quite different for children.

Why do we Need Tests for Children at all?

The tests used in any children group can be attributed with several functions. Some of them can be corroborated here for the knowledge of the test maker and taker both. They are:

- To help students in making choices and decisions during critical junctures of their life and to choose vocations, etc.

- It helps the clinician to uncover the potentials, abilities, and skills of the child and to provide many opportunities to develop them.
- The teachers can objectively assess the interests and capacities of the child and can restructure the courses, reframe the curriculum, and set some of the possible alternative for the child to choose among the set of extra co curricular activities.
- Psychological testing can help especially in an academic setting for establishing a homogeneous setting by assessing the child and help the child in getting in to a particular setting according to the potentials, he/she is lauded with.
- Psychological testing helps in diagnosis of children with any kind of developmental disorder, emotional or behavioral disorder, or children with arrested mental development. It can also give us useful insights regarding the student's inter-psychic balance.
- Tests have a lot of diagnostic, prognostic, and therapeutic implications which a researcher/clinician needs to keep in mind when assessing a child.

What should we test then?

In response to the question what should we be testing or assessing, I would like to borrow the prescription given by Johnson and Bommarita (1971). They include cognition, personality, perception of the environment, self-concept, environment, motor skills, brain injury and sensory system, physical attributes, and social behaviour in their system.

In a country like India, the children are bombarded with vicissitudes of experiences, irresistible and compelling influences of western culture and mass media and communication. Their developing psyche is quite plastic and formative. With due regard to the developmental malleability the environment has a lot of influence on children. Children are force-fed with the product of 3-language formula and huge tasks of schools with the growing needs and aspirations of their respected parents every time they grow up to a higher ladder. India is a developing country and the children grown in this country differ from the other children of other developed countries. In a county where most people are still rotting in poverty, children are neglected and very less regard is given for unfolding all of their innermost faculties and potentials. Therefore, the developing needs and their basic interests are to be studied more carefully. A proper psychological testing can only enable any sincere and prudent steps in the development of any plans/strategies for children.

The wide difference in the socio-cultural context of India from the west, influence of the rapid socio-cultural transformation and the culture specific aspects about a child's temperament are quite important when making any plans or policies regarding the mental health of children. G.G. Prabhu (1987) has also talked about the lack of recognizable tradition of evaluation and assessment in the areas of child mental health. Paradoxically when the needs are so much, the clinical practitioner lacks the appropriate tools and skills in assessing the various dimensions of a child's psyche and behavior. Initiatives taken by the health care professionals in the development of standardized tools and assessment procedures are quite discouraging and not up to the mark. Psychological testing has been an interesting area for the psychiatrists but the practice of testing has been generally limited to the few clinical psychologists in India. This problem of lack of serious testing and assessments has been percolating for decades and this problem has been exacerbated by the lack of trained professionals for the using them.

Some of the tools developed in India by the Indian researchers over the decades of research and clinical work for children on the Indian soil are noteworthy. We should give a furtive glance at some of the basic tests/scales developed for children and adolescents in India. Based on the categories of testing and the dimensions tested they can be divided as are discussed under various types.

(A) Intelligence:

Intelligence has been defined by many, but the fruit of intelligence is reflected in the performance of a given individual. So many tests are devised both in west and in our own country for assessing the intelligence and the types of intelligence in a child. For decades, researchers have been quite busy developing tests/scales or batteries for testing intelligence. The reason these tests have gained acceptance and some fortunately, recognition is that clinicians have started recognizing the value of an intelligence test for several things. Now even schools have started enrolling children based on intelligence scores only.

The various tests that have gained gradual acceptance and fame has began with C.M. Bhatia's performance battery of testing intelligence (Bhatia, 1955). Therefore, the major revolution of testing in India has been dating back to 1950's and one of the pioneers in that enshrining tradition is Dr. Bhatia only. There are at present several standard tests/scales available for testing intelligence function of any group of children for varied age range. The age ranges are varying from each other. One of the tests is a modification of modified Goddard Form Board Test, that purports to assess the performance ability of the child with the age range of 8-12 years. Some other tests are adaptations that are made to test the same functions in our setting by taking into consideration our context and the differential growth/developmental experiences of an Indian child. Some of them are Stanford Binet Scale in Hindi adapted by S.K. Kulshrestha (1971) and in Kannada and Marathi by V.V. Kamath ; Goddard's form board test by B.C. Patel meant for testing children with the age range of 6-10yrs by performance. Another powerful adaptation of Cattell's Culture Fair Intelligence Test (2and3) for 8 or more year's children through mathematics was done by S. Rao.

Another well-known scale that has gained acceptance by several clinical psychologists/ neuro-psychologists in India is the adaptation of Wechsler's Intelligence Scale for Children (WISC) by A.J. Malin. It is quite similar to the original version of WISC and includes many similar questions canalized according to the education pattern and awareness level of an average Indian child. The reason of adapting a foreign test has been avidly reflected by the writings of Malin (1969). He contends, "To close the doors to all foreign tests on the plea that indigenous constructions only can do full justice to the Indian environment would not only deprive us of the latest advances in psychometrics, but also would scarcely commend India for a scientific outlook". The solution as he continues, says lies in inculcating a broader scientific outlook.

Malin's test of intelligence for children is made for 5-15 years of children. Some of the basic dimensions that it purports to measure are information, comprehension, arithmetic, similarities, vocabulary, digit span, picture completion, picture arrangement, block design, object assembly, coding, and mazes. Norms are provided up to 5-15 years of age. Some of the practical difficulties lie with the test application like the language barrier again. Though he has contended that the language of India is pluralistic, so the adoption of English will solve the problem, still the problem in translating each question and then interpretation is a little cumbersome for the clinician. Another pitfall is that it does not provide separate norms for girls and boys in accordance with their age and educational levels.

Tests can be divided on the lines of group vs. individual tests and performance and verbal functions intending to assess.Tests which are individualized, standardized and test through performance are problem solving test by L.N. Dubey, Draw-a Man Test by Promila Pathak (1987) meant for 6 years or more, human figure drawing/draw a man test by A.N. Mishra (1970) for 6-10 years in Hindi. Sharma's draw a bicycle test of intelligence is for 11-16 years. Problem solving ability test by L.N. Dubey is for 12-17 years ages is a nice test for analyzing problem solving capability.

The tests that are meant for group, and assess both verbal and performance functions of a child are test of general intelligence by Prayag Mehta (1962). Another test (general mental ability test for children (7-11 years) is devised by Srivastava and Saxena. Group test of intelligences are many and they are devised with the whole function of assessing intelligence of a group of children at school or for research. Mixed type group test of intelligence is a good test devised by P.N. Mehrotra that include both verbal as well as non-verbal tests. Another such test is devised by S. Jalota (1972) for 11-16 years and tests both verbal as well as performance. Another test developed in Hindi called Samoohik Mansik Yogyata Parikksha by R.K. Tondon (1961) need mention here

Among all these tests, C.M. Bhatia's performance battery is the best test available for assessing children with the tests incorporated. Most of the tests are performance oriented, to catch and sustain attention of children in tests. Undoubtedly this is the only test which provides norms for both literates and illiterates, for every age level and years of education in consideration. It especially provides information for a child who is handicapped on verbal tests, attractive due to its novel and intriguing manipulative activities and provides opportunities for observing the clinical situations and data. It incorporates 5 tests within its system namely Koh's block design test, Alexander's pass-a long test, pattern drawing test, immediate memory test, and picture construction test. It provides two scores as performance quotient and verbal quotient and averaged together we get the IQ of the child. It is worth mentioning here that NCERT had published a book entitled, "Indian Mental Measurement Handbook: Intelligence and Aptitude Tests" (NCERT, 1991). It provides a detailed description of about 40 tests relating to intelligence, creativity, and aptitude. All these tests are either developed specifically for Indian population (including children) and each test is reviewed is two eminent psychologists / educationist. It is a good source for someone looking for tests for Indian children.

(B) Personality and Temperament

Children's temperament is reflexive and modifiable from time to time. Therefore, we need good quality tests for assessing the temperament of a child. Some of the tests that have come across for assessing the child's temperament need mention over here. Malhotra's Temperament Schedule (1988) is one of the best tests available for assessing the child. It is made for children with the age range of 4-14 years. It has certain dimensions on which it tests the child, these are Sociability (Approach-Withdrawal, Adaptability, Threshold of responsiveness), Emotionality (Moodand Persistence), Energy (Activity, Intensity), and Attentivity (Distractibility). By testing these nine dimensions, they contend that they can test the temperament of the child in general. Another important test for assessing children's personality is related to the projective techniques of theme interpretation, Children's Apperception Test by Uma Choudhary (1985). It is an adaptation of the original CAT. The author herself accepts the lack of freedom when adapting a test as she has felt during making the CAT pictures by comparing with the original version. Therefore, all of the cards are modified according to the Indian children's mindset. It contains10 pictures of animals and standardized over the school children of Calcutta and West Bengal and other northeastern states.

Battery of Pre-Adolescent Personality Tests by Pareek, Rao, Ramalingasway, and Sharma (1975) is also not worthy. This includes a list of tests like Pre-Adolescent Adjustment Scale (PAAS), Pre-Adolescent Dependency Scale (PADS), Pre-adolescent Class Trust Scale (PACTS), Pre-Adolescent Initiative Questionnaire (PAIQ), Pre-Adolescent Activity Level Scale (PAALS), and Pre-Adolescent Level of Aspiration Test (PALAT). As the authors claim it can be utilized for individual as well as group diagnosis as an index of mental health, for guidance and counseling, and for research in pre-adolescent and adolescent behavior. Norms were developed taking standardization sample from 3 cities of India, namely Delhi, Calcutta, and Coimbatore with the possible reason that these cities represent 3 dominant parts of India.

Other tests testing the various dimensions of temperament, self or various traits are worthy of mention. They are Children's Personality Questionnaire by Kapoor and Rao (1972) for 8-12 years child in Hindi as an adaptation. Another scale is a dimension of temperament scale by N.K. Chadha and S. Chadna (1984) available in both Hindi and English. How children do seek attention and approval of the elderly is tested by children's approval seeking test by N.K. Tripathi and R. Ambast (1984). Children's self-concept scale is one of the most ambitions scales prepared for testing what children think about them by S.P. Ahluwalia (1986). For appraising the interest of the child, we can take the help of an interesting and quite well known tool named as Chattergie's Interest Preference record (Chattergie's, 1960) which test the interest of the child through performance.

Locus of control scale for children by Roma Pal (1995) is a test for assessing the locus of control.

On an average test for assessing temperament, exclude one quite significant dimension of a tool of comprehensiveness. They even include only very few dimensions of a child's psyche and behavior, perhaps due to the small amount of research done on them. There is a dearth of test instruments for children's assessment of personality. For testing the personality of children, Pathak has adapted a very useful test named as draw a person Test of the original version by Goodenough. Particularly as a projective test, it gives special insights to the clinician about a child's personality.

For studying the self-esteem, we can take the help of a test developed by Vinutha et al., (1989).This test was standardized on a sample of 368 boys and girls using Kannada and English versions of the inventory.

(C) Maturity:

One of the commonly used tests for assessing social maturity levels is the Vineland's social maturity scale (VSMS) adapted by A.J. Malin (1992). This scale is developed in the Nagpur child guidance clinic. This scale has limited its age range up to 15 years of age unlike the original version that claims to test up to 25 years of age. Even scoring is not as easy as the original. It has other lacunae, as it lacks the original dimensions of testing, based on which parents are told about the specific developments of their child in various spheres, so it takes the help of the original version. So this puts a doubt mark again the applicability of the dimensions and their age scores on our children. The dimensions it seeks to test are self-help (general), self-help (eating), self-help (dressing), locomotion, occupation, communication, self-direction, and socialization.

Some of the other tests are Stewart Social Maturity Scale by T.V. Rao and A.J. Stuart (1976), Social Maturity Scale by R.P. Srivastava (1983) meant for 0-25 years, as latter one has a little superiority over the VSMS. Social maturity scale has also another scale for this function. All these tests have one thing in common i.e. they try to measure the social maturity of the children by taking a behavioral account of the child from the parents/care takers. Rao's Social Maturity Scale (Rao,1998), assesses social maturity and gives scores on three dimensions viz., personal adequacy (work orientation, self-direction, ability to take stress); interpersonal adequacy (communication, enlightened trust and cooperation); and social adequacy (social commitment, social tolerance and openness to change). It takes about 45 minutes for administration.

(D) Curiosity and Liking: As children are curious and they will never leave anything new and manipulative, so they need to be tested to know the practical ability of the child in a situation. Therefore, Rajiv Kumar has devised a test for analyzing the curiosity level of the child. It is in Hindi and standardized over Indian children. The test for liking is only one at present, as no serious look has been given to the matter of what the child likes or not. Therefore, it gives clues regarding the styles parental upbringing and researches undertaken on them. Student liking scale developed by Malhotra and Passi (1985) is a likert type scale developed for the purpose of measuring student's liking for teacher behaviour are assessed in this scale. These are: i) student liking for teacher behavior inside the class, ii) student liking for teacher behaviour outside the class, iii) student liking for teacher behaviour with colleagues, iv) student liking for teacher behaviour with school management. It is a thirty item scale and percentile norms are provided.

(E) Study habits: After liking another important function of everyday life that concerns with the utmost growth and development is STUDY. Some of the tests developed for assessing this function are study habit and reading interest inventory by Jai Prakash.It is in Hindi and not only shows the level of interest, but also the various personality dimensions of a child. Test of study habits and attitudes by C.P. Mathur (1985) is another test that tries to test the habits and attitudes of the child in the areas of study, reflecting a lot on his personality.

(F) Adjustment Functions: Adjustment problems have been one of the common problems with children and which often brings them to a clinician for assessment and evaluation.

Therefore, the tests that are developed for assessing this function are Adjustment Inventory for School Children (AISC) by A.K.P. Sinha and R.P. Singh (1984). Bhagia school adjustment inventory by N.K. Bhagia (1967) in Hindi is one of the common tests used in schools. There is another scale available also for assessing the functions of adjustment in children which is known as Adjustment Inventory. It was developed by V.K. Mittal (1965) and is available in Hindi. Emotional stability also provides a useful measure of the adjustment of a child. Problem behaviour checklist by Veemala Veeraraghavan and Dogra (1999) is a nice test testing the various psychopathologies in a child or group of children. It's a standardized test for assessing the adjustment related problems of a child unlike the foreign, test available for assessing the adjustment function in totality like Child Behavior Rating Scale (CBRS).

(G) Anxiety: there are so many tests developed for measuring the anxiety level, types of anxiety, sources of anxiety, etc. of the child in India. Two well-known tests of Sarason's general anxiety scales for children (GASC) and test anxiety scale for children (TASC) are adapted in Hindi and Punjabi languages by Nijhawan (1971). These scales are simple, easy to score and have been reliably used in several research studies. GASC has been used in several ways, but TASC has been used for assessing the level of anxiety before any scholastic or achievement performance test (Nijhawan, 1971). TASC has also been developed by A. Kumar (1982) for 6ht to 8th grade children in Hindi. Academic anxiety scale for children is another test developed for the same function by A.K. Singh and A. Sen Gupta (1986) in Hindi. Thakur's Death Anxiety Scale (1984) is another test for assessing the anxiety level of children associated with the concept of death. It provides vivid questions for assessing this trait. Fear in children can be assessed perfectly by only one tool available for assessing it. This test is developed by C.B.Dwivedi (1977) is for 6-13 years of children. Frustration tolerance and the anxiety produced thereafter is the subject of one test developed for children by S.N.Rai. All these tests are quite similar to each other and are not drastically different.

(H) Developmental screening: There is always a great need for developing some valid and comprehensive developmental screening test or checklist. In response to the strongly felt need, M.Kapoor has devised a checklist (Developmental Psychopathology Check List). It incorporates six basic dimensions for screening purpose. They are developmental history, developmental problems, psychopathology (hyperkinesis, conduct disorders, learning problems, emotional disorders, obsessive compulsive disorders, somatic problems including hysteria and psychosis), psychosocial stressors, temperamental profile, and supportive factors. As the author contends, it can be effectively used across age groups, gender, both cross-sectionally and longitudinally, and is specially simplified to suit the Indian children.

Developmental screening test is a test developed by J. Bharat Raj (1983) at all India institute of Speech Pathology and Hearing, Mysore. This test has a simplified version with the age range of 3 months to 15 years. It is found to be quite useful for and satisfactory having high validity and reliability in urban samples. Another Developmental Screening Test has been devised by NIMH in 1988. Gessel's Developmental Schedule has been adapted by Bhakoo et al., (1977) and Muralidharan. Developmental Assessment Scales for Indian infants (SASII) revised by P. Pathak (1997) is also available. Norms for infants from birth to 30 months are provided. It is modeled after Bayley's Scales for Infant Development.

(I) Parent Child Relationship and Attitude of Children towards Parents: Several parent child relationship scales have been developed over the decades of research but only a few of them are reported here. One of these is developed by S. Malhotra (2002). How children perceive parents can be tested by children's report of parental behaviour inventory developed by Uma Saxena (1993). Home environment inventory by Mishra (1989) assesses home environment. It has 100 items and gives scores on ten dimensions viz., control, protectiveness, punishment, conformity, social isolation, reward, deprivation of privileges, nurturance, rejection and permissiveness. Percentile norms are given.

(J) Creativity: creativity is another possible dimension of testing among children. Creativity is a multidimensional (verbal and non verbal) 'attribute differently' distributed among people and includes chiefly the factors of seeing problems, fluency, flexibility, originality, inquisitiveness and persistence. There are very few tests available for these though, but they prove to be helpful. The first test namely, Passi Tests (Passi, 1979) of Creativity (H/E) are developed for the purpose of measuring creativity in school children. In all six tests, namely: i) the seeing problems test ii) the unusual uses test iii) the consequences test, iv) the test of Inquisitiveness v) the square puzzle test and vi) Blocks test of creativity are included in the test battery. Another test is Majumdar scientific Creativity Test (MSCT) which tests also the components related to scientific creativity among children. Verbal test of creative thinking by Mehdi (1985) is verbal test which is a part of total battery which consists of both verbal and non-verbal tests. The verbal test of creativity includes four sub-tests, namely consequences, unusual uses, similarities and product improvement tests.

(J) Miscellaneous: for studying the various other traits as well, psychopathologies in children several tests have been developed at several parts of India. Some of those tests are published and some of them are unpublished. One of the tests developed by Mishra and Tripathi (1990) is prolonged deprivation scale (PDS) in Hindi and can be used for any age group. This test has been successful in analyzing the developmental lags produced in children due the various deprivations, as in India still millions of people are rotting in poverty. Child Psychopathology Measurement Schedule, is one of the other tests that have been devised by Savita Malhotra for addressing the need of a well-standardized, reliable, culturally appropriate and valid instrument. This is the adaptation of Child Behavior Checklist by Achenbach and Edelbrock. Student Liking Scale developed by Malhotra and Passi (1985).

Considering the growth of various learning related problems in children, two tests are developed in India for children. One of such tests is by Kapur, (1995) which consists of eight dimensions. They are test of general abilities (includes WISC), attention, percepto-motor abilities, visual discrimination, auditory discrimination, memory, language skills, and arithmetic skills. Again, she says that following the test, a profile of strengths and weaknesses is drawn for the individual child and a remediation program tailored to suit to the needs of the child is prepared.

Learned helplessness scale has been developed by Kohli and Dhar, et al. (1987). for assessing the dependence proneness of the child. It contains 15 items and has been reported to have high reliability and validity (Dhar et al., 1987).

Another test which need mention here is the Indian adaptation of Rosenzweig's Picture – Frustration Study (Children Form) by Pareek and Rosenzweig (1989). It can be used for a variety of purposes e.g. clinical, and for the examination of dynamic patterns of child's behavior etc. It is applicable to children of 4-13 years of age.

Problems and Concerns

After this whole review of test developed in India for children it can safely be concluded that the test developed in India are not quite deficient, but they need to take a comprehensive differential approach. Tests should be oriented clear. In several tests, some fussy aspects are lying. Even in practical situations, we face many difficulties in applying these tests on children, because of their length and monotony. Paper – pencil test are quite boring and even have many precautions to be taken. There are so many tests on intelligence that are primarily meant for verbally fluent children, but very few tests are oriented towards creating non-verbal as well as interest arousing contents.

Very few tests take into consideration the colors, all are black and white tests, which create monotony and may influence the results of the test. There are several tests which are misused; even sometimes the clinician himself is quite confused as to how to use them. If strict control is not established, then objectivity may be lost from the test results. There is very less flexibility in the administration of the test, as in practice and actual situations we cannot make all things constant. The dynamics of behavior and temperament of children may falsify the test results by manipulating it. The lack of standardized tools for assessing memory, and various other psychopathologies is one of the common problems encountered in a practical situation.

What our researches should focus now?

There are wide varieties of areas that are waiting to be explored, and if done judiciously, they may bring us promising and lucrative benefits. Our research and practice should now focus on developing authentic, and our context specific tests to meet the demands of our Indian subcontinent. We should all try by establishing an intellectual pool for developing resources and generating initiatives. Otherwise, as observed by Zeigarnik (1972) we may face the same situation where test results will produce only end-results, while the work processes of the subject –the individual features of intellectual activity, the qualitative aspects of disturbance and the multifarious qualities of his activities will remain hidden. Dr. C.M. Bhatia's (1984) observation need a special mention here that "the tests we use in Indian setting, borrowing from others are a positive disservice to the subjects tested and to the clinical psychologists and psychiatrists who use them." Therefore, we should reorient ourselves to see freely with open eyes towards the needs and demands and should try in all effort to fulfill them.

The list of areas that we should attend more carefully now is:

- Memory, information processing, and retrieval
- Better learning techniques, Attention tests
- Attitudes (towards school, friends, family, environment and the whole world).
- Tools for community work and various other tools for assessing specific needs of that population
- Diagnostic interview with children
- Communication problems
- Shyness, timidity, and self-reservation
- Fear inventories and irrational fears
- Depression, sadness, winter blues
- Children's global functioning and adaptation, Strengths and difficulties

- Obsessive-compulsive problems
- Autism, mental retardation, hyperactivity and attention deficit, and various other pervasive developmental disorders
- Schizophrenia psychotic disorders, formal thought disorders and the interview methods.
- Emotional maturity and stability
- Children's love, affection and attachment.
- Achievement motivation, general motivation, and child's aspirations.
- Scales for children with some kind of organic disorder, heart problem (operated), brain injured, other physical handicaps, cancer and injury, etc.
- Expectations from the world, wishes and desires.
- Feelings of children and the psychological states of children in/after trauma.
- Decision making, risk taking and achievement motivation..

Prospects and Promises for Future:

There is a need for cooperative effort between the academic psychologist, the clinical psychologist and the psychiatrist and a psychometrician is required. Therefore, these three professionals cannot achieve the great goal of making the armamentarium of testing stronger single handedly, as there is a constant need to furnish each other's knowledge and to collaborate with other health professionals like psychiatrists, social worker, and speech pathologists and audiologists, cardiothoracic and vascular surgeons, and pediatrician. Even at times, we do need the help of rehabilitation specialist and oncologist. Therefore, what we need now is to take a very broad cross-cultural need based approach, and the solution always rests on the solution based perspective taking. At the same time the practitioner, need to inculcate and grow a perspective taking ability to understand the growing need of the *Homo sapiens*.

REFERENCES

Ahluwalia, S.P. (1986) *Children Self Concept Scale.* Agra: National Psychological Corporation.

Bhagia, M.N. (1967) *The School Adjustment Inventory.* Delhi: Mansayan. Chada, N.K. and Chandna, S. (1984) Dineenjian of temperament Scale. Agra : NPC.

Bharat Raj. J. (1983). *Developmental Screening Test (DST).* Mysore: Swayamsiddha.

Bhatia, C.M. (1955) *Performance intelligence test battery,* Bombay: Oxford.

Bhatia, C.M. (1984). Psychological Testing in India- a Retrospect and Prospect, Letter to the Editor, *Indian Journal. of Clinical Psychology*: 53:56.

Chatterji, S. (1960) *Chatterji's Non-Language Preference Record Examiner's Manual,* Patna: Author.

Choudhury, U. (1985). *An Indian Modification to the Children's Apperception Test.* New Delhi : Mansayan.

Dhar, U., Kohli, S. and Dhar, S. (1987) *Manual for the Learned Helplessness Scale. Bhiwani: Haryana Council of Psycological Reserach.*

Dwivedi, C.B. (1977) *Manual of Directions and Norms for Fear in Children Inventory,* Varanasi: Rupa Psychological Centre.

Jalota, S.S. (1972) *Manual of Group Test of General Mental Ability.* 225, Sector 16-A Chandigarh.

Johnson, O.B., and Bommarita, J.W. (1971). *Tests and measurements in child development: a handbook.* San Francisco: Jossey-Bass Inc.

Kapoor, S. and Eao, N. (1972) *Children Personality Questionnaise form B.* 1 Uinois : IPAT.

Kapur, M. (1995). Developmental Psychopathology Check-list for Children (DPCL). In M. Kapur, (1995). *Mental Health of Indian Children.* New Delhi: Sage.

Kapur, M. (1995). *Mental Health of Indian Children.* New Delhi: Sage.

Kulshrestha, S.K. (1971) *Stanford-Binet Intelligence Scale* (3rd Eds.) (1960) Hindi Adaptation, Allahabad: Manas Sewa Sansthan.

Kumar. A. (1982). *Global Anxiety Scale for Children.* Agra: National Psychological Corporation.

Malhotra, S. (2002) *Child Psychiatry in India: An Approach to Assessment and Management of Childhood Psychiatric Disorders,* New Delhi: McMillan.

Malin, A.J. (1969) *Malin's Intelligence Scale for Indian Children (MISIC), S.* Malhotra, and A. Malhotra, (1988). *Malhotra's Temperament Schedule (MTS).* Agra: National Psychological Corporation.

Mathur, C.P. (1985) *Test of study habits,* Agra: National Psychological Corporation.

Mehdi, B. (1985) *Verbal test of creative thinking,* Agra: National Psychological Corporation.

Mehta, P. (1962) *Group Intelligence Test.* New Delhi: Mansayan.

Mishra, A.N. (1970) *Human Figure Drawing-A-Man Test for Children.* Ballia: Sunita Misra.

Mishra, G.; Tripathi, L.B. (1990), *Prolonged Deprivation Scale (PDS).* Agra: National Psychological Corporation.

Mishra, K.S. (1989) Manual for Have Environment *moventory.* Lucknow : Ankur Psychological Agency.

Mittal, V.K. (1965) *Adjustment inventory School / College Form.* Meerut: Manovigyyan.

Molhotra, S.P. and Passi, B.K. (1985) *Student Liking Scale,* Agra: National Psychological Enlarged Edition, by J. Bharath Roy, Mysore: Swayamsiddha Prakshana.

NCERT (1991) *Indian Mental Measurement Handbook: Intelligence and aptitude,* New Delhi: Natoinal Council of Educational Research and Training.

Pal, R. (1983) *Locus of control (Internal-External Scale).* Agra: Psychological Research Cell.

Pareek, U.; Rao, T.V; Ramalingaswamy, P. and Sharma, B.R. (1975). *The Battery for Pre-Adolescent Personality Test.*

Pareek,U and Rosenzweig, S. (1989) *Manual of the Indian adaptation of Rosenzweig picture frustration study (Children Form),* Delhi: Mansayan.

Passi, B.K. (1979). *Passi Tests of Creativity,* Agra: National Psychological Corporation.

Pathak, P. (1987). *Draw-a Man Test for Indian Children Pune : Anand Agencies.*

Peshwaria, R.; Venkatesan, S. (1992). *Behavioral Assessment Scales for Indian Children with Mental Retardation, (BASIC-MR) Part-B.* NIMH, Secunderabad.

Prabhu, G.G. (1987). Child and adolescent mental health research in India: An overview. *NIMHANS Journal,* 5, 5-10.

Rao, N. (1998) *Manual for Rao's social Maturity scale, Agra : NPC.*

Rao, T.V. and Stewart, A.J. (1976) *Stewart Maturity Scale; Indian Adaptation.* Delhi:Mansayan.

Singh, A.K. And Gupta, A.S. (1986) *Manual for Academic Anxiety Scale for Children.* Agra: National Psychological Corporation.

Sinha, D., Varma, M. (1971). *Manual for Moral Judgement Test (MJT).* Agra: National Psychological Corporation.

Tandan, R.K. (1961) *Samoohik Mansik Yogyata Priksha.* Moradabad: Psychological Research Centre.

Veeraraghavan, V.; and Dogra, A. (1999). *Problem Behavior Checklist (PBCL),* New Delhi: Psycho-Educational Testing Centre.

Wig, N.N.; Verma, S.K; Pershad, D. (1983). Development of Psychological Tests in India: An Overview of the Current Situation. *Indian Journal of clinical psychology*, 10: 429-437.

Zeigrnaik, B.V. (1972) *Experimental Abnormal Psychology* (Translated by Timothy C. Brock) New York: Plenum Press.

SECTION–IV : CHILDHOOD DISORDERS AND INTERVENTION

15. Childhood Disorders and Interventions
16. EMDR: Therapeutic Prospects in Child Psychopathology

15

Childhood Disorders and Interventions

—Harprit Kaur, Jasneet Kaur and Such Kaur

Mental disorders are conceptualised as clinically significant behavioural or psychological syndrome or pattern that occur in an individual, and that are associated with present distress (e.g. a painful symptom) or disability (i.e. impairment in one or more important areas of functioning) or with a significantly increased risk of suffering, pain, disability, or an important loss of freedom (DSM-IV, American Psychiatric Association, 1994). In addition, this syndrome must not be merely an acceptable and culturally sanctioned response to a particular event. It must currently be considered a manifestation of a behavioural, psychological, biological dysfunction in an individual.

In past two millennia, many nomenclatures have been developed that differ in their relative emphasis on phenomenology, etiology, and course as defining features. Moreover, various systems have categorised the mental disorders in their own manner. The most important and widely used systems for mental disorders are: *"Diagnostic and Statistical Manual of Mental Disorders"* Currently DSM IV-TR is use [DSM, American Psychiatric Association, 1994] and *"International Statistical Classification of Diseases and Health Related Problems"* Currently ICD-10 is in use (ICD, World Health Organisation, 1992). The American Psychiatric Association collaborated with the New York Academy of Medicine to develop a nationally acceptable psychiatric nomenclature that would be incorporated with the first edition of the American Medical Association's Standard Classified Nomenclature of disease. This nomenclature was designed primarily for diagnosing patients with severe psychiatric and neurological disorders. DSM-I contains a glossary of description of the diagnostic categories and manual of mental disorders to focus on clinical utility. DSM-II was similar to DSM-I but eliminated the term reaction and it was made compatible with the ICD system prevalent at that time. The third edition i.e. DSM-III represented major advance in the diagnosis of mental disorders and greatly facilitated empirical research. American Psychiatric Association appointed a work group to review DSM-III, which lead to the development of revised version of DSM i.e. DSM-IIIR in 1987. Then came DSM-IV in 1994. Both DSM III and IV were multi-axial system, that evaluated the patient along several variables, contained five axis which comprised the entire classification of Mental disorders, Personality disorders, Physical disorders, Mental Retardation, Psychosocial and Environmental problems. The major categories of childhood disorders are mentioned in DSM-IIIR (APA, 1987) and ICD-7 (WHO). In both of them, these disorders are described and explained with clinical symptoms and there diagnostic criteria.

ETIOLOGY

Causation of childhood disorders may be categorized as Pre, Peri, and Post-natal factors or as genetic - biological factors and the psychosocial factors.

Pre-natal Factors are the factors which operate before birth and which influence the child's health. Many research studies have shown that adverse influence during pregnancy may cause impaired development in the child after birth. Food deprivation (Creasy,1991); alcohol intake (Faden, Graubard and Dufour, et.al.,1997); smoking (Eyler et.al.,1998); and drugs during pregnancy (Tuthill et.al.,1990) may result in adverse birth outcomes, such as preterm birth and low birth weight. Prenatal factors also influence general physical development of child. Studies have shown that the variation in the fetal physiological environment, appear to have effect on brain development, which may lead to neonatal brain disease or psychopathology later in life. Exposure to high levels of radiation on pregnancy has been related to mental retardation (Otake and Schull, 1984). Other prenatal factors linked with later development, in particular schizophrenia and major affective disorders, include malnutrition (Hoek, Brown and Susser, 1998; Geddes, 1999) and influenza (Machon Madnick and Huttunen, 1997). Children are born with high risk for schizophrenia, if their mothers experience severe maternal stress in pregnancy (Van Os and Selten, 1998).

Peri-natal Factors are those factors that are present during child birth and may be responsible for later child psychopathology. Anoxia (lack of oxygen during birth) may predispose to brain damage and neuropsychiatric disorders. Premature delivery and even the excessive use of drugs during delivery can lead to brain dys-functioning. Children inherit the biological make-up which may predispose them directly or indirectly to various disorders. The most common birth difficulty and low birth weight associated later mental disorders are Mental retardation (M.R.), attention deficit-hyperactivity disorder (A.D.H.D), and emotional disturbances. It is also important to note that the extent of combination of both pre and peri-natal factors will determine the later psychopathology in a child.

Post-Natal Factors are those factors that occur just after birth. The neonate being vulnerable may be exposed to a variety of problems. A frequent complication in the 1st week of life is neonatal jaundice which has various causes. Jaundice due to blood group in-compatibility may cause brain damage. Other possible causes may include any trauma, infection and under-nutrition. Researches have shown that if the mother is under any trauma (e.g. death of near one) or does not take proper diet, this will definitely affect the health of the child.

Genetic and Biological Factors: The basic biology and the dynamic organic nature of the human body are fundamental determinants of health. The focus is on the genetic endowment of an individual, the functioning of the various body systems and the process of development and maturation. Biological risk factors can be either innate (e.g. Down syndrome) or acquired (eg. brain damage due to severe head injury). Biological risk factors can affect healthy child development at several levels. Risk factors are not independent variables operating in a vacuum but may interact in an additive fashion (Szatmari et.al., 1994). Different types of biological and genetic risk factors are given below:-

(a) Genetic and Chromosomal Syndrome: such as Down Syndrome, Fragile 'X' Syndrome, and Tuberous Sclerosis. Individually these disorders may be rare, but there are many single gene disorders and chromosomal abnormalities that affect the brain (Costa, Scriver and Childs,1985).

(b) Drug abuse during pregnancy: low doses of alcohol, tobacco and illegal prescription drugs have a harmful effect on developing foetus (Singer, Garber and Kliegman,1991; Slotkin,1998).

(c) Prematurity: premature births are defined as births that occur before 36- weeks' gestation. Most of the premature children do very well and have minimal disabilities (Saigal et.al.,1990; Lorenz et.al.,1998). However, some have very special needs in terms of learning problems, physical disabilities, sensory deficits and attention deficits (Saigal et.al., 1991, 1991a; Szatmari et.al.,1990).

(d) External influences on brain development: studies have shown that stress during pregnancy as well as maternal and early infant nutrition can affect the development of fetal and infant brain. Animal models suggest that stress during pregnancy can affect the intrauterine hormonal environment which may then place the infant at later risk of depression (Schneider et.al.,1998; Sandman et.al.,1997; Anisman et.al., 1998).

(e) Gender: studies have shown that boys are at greater risk than girls for the development of several developmental disorders such as autism (Bryson, Clark and Smith,1988) and certain types of behavioural conditions as well as attention deficit and conduct disorder (Offord, et. al.1987).

(f) Developmental disabilities: these disorders have a biological basis with strong genetic causation. These disorders are characterized by delayed acquisition of certain skills and uneven pattern of development.

In addition to pre; peri; post-natal and genetic factors, there are some other causes behind childhood disorders, these are called *Psychosocial Factors*. Psychosocial factors are those psychological and social factors that affect a child's psychological make up and hence lead to distorted cognitions and maladaptive behaviour. Major psychosocial factors that affect child's development are :- socio-economic status, distorted family relationships, emotional instability, lack of security, child rearing practices, communication patterns in a family, family composition, school environment, peer group, labelling practises etc. Like pre; peri; and post natal factors these factors also play an important role in the etiology of childhood disorders. They may be the precipitants, or responsible for maintaining the dysfunctional behavioural patterns. The family, school, playmates, socio-cultural environment on the one hand and the child's temperament on the other creates the milieu in which the child lives and grows. Any stressor in it or the absence of support in any of these area's , will become the cause for child psychopathology.

DIFFERENT CHILDHOOD DISORDERS

The important childhood disorders are as follows:

- Mental Retardation
- Learning Disabilities
- Attention Deficit Hyperactive Disorder (ADHD)
- Autism
- Conduct Disorder
- Schizophrenia
- Anxiety
- Depression
- Other Childhood Disorders
  - (a) Selective Mutism
  - (b) Enuresis and Encopresis
  - (c) Tics

(d) Pica
(e) Impulse Control
(f) Somatization
(g) School Refusal
(h) Dissociation

Mental Retardation (M.R.)

Mental retardation or intellectual disability is significantly sub-average intellectual functioning existing concurrent with low level of adaptive behaviour, present from birth or before the age one becomes adult, causing limitations in the ability to perform normal activities of daily life. Psychological classification of M.R. is based on I.Q., whereas medical classification is etiologically based.

Main clinical features of M.R. are physical and neurological abnormalities; unusual facial features; too large or too small head; deformities in hands and feet; cognitive impairment and language deficiencies; behavioural problems – explosive outbursts, temper tantrums and physically aggressive behaviour; impaired ability to communicate and control impulses; other signs of serious illness – seizures, lethargy, vomiting, abnormal urine odour and failure to feed and grow normally.

WHO surveys have revealed that about 3% of the total population are considered to have mental retasdation It is a lifelong condition. Level of Mental Retardation determines the expected functioning. A *mildly retarded* (IQ 52-69) individual can develop social and communication skills in the first six years; motor coordination is slightly impaired; and is often not diagnosed until later age. During the same time, a *moderately retarded* (IQ 36-51) can talk or learn to communicate; but the social awareness is poor; and motor coordination just fair. A *severely retarded* (IQ 20-35) on the other hand can say a few words; is able to learn some self help skills; but motor coordination is poor. A *profoundly retarded* (IQ less than 18) exhibits extreme cognitive limitations and little motor coordination. By 20 years of age, the mild MR can learn up to about 6th grade level and can be expected to learn appropriate social skills. The moderate MR learns some social and occupational skills; and may progress to elementary school level. The severe MR may just learn to talk or communicate; and learn simple health habits by this time. The profound MR however will still have poor motor coordination and limited communication skills. In terms of social and vocational maturity the mild MR achieves social-vocational skills for self support but during times of economic or social stress may need guidance and assistance. The moderately retarded can support self by performing unskilled or semiskilled work under sheltered conditions. However severe MR at best may partially contribute to self care under supervision. The profound MR achieves very limited self care and usually needs lifelong nursing care.

M.R. is a condition and not a disorder, so it cannot be treated but can only be managed. The management of M.R. involves *multi-dimensional approach* that includes psycho-education, psycho-therapeutic and psycho-pharmacological interventions, as per the need of specific case and level of retardation. Pharmacotherapy in management includes various anti-depressants, anti-psychotics, and anti-anxiolytics. Psychotherapies include individual therapies like play therapy, operational therapies, music and art therapies as well as group therapies and family therapies. Behaviour modification, observational learning, service based support system, and various individualized educational programmes may also be incorporated.

Learning Disabilities (L.D.)

According to Association for Children and Learning Disabilities, "Learning difficulties is a chronic condition of presumed neurological origin which selectively interferes with the development, integration and/or demonstration of verbal and/or non-verbal abilities." The term "specific learning disability" was introduced only in 1963 by Samuel Kirk a famous special educator.

Although learning disabilities may occur concomitantly with other handicapping conditions (such as sensory impairment, M.R.) or with extrinsic influences (such as cultural differences), it is a disabling condition in its own right. Children housing learning disabilities usually have I.Q's within the normal range but they have trouble processing sensory information which interferes in their academic activities at school. There are a variety of skills affected by learning disabilities, some of which are given in Table 1.

Table 1. Different disabilities associated with different skills.

Skills of Disabilities	*Different Disabilities*
I. Language	(a) Reading Disorder
	(b) Disorder of Written Expression
	(c) Mathematics Disorder
II. Motor Skills	(a) Developmental Coordination Disorder
III. Communication Disorder	(a) Expressive Language Disorder
	(b) Mixed Receptive-Expressive Language Disorder
	(c) Phonological Disorder
	(d) Stuttering

Clinical symptoms of learning disabilities at pre-school and school age in children are shown below:-

- **Signs at Pre-School Age**
  - (a) Delay in understanding and or using spoken language.
  - (b) Difficulty understanding simple instructions.
  - (c) Lengthy pause before naming objects and colours.
  - (d) Limited awareness or interest in books.
  - (e) Difficulty colouring or drawing.
  - (f) Problems with motor coordination.
- **Signs at School Age**

  The following are the symptoms/ signs of learning disability at school age–
  - (a) Difficulty understanding and following instructions.

Skills of Disabilities	*Different Disabilities*
	(b) Trouble remembering what someone has just told.
	(c) Failing to master reading, spelling, writing or maths skills, and therefore fails in doing school work.
	(d) Frequently looses or misplace homework, school books or other items.
	(e) Lacking motor coordination when walking, playing sports, holding a pencil etc.

Prevalence studies shows that 10-16% of school age children are estimated to have special diagnostic and remedial needs of Learning disability (L.D.) In India, Ramaa (1992), identified 14 dyslexic children out of 550 school going children (age range 9 to 11 yrs).

Children with this disorder have residual difficulties but complete inabilities in learning are rare. Visual/Spatial perceptual problems are marked. Problematic mathematical skills in areas such as space, direction, and calculation facts (e.g. +, ñ , x, ˜) due to confusion with the mathematical signs may be present. Reversals or rotations of letters (e.g. 'p' and 'q', 'b' and 'd'), reversals or rotations of numbers (e.g. '5' and '2', '9' and '6'), reversals of words (some 'mirror' writing), confusions with words e.g. when writing - using a word that is similar in appearance to the required word, confusion with left and right (in space, direction or position), are also seen.

For success, persons with learning disabilities require specialized interventions at home, school, community and workplace settings, appropriate to their individual strengths and needs, including specific skill instruction; the development of compensatory strategies; the development of self-advocacy skills; and appropriate accommodations.

Management of L.D. includes various *educational remediation* like direct instructions and practice with letter sound

sound association, word recognition tasks and reading comprehension. *Medication* includes various stimulants such as anti-anxiety medication, motion sickness medication, vitamins, and special diets. *Psychosocial approach* to L.D. includes supportive psycho-therapy, parent guidance and training, social skill training, and behavioural modification approaches. Overall management and treatment program should also include attention to associative disorders such as language and psychiatric disorders.

Attention Deficit Hyperactive Disorder (A.D.H.D.)

A.D.H.D. is characterized by developmentally inappropriate levels of inattentiveness, impulsivity, and hyperactivity that appear in at-least two contexts (e.g. home, school), and is present for at-least six months before the age of 7 yrs (American Psychiatric Association, 1994). There are three subtypes of A.D.H.D. These are the *Predominantly Hyperactive – Impulse type; Predominantly Inattentive type* and *Combined type.* A.D.H.D. was first described by Dr. Heinrich Hoffman in 1845.

Major clinical features are their inability to pay attention/ difficulty with attention, hyperactivity and impulsivity. They are much more active than most children of their own age. Children with A.D.H.D. seem to have unlimited energy and find it difficult to keep there mind on one thing, get bored easily and hence attention shifts from one thing to another. Their school work is messy and room is scattered. Many show communication problems and exhibit restlessness as they tap their hands and shake their feet. Children who are impulsive often talk when it is not their turn. Children with A.D.H.D. find it difficult to follow even the simple instructions. They show proneness to accidents as they over do dangerous acts without thinking about the situation. They are often irritable and emotional difficulties are frequently common. Learning problems or the behavioural difficulties are common in them.

Prevalence rate is 3-5% in elementary school children. Boys have greater incidence than girls and ratio is 3:1 and the disorder is most common in first born boys.

In majority of cases, the disorder is relatively stable through early adolescence. Symptoms tend to continue during late adolescence and adulthood, although a minority experience the full complement of symptoms of A.D.H.D. into mid-adulthood.

Management of A.D.H.D. involves a *Multi-model approach*– which combines medical and psychosocial management. Moreover, researches indicate that this approach is more effective than any single form of intervention. This approach is a coordinated effort of a team comprising of the clinical psychologist, educators, counsellors, and of course the parents. Management is based on specific outcome goals depending on the age of the child, severity of symptoms and nature and degree of associated problems. Medication for A.D.H.D. involves various stimulants like Methylphenidate, Dextro-amphetamine, Anti-hypertensive, Tri-cyclic antidepressants etc. Psychosocial interventions include – parent training, child training, and role of teachers.

Autism

Autism is a complex disorder of the central nervous system that has the following three defining core features: impairments in social interaction, and communication, behaviour with narrow and restricted interests.

Autistic disorder is sometimes referred to as early infantile autism, childhood autism, Kanner's autism. Major symptoms of childhood autism are-deficits in social behaviour, impairment in non-verbal communication, impairment in understanding and development of speech, child can show ritualistic or compulsive behaviours and can show intense attachments to odd objects (e.g. Small plastic toys etc.), shows unusual responses to sensory experiences, have disturbance in mobility, can show intelligence and cognitive deficits, can show behavioural symptoms also e.g.: aggressive or self injurious behaviour, extreme under-activity, short attention span, abnormalities in eating and sleeping. DSM-IV suggests the prevalence of autistic disorder varies from 2-5 per 10,000 children (American Psychiatric Association, DSMIV, 1994).

The onset for autism is before 3yrs of age. Some cases have shown normal development for the first year (or even 2 year). Autistic disorder follows a continuous course. By school age, children and adolescents, developmental gains in some areas are common but small percentage of individuals go on as adults to live and work independently. In about 1/3rd of cases, some degree of partial independence is possible.

Many different *biomedical treatments* are used in autism. Medications used in autism are psychoactive. These may include antipsychotic drugs, antidepressants, stimulants like methylphenidate and amphetamines. *Behavioural therapies* are the most beneficial programme for autistic children which help in improving communication, learning, adaptive skills and appropriate social behaviours. Parental education is also an effective method of intervention for the autistic children *Complementary therapies* include art therapy, music therapy, animal therapy and sensory integration therapy. These therapies are typically used in addition to *behavioural* and *educational approaches.*

Conduct Disorder

Conduct disorder is a disorder of childhood and adolescence that involves chronic behaviour problems, such as defiance, impulsivity, or antisocial behaviours, drug abuse, and/or criminal activity. Classification of conduct disorder is a controversial and unsettled issue in mental health (Cantwell and Baker,1988; Frick, Lahey, Applegate et. al., 1994), but depending upon the constellation of symptoms, conduct disorder might be diagnosed based on predominantly irresponsible, delinquent behaviour such as truancy and running away, covert violations of the rights of others such as non-confrontative theft, or overt physical aggression such as assault or rape. Conduct disorder is often associated with A.D.H.D. In addition to above mentioned symptoms other noticeable clinical symptoms of conduct disorder are – heavy drinking, lying to get a favour or avoid obligations, vandalism, bullying, fighting etc. (DSM-IV, American Psychiatric Association,1994). Prevalence of conduct disorder is approximately 9% for males and 2% for females younger than 18 years (DSM-IV, American Psychiatric Association, 1994).

Clinical course and prognosis for conduct disorder vary from mild form to severe form of conduct disorder. With proper management mild forms show improvement over time, whereas more severe forms tend to be chronic (DSM-IV, APA,1994). Aggressive conduct disorder type has the worst prognosis (Kelso and Stewart,1986).

Management and treatment plan for youth with conduct disorder include short and long-term inpatient psychiatric units, residential and day treatment centres, correctional facilities, and out patient settings. Both psychotherapies and pharmacotherapy are used to a greater or lesser extent depending on the treatment setting and the clinician's orientation. Different *psychotherapies* that are commonly used are – behaviour therapy, family therapy, individual and group therapy, parent management training, cognitive therapy, problem-solving skills training, family-focussed treatments, peer relations and school-based interventions etc. Various drugs that are used effectively are haloperidol (Werry and Aman, 1975); Lithium Carbonate (Campbell et. al., 1984, 1995); Propranolol; Selective Serotonin Reuptake Inhibitors (SSRIs); Clonidine (Kemph, DE Vane, Lewin et. al., 1993); Trazodone; Risperidone; Buspirone etc.

Schizophrenia

Psychiatric symptoms in non-mentally retarded children were first recognised and published by De Sanctis in 1906 and he termed this illness as *Dementia Praecoxcissima* – (based on the classic symptoms of Dementia Precox of Kraepelin). Five percent of adult cases of schizophrenia had onset as early as 7th year of age (Bleuler, 1911). Loretta Bender (1942) regarded schizophrenia as biological process activated by a physical crisis.

Clinical features/symptoms of childhood schizophrenia are same as adult schizophrenia. Same as psychosis in adults, schizophrenia in children is characterized by hallucinations, delusions, and affective and thought disturbances that occur during the active phase [DSM-IV, APA, 1994]. Other common objective symptoms are – loss of contact with reality, reduced activities, speech disturbances, blunted affect, moodiness, low social development, soft neurological signs etc. The diagnosis of childhood schizophrenia is more difficult than the diagnosis of adult schizophrenia particularly because the active phase may appear after a long prodrome period of non-specific symptoms and when they do appear, the child with limited vocabulary may be ill equipped to elaborate. Further it may be difficult to distinguish positive symptoms from creative imagination of an intelligent child. Schizophrenia with onset in childhood is estimated to be 50 times less prevalent than that with onset in adulthood (Karno and Norquist,1989).

It is now widely agreed that schizophrenia of childhood onset is of severe form, chronic in nature and shows poor response to neuroleptics than the adult variety. Normal early development, normal pre-morbid personality and good intelligence are parameters of better prognosis.

Various types of therapies and treatments including antipsychotics, L.S.D., hormones and electro-convulsive therapy have been tried but no specific treatment is known and controlled studies for various therapies hardly exist. Assessment of an individual child's strengths, weaknesses, and environmental resources is critical in planning. Various drugs like Phenothiazines, Butyrophenones, Thioxanthenes, Dibenzoxazepine, Barbiturates and Stimulants etc. are frequently used with E.C.T. (in rare cases) to treat children with schizophrenia. Psychotherapies like – behaviour therapy, speech therapy, aversion therapy, perceptual motor training, cognitive therapy, operant conditioning, for teaching self care and simple communication skills, are used.

Anxiety

Anxiety as an emotional state is universal in occurrence. It can be described as an intense and fearful response to an ordinary event, an exaggerated fear of future events or even a feeling of dread and impending doom, quite unrelated to any external events. A feeling of helplessness and inability to cope accompanies the above response.

Symptoms of anxiety are seen in two major areas namely physical symptoms and psychological symptoms. Physical symptoms are muscle tension, sleep disturbances, eating disturbances, illness behaviour, nausea, excessive sweating, fumbling in speech etc. and psychological symptoms include restlessness, irritability, difficulty concentrating or mind going blank etc. [DSM-IV, APA, 1994].

There are different subtypes of anxiety based disorders and these are shown below:-

I. Generalized Anxiety Disorder (G.A.D.)	:	Children with this disorder experience extreme, unrealistic worry that does not seem to be related to any recent event.
II. Separation Anxiety Disorder (S.A.D.)	:	S.A.D. confine typically to younger children who are extremely unwilling to separate from major attachment figures or from home [DSM-IV, APA, 1994].
III. Phobias	:	Phobias are unrealistic and excessive fear of some situation or object.
IV. Post-Traumatic Stress Disorder (P.T.S.D.)	:	P.T.S.D. develops after experience of a very stressful event, includes anxiety and flashbacks-nightmares of event.
V. Obsessive Compulsion Disorder (O.C.D.)	:	Its essential features are recurrent obsessions (intrusive thoughts) and compulsions (repeated behaviours) that are time consuming and cause marked distress or significant impairment in daily functioning.

Recent epidemiological studies have demonstrated that anxiety disorders are the most common psychiatric problems encountered in childhood. Kashani and Orvashel (1988) found the rate of childhood anxiety disorders is as high as 17.3%.

The management and treatment program depends upon the type of anxiety disorder a child is suffering from. But for all anxiety disorders, both *medication* as well as *psychotherapies* are used. Different psychotherapies like – behaviour modification, parent-child interaction therapy, cognitive behavioural treatment strategies, flooding, systematic desensitization, as well as parental counselling are commonly used with some minor tranquilizers and antidepressants like clomipramine etc.

Depression

Mood disorders are abnormalities or fluctuations related to our different moods or affect. The uncontrolled grief, sadness, or sorrow is *depression* whereas extraordinarily elevated mood is *Mania*. Children mainly experience depression while separating from their parents, especially-mothers, and they show this behavioural alteration in three successive phases – 'Protest ; 'Despair' ; and 'Detachment'.

To identify childhood depression, without any evaluation, is very difficult – as children don't have enough communication material to explain their mood swings (Cantwell and Carlson,1983; Weller and Weller, 1984, 1986, 1986a). And due to this fact, children with depression are more likely to show phobias, separation anxiety disorder, somatic complaints and behaviour problems. With psychotic depression children are more likely to report hallucinations whereas adults report delusions. Children with depression show withdrawal, unhappiness with weeping episodes, disturbed sleep, low self image and feeling of being unloved, and also show aggressive behaviour with self destructive thoughts (Poznaski Karahenbull and Arull, 1976). Other than these, they depict "depressive themes" in dreams and fantasy, "verbal expression" of unhappiness, worthlessness, unattractiveness, and "disturbed behaviour manifestation" of anorexia, psychomotor retardation or delinquent behaviour (Cytryn and Mc Knew,1974).

Exact prevalence of depression in children is unknown, but, several studies provide useful data of its occurrence. The percent of children had major depression (Kashani et.al,1983) whereas its prevalence is less than 1% in pre-schoolers.

Childhood depressives have a high risk of recurrence but timely treatment and appropriate follow-up can control it reasonably well. But if child has long established symptoms and positive family history then the prognosis becomes poor. Adolescent depression is marked by identity crises and has high risk of suicide attempts.

Severity of child's depression and its causes, helps to decide whether that child needs medication alone, or psytho-therapy alone, or the combination of both. Medication provides help to correct the chemical imbalance within brain. On the other hand, psytho-therapy will help the child alter negative thought patterns and better cope with stressors. For pre-scholars play therapy including family therapy is used for effective results. Cognitive behaviour therapy (C.B.T.) is also most commonly used therapy. After its completion children get benefits from scheduled or "as-needed" booster sessions. Tri-cyclic antidepressants (T.C.A.s) are most commonly prescribed medication to treat depressed children (Weller et.al,1982). Selective Serotonin Reuptake Inhibitors (S.S.R.I.), like Prozac, Zoloft etc have broadened the area of medication treatment for childhood depression. But associated psychological intervention is imperative to deal with self-esteem issues and to provide a positive view of future and significant others.

Other Childhood Disorders

Besides these childhood disorders there are many other disorders of psychogenic origin that children can exhibit. Some of them are described below

Selective Mutism – It is characterized by persistent failure to speak in specific social situations (e.g. School or with playmates). Main clinical features of this disorder are:- consistent failure to speak in specific social situations despite speaking in other areas; the disturbance interferes with educational and occupational achievement or with social communication; the duration of disturbance is at least one month(not limited to the first month of the school); the failure to speak is not due to lack of knowledge of, or comfort with, the spoken language required in the social situation; the disturbance is not better accounted for by a communication disorder (e.g., stuttering) and does not occur exclusively during the course of a pervasive developmental disorder, schizophrenia, or other psychotic disorder. Children with this disorder have difficulty in maintaining eye contact and they have a tendency to have a blank facial expression. They usually make stiff and awkward body movements. Treatment for selective mutism depends a lot on the subject, their age and other factors. Stimulus fading is very common with younger children and systematic desensitization is used with older children and teenagers.

Enuresis and Encopresis both are elimination disorders. *Enuresis* is the medical term for bed-wetting during sleep. Bed-wetting is fairly common and is often just a developmental stage. Bed-wetting is more common among boys than girls. Causes of enuresis include genetic factors, stress, slower than normal development of the central nervous system, hormonal factors, urinary tract infections, abnormalities in the urethral valves in boys or in the urethra in girls or boys, abnormalities in the spinal cord or a small bladder. Enuresis is involuntary discharge of urine during sleep. Nocturnal enuresis is present in about 15 to 20 percent of otherwise healthy 5-year-old children, 7 percent of healthy 7-year-olds, 5 percent of healthy 10-year-olds, 2 to 3 percent of 12 to 14-year-olds and 1 to 2 percent of normal children at age 15. For the treatment of enuresis general behaviour approaches are used. Parents are taught to establish motivation for dry nights and they should manage their child's fluid intake. Children with this disorder are trained to wake up during need and in severe cases medication is prescribed by the physician.

Encopresis refers to the repeated passage of faeces into inappropriate places (e.g. clothing or floor) after age four. This stool or faecal soiling usually has a physical origin and is involuntary – the child does not soil on purpose. In the United States, it is estimated that 1-2% of children younger than 10 years are affected by encopresis. Many more boys than girls experience encopresis; approximately 80% of affected children are boys. In the great majority of cases, encopresis develops as a result of chronic constipation. Combination of behaviour therapy and medication proves effective in the treatment of encopresis. It is very important that parents and other caregivers keep a complete of the child's medication use and bowel movements during the treatment period. This record can be very helpful in determining whether the treatment is working.

Another childhood disorder is – ***Tics*** – which is characterized by sudden, repetitive movement or sound that can be difficult to control. Tics that involve movements are called *motor tics* and those that are sounds are called *vocal tics.* Tics can either be *simple* or *complex.* Shoulder shrugging is one of the most common simple motor tics- other includes – nose wrinkling, head twitching, eye blinking, lip biting, facial grimacing, repetitive or obsessive touching, kicking, jumping etc. common vocal tics include – coughing, throat clearing, grunting, sniffing, barking, hissing etc. Most tics are temporary and are known as *transient tics,* they tend to last for less than 3 months. In rare cases tics persist for an extended period of time, which is known as *chronic tic disorder.*

Other is – ***Pica*** - is a medical disorder characterized by an appetite for largely non-nutritive substances (e.g., coal, soil, faeces, chalk, paper, soap, ash etc.) or an abnormal appetite for some things that may be considered foods, such as food ingredients (e.g., flour, raw potato, starch, ice cubes etc). These actions must persist for more than one month at an age where eating such objects is considered developmentally inappropriate. Pica is seen in all ages, particularly in pregnant women, and small children, especially children who are developmentally disabled, where it is the most common eating disorder. Pica in children can be dangerous. Eating non-nutritive substances lead to poisoning, this can lead to greater risk of gastro-intestinal obstruction or tearing in the stomach. Treatment emphasizes psychosocial, environmental, and family guidance approaches. Medication also proves helpful in reducing the abnormal eating.

Impulse Control disorders are behavioural disorders characterized by a failure to resist an impulse drive temptation to perform an act that is harmful to the person himself or to others. Different impulse control disorders have different sex ratios but all have similar ages of onset i.e., generally childhood or adolescence, and have a chronic course (Cupchick, 1992). This category of disorders includes Intermittent Explosive Disorder, Kleptomania, Pyromania, Pathological Gambling and Trichotillomania. These disorders have been viewed by researchers in two perspectives, namely Obsessive Compulsive Spectrum Disorders (Hollander and Wong, 1995; Biennenu et. al. 2000), and Affective Spectrum Disorders (Hudson and Pope, 1990; McElrey et. al. 1994). A Biopsychosocial Model of etiology is propagated for these disorders. A combination of behavioural and pharmacological approaches proves effective in its treatment (Peterson et. al. 1994).

School refusal is one more disorder, which is a problem that is stressful for children, families and school personnel. Failing to attend school has significant short and long-term effects on children's social, emotional, and educational development. School refusal is considered more of a symptom than a disorder and can have various causes. It often is associated with comorbid psychiatric disorders such as separation anxiety, social anxiety and depression. Undiagnosed leaning disabilities or reading disorders may also play a significant role in the development of school refusal. School refusal may happen at any age but most typically occurs in children aged 5-7 years and in those aged 11-14 years. It is important to identify problems early and provide appropriate interventions to prevent further difficulties. Treatment includes education-support therapy, cognitive- behavioural therapy, systematic desensitization, exposure therapy, operant behavioural techniques, parent-teacher interventions and pharmacotherapy.

Somatization is one more disorder that is defined as the manifestation of psychological difficulty or distress through somatic symptoms, a tendency to experience and communicate somatic distress and symptoms unaccounted for by pathological findings, to attribute them to physical illness and to seek medical help (Lipowsky, 1988). Common clinical symptoms showed by children are – tiredness, dizziness or blackouts. Prevalence studies of children and adolescence have found that parents of 11% of girls and 4% of boys aged 12-16 years either report somatic symptoms in their children or perceive them as sickly (Offord et. al. 1987). Treatment for somatisation in children involves cognitive behavioural therapy and family techniques as well as sensitive psychological sound advice by paediatricians. The role of anti depressant medication for childhood somatisation deserves further study.

Interventions

Management of various childhood disorders include techniques or psychotherapies like - Play Therapy, Speech Therapy, Behaviour therapy or Behaviour Modification Therapy, Cognitive-Behavioural Therapy etc. But before making management plan, therapists must view some aspects which can affect the effectiveness of a particular therapy; particularly these are,

- Mental age appropriateness of expected behaviour.
- Well defined goals.
- Small reachable goals.
- Brief crisp instructions to child.
- Repetitive-consistent expectations.
- Differential reinforcement.
- Acceptable alternative behavioural definition.
- Record keeping.
- Quality time.

After making a management plan, therapists apply various intervention techniques to children with different disorders. Commonly used therapies for children with maladjusted behaviour are:-

I. Play therapy

II. Behaviour modification therapy

III. Cognitive behaviour therapy

Play Therapy

Play therapy is a clinical intervention in which the major tool is – *"Play"* - for finding out the causes of childhood disorders and for their treatment as well. Play is to a child what verbalization is to an adult. Play is a child's natural way to explore their own world; to find solutions to problems; a process of healing; letting thoughts and emotions come to the surface during play. So, play therapy matches the dynamic inner structure of the child with an equally dynamic approach. Therapeutic play basically serves the purpose of communication to children. In play therapy toys are viewed as the child's language. During play therapy children are assisted to expose, to live out their disturbing emotions, conflicts or traumas; express the experience and the associated feelings. This process allows the therapist to experience, in a personal and interactive way, the inner dimensions of the child's world.

'*Active play therapy*' was propagated by Solomon (1938), for impulsive acting out children so that they could express rage and fear through the medium of play resulting in the abreactive effect of redirecting acting out into socially appropriate play-oriented behaviours. Play therapy evolved into "*relationship therapies*" under the influence of Otto Rank, and later on Allen (1942), and later Moustakas (1959), modified it for dealing with separation individuation issues wherein the secure relationship with the therapist formed through play became a safe base from which inter personal situations may be mastered. Another shift in its conceptualisation was evident when the client-centered approach to therapy developed by Carl Rogers was incorporated into play therapy by Virginia Axline (1947). It was believed that imbalance between child and his environment when resolved through play result in dissipating emotional disturbances and facilitates natural self-improving growth.

In elementary schools and as educational play therapy, the academic conceptual pursuits are acquired and assimilated with the assistance of the concrete and natural world of play. By using play, the teaching and talking is with children rather than 'to' children; i.e., play becomes the medium or the adjunct to the learning environment. To gain acceptance of the programme from parents as well as school personnel without believing it to be a "therapy" for "deep psychological problems"; it may be labelled as play media programme, counselling with toys, emotional growth through play, development growth through play, or the like. The play therapist takes on a systematic interdisciplinary team approach and may provide crisis intervention, while primarily taking a preventive and developmental perspective to facilitate normal child growth and understanding of self. The programme may be modified for special groups like gifted children, mentally retarded, or physically disabled children, children with learning disabilities or speech deficits, or with social-emotional maladjustments. These special children then can be effectively integrated into the normal schools.

The choice of orientation in therapy is the fit between the child's problem and hence the need; and the expertise cum convictions of the therapist (Kaur, Chavan and Lokraj, 2005). Each form is effective if used appropriately. Three modifications which have gained popularity in the recent times are – *Filial play therapy, Sand play therapy* and *Cognitive Behaviour play therapy.*

In ***Sandplay therapy***, '*sandtray*' is the vehicle, '*sandplay*' is the activity and '*sandworld*' is the product. The client is given the possibility, by means of figures and the arrangement of the sand in the area bounded by the sandbox, to set up a world corresponding to his or her inner state. The process of touching the sand, adding water, making scenes, seems to elicit the twin urges of healing and transformation which are goals of therapy. The essentials of sand play therapy are a specially proportioned sandtray, a source of water, shelves of miniatures of multitude variety: people, animals, buildings, bridges, vehicles, furniture, food, plants, rocks, shells the list goes on-and an empathic therapist who provides the freedom and the protection that encourages children to experience their inner, often unrealised, selves in a safe and non-judgmental space. In traditional play therapy, the trained play therapist meets with parents or care takers first and then works on his/her on with the child for a number of weeks or months. Every six weeks or so the play therapist meets with the parents to give feedback and discusses the child's needs and progress.

Filial therapy is child-centered play therapy wherein the parents are not just the co-therapists but are the primary sources of therapeutic influence. This modification was developed by Bernard and Louise Gurney in 1960's and is particularly popular in UK. The parents acquire the skills and the rationale behind the goals of therapy and the process of change is mediated by play at home. The therapist closely monitors the process through constant feedback interactions with parents but the focus remains on the themes and their interpretations to the parents. The review is through audio or video recordings, or notes taken immediately after the play session. Sessions of child with the therapist are also primarily conducted by the parent. The therapist firstly assesses the parents, then provides training, then conducts few joint sessions in which he slowly decreases his active role, and finally the parents take over. Joint sessions may be incorporated if and when the need arises. The play sessions are such quality time that they may continue after the problem has been removed, just for enhancing the parent child relationship.

Cognitive Behaviour Play Therapy (CBPT) involves adaptation of the Beckian cognitive therapy and principles, for use with the preschoolers. Medium is play, principles of reinforcement are maintainers, yet play is directed towards modifying faulty cognitive interpretations and developing adaptive cognitive schemas. The content is kept specific to the developmental stage. CBPT typically contains a modelling component through which adaptive coping skills are demonstrated. Through the use of play, cognitive change is communicated indirectly and more adaptive behaviours can be introduced to the child.

Be it practiced in any form, play therapy has an initial, middle and the final phase, requiring adequate termination process, just as in any form of adult psychotherapy.

Behaviour Therapy

Behaviour Therapy is a combination of various techniques, focussing on the treatment of disruptive behaviour in children and adults. Behaviour therapy model believes that like all other learned behaviours, maladaptive behaviour is also learned, and so on the basis of learning principles i.e. extinction of learned behaviour is possible, as well as new adaptive behaviours can be relearned. Hence behaviour therapy is based on *Learning or Conditioning Principles.* Main focus of behaviour therapy is on overt behaviour – which is present in the form of symptoms, syndrome and disorders. Behaviour therapy is basically oriented towards behaviour modification. So, it is also known as behaviour modification technique. Behaviour modification techniques are used both for increasing desirable behaviours and decreasing undesirable behaviours. Behavioural approaches offer ways for understanding and managing behaviour problems without recourse to hypothetical concepts or explanations in terms of 'inner states'. Approach to behaviour management combines psychological, educational and social approaches. Principles for managing behaviour problems are:

- Behaviour problems are skills which are learnt.
- They are functional.
- They cannot be understood in isolation of entire person or environment in which problem occurs.
- They are influenced by environmental factors that is, antecedents and consequences.
- No magic cure.
- No simple solutions.
- No readymade 'packages'.
- A long term undertaking.

Above mentioned are basic assumptions that must be kept in mind by a therapist. Behavioural management plan includes a proper process that is made of different steps. Steps for behaviour modification plan can be:

1. Identification of Problems: Identification of problems involves identifying the problem behaviours or the target behaviours or the deficit/maladaptive behaviours or priority behaviours in children for which treatment is sought few examples are given in Table 2, which can be helpful in understanding the process of identifying problem behaviours or target behaviours and for keeping record of the progress.

TABLE 2. Identifying target behaviours

Sl.No.	*Problem Behaviours*	*Priority*	*Deficit/ Maladaptive Behaviour*	*Target Behaviour*	*Detail*
Examples	Abuses; does not respect parents; lies.	Respect parents, no abuses, lies.	Low moral development	Say "ji", Inform when going out	Keep record of times when done/not done target tasks

As per the example above after the mastery of current target behaviours, new targets towards the removal of problem behaviours would be identified. Reinforcements would be given and role modelling may be incorporated. Further assignments like stories with morals, small tasks with moral conflicts may be given towards enhancing morality.

2. Defining target behaviours: After identifying the problem, next step for the therapist is to define the problematic behaviour or the target behaviour. The maladaptive behaviour should be defined in a hierarchical manner and in small steps.

3. Behaviour recording: In Behaviour recording a therapist records the targeted behaviour in the form of its *frequency, duration, interval, time sampling.*

4. Functional analysis: Functional analysis involves the A-B-C of the functioning of maladaptive behaviour. 'A' means antecedents i.e. events occurred just before the targeted behaviour; 'B' means behaviour's frequency, duration and intensity; 'C' means consequences i.e. the events that occur just after the targeted behaviour. So, in functional analysis the therapist finds out the causes and the results of the targeted behaviour.

5. Treatment procedures and their evaluation: treatment procedures are oriented towards *decreasing the undesirable behaviour* and *increasing the desirable behaviour*. There are different ways of modifying the targeted behaviour, some of the important proedures are given in Table 3.

TABLE 3. Procedures for modifying problem behaviours

Increasing desirable behaviour	*Decreasing undesirable behaviour*
(a) Reinforcements-that can be in the form of Primary (food etc), Secondary (money etc), Social (praise etc).	(a) Restructuring environment i.e. controlling the stimulus that is the cause of maladaptive behaviour.
(b) Presentation of reinforcers can be contingent, immediate, consistent and clear. On the other hand reinforcers	(b) Extinction i.e. controlling the feedback of that maladaptive behaviour so that it could be removed/extiguished from the

Increasing desirable behaviour	*Decreasing undesirable behaviour*
can be presented in continuous form or intermittent; ratio form or interval form; fixed form or variable form.	behavioural repestoire.
	(c) Punishment i.e. aversive feedback for undesirable behaviour
	(d) Differential reinforcement

The widely used behaviour modification techniques for children are described in Table 4.

TABLE 4. Important behaviour modification techniques

	Behaviour modification techniques	*Meanings*
I.	Reinforcement techniques	In it different types of reinforcers like reward and punishment are provided. This technique proves more effective when used by the parents as well as the therapist and when reinforcer is appropriate.
II.	Token economy	In this 'Tokens' are given by the therapist to the child for the desirable behaviour and when the child collects the particular number of tokens then the child can exchange those with anything of his/her choice.
III.	Modelling/imitation	It is a very common and general technique of teaching children-how to behave in a particular way by watching significant others and copying them.
IV.	Behavioural contract	In this a contract is made between the therapist and the client (child) that contains the expected behaviour of the child by therapist and the reward desired by the

	Behaviour modification techniques	*Meanings*
		child. In this the therapist works as a mediator for the child and the parents.
V.	Systematic desensitization	In it a hierarchy of the stimulus is made by both client and therapist. Therapist teaches relaxation techniques to the client and then exposes him (imagined or actual) to feared-stimulus object, and helps him gain mastery over it.

Cognitive behaviour therapy

Cognitive Behaviour therapy is the combination of cognitive therapy as well as behaviour therapy. Cognitive behavioural therapy model (CBT) is based on the assumption that, through practice and reward, changes in key areas of children's cognitive processing will result in behavioural changes Spiegler and Guereremant (1998). Cognitive behavioural strategies with children and adolescents include behavioural performance-based procedures as well as cognitive interventions to produce changes in thinking, feeling and behaviour. The model places greatest emphasis on the learning process and the influence of the contingencies and models in the environment while recognizing the importance of the individual's cognitive style in the development and remedying of psychological distress. CBT integrates cognitive, behavioural, affective, social and contextual strategies for change. (Spiegler and Gueserement, 1998).

The attitude of the cognitive behavioural therapist, working with children and adolescents can be described using the terms "Consultant; Diagnostician; and Educator". As consultant, the therapist is a person who does not have all the answers, but one who has some ideas worthy of trying out and some ways to examine whether or not the ideas have value for the individual client. The therapist as consultant strives to develop skills in the client that include thinking on his/her own and moving towards independent, mature problem-solving. In diagnostician's attitude the therapist collects data and judging against a background of knowledge of psychopathology, normal development and psychologically healthy environments, makes meaningful decisions. Lastly, the therapeutic attitude of cognitive-behaviour therapists is as an educator: the term educator communicates that we are talking about interventions for learning behaviour control, cognitive skills, emotional development and optimal ways to communicate to help someone to learn. The mental attitude of the cognitive-behavioural therapist working with children and adolescents is one that has a collaborative quality (as consultant), integrates and decodes information (as diagnostician) and teaches through experiences with involvement (as educator).

Cognitive-behavioural approaches to interventions for children and adolescents have been applied in a variety of areas, like anger and aggression; Attention Deficit Disorder with Hyperactivity (ADDH); anxiety; and depression.

The issue of motivation for change has yet to be fully addressed in most cognitive-behavioural interventions. Presumably, cognitive processes and changes are motivated by the positive consequences that are attained and the negative consequences that are avoided. The social reinforcement provided by the therapist can be a major source of motivation for children. If a positive therapeutic relationship develops, children can become more accepting of therapists' perceptions of events and can be more open to reframing their own interpretations of events. Another nonspecific factor that affects treatment outcome involves the reactions and consequences provided after contact with the therapist by significant others in the children's lives. This is how the cognitive-behavioural therapy should actively intervene with key individuals in the child's social environment to maintain therapeutic change. For detailed readings on interventions interested readers can consult Spiegler and Gueremant (1998), Martin and Pear (1996), Kazdin (2001) or any other text.

To conclude, although wide range of child psychopathology exists but one may label a child with utmost caution simply because the label sticks somewhere even though child might have been cured. The success rate of management is high since the child is in formative years. The best approach remains the 'multi modal approach' with creative age specific adaptations.

REFERENCES

Allen, F. (1942). *Psychotherapy with Children*. New York: Norton.

American Family Physician, (2003). *School Refusal Behavior*, 68:1555-1560, 1563-1564.

American Psychiatric Association, (1980). *Diagnostic and Statistical Manual of Mental Disorders*, (Edn. 3rd), Washington D.C.: American Psychiatric Association.

American Psychiatric Assoaition (1987) *Diagnostic and tatistical manual of mental disorders* (3rd rev. ed.), Washington DC: Author.

American Psychiatric Association (1994) *Diagnostic and statistical manual of mental disorders* (4th ed.), Washington D.C. : American Psychiatric Association.

Anisman, H., et.al. (1998). Do early-life event permanently alter behavioural and hormonal responses to stressors? *International Journal of Developmental Neuroscience*, 1, 149-164.

Arun, P. and Kaur, H.(2002). Psychological Treatment of Impulse Control Disorders of Childhood. *Indian Journal of Clinical Psychology*, 29, 54-59.

Axline, V. (1947). *Play Therapy*. Boston: Houghton-Miffin.

Bender, L. (1942). Childhood Schizophrenia. *The Nervous Child*, 1, 138-140.

Bhatia, M.S., Dhar, N.K. (1996). A *Comprehensive Textbook of Child and Adolescent Psychiatry*. New Delhi: CBS Publishers and Distributers.

Biennenu, O.J., Samuel, J.F., Riddle, M.A., Hoehu–Saric, R., Liang, K.Y.Y. Cullen, B.A., Grados M.A., and Nestadt, G. (2000). The relationship of obsessive – compulsive disorder to possible spectrum disorders. Results from a family study. *Biological Psychiatry*, 48, 287-293.

Bleuler, E.(1911). *Dementia Praecox or the Group of Schizophrenias*. Translated by J. Zinkin–New York International Universities Press.

Bryson, S.E., Clark, B.S. and Smith, I. (1988). First report of Canadian epidemiological study of autistic syndromes. *Journal of Child Psychology and Psychiatry and Allied Disciplines,* 29, 433-446.

Campbell, M., Small, A.M., Green, W.H., et.al. (1984). Behavioural efficacy of haloperidol and lithium carbonate. *Archives of General Psychiatry*, 41, 652-656.

Campbell, M., Adams,P.B., Small,A.M.,et.al.(1995). Lithium in hospitalized aggressive children with conduct disorder: A double-blind and placebo-controlled study. *Journal of American Academy of Child Adolescent Psychiatry*, 34, 445-453.

Cantwell, D.P., and Barker, L. (1988).Issues in the Classification of Child and Adolescent Psychopathology. *Journal of American Academy of Child Adolescent Psychiatry*, 27, 521-533.

Cantwell, D., Carlson, G.A.(1983). *Affective Disorders in Childhood and Adolescence*. New York: S.P. Medical and Scientific Books.

Costa, T., Scriver, C.R. and Childs, B. (1985). The effect of mendelian disease on human health : a measurement. *American Journal of Medical Genetics,* 21, 231-242.

Creasy, R.K. (1991). Lifestyle influences on prematurity. *Journal of Developmental Physiology*, 15, 15-20.

Cupchik, W. (1992). Kleptomania and shoplifting. *American Journal of Psychiatry*, 149, 1119-1120.

Cytryn, L. and Mc Knew, D.H. (1974). Factors influencing the changing clinical expression of the depressive process in children. *American Journal Psychiatry*, 131, 879-881.

De. Sanctis S. (1906). On some varieties of dementia praecox. Translated by M.L. Osborn. *In: Modern Perspective*, New York, Brunner/Mazel, 1971. pp. 590-609 (Originally published in Rivista Sperimentale di Freniatria 32,141-165).

Eyler, F.D., Behnke, M., Conlon, M., Woods, N.S. and Wobie, K. (1998). Birth outcome from a prospective, matched study of prenatal crack/ cocaine use: II interactive and does effects on neurobehavioural assessment. *Pediatrics*, 101, 237-241.

Faden,V.B., Graubard, B.I., and Dufour, M. (1997). The relationship of drinking and birth outcome in a US national sample of expected mothers. *Paediatric and Perinatal Epidemiology*, 11, 167-180.

Frick, P.J., Lahey, B.B., Applegate, B., et.al. (1994) DSM-IV field trials for the disruptive behaviour disorders : symptoms utility estimates. *Journal of American Academy of Child Adolescent Psychiatry*, 33, 529-539.

Garber, S.W., Garber, M.D., Spizman, R.F. (1987). *Good Behavior*. New York: Villard Books.

Geddes, J. (1999). Prenatal and perinatal risk factors of early onset schizophrenia. *British Medical Journal*, 381, 426-442.

Gelfand, D.M., Hartman, D.P. (1984). *Child Behavior Analysis and Therapy*. Second Edition. New York: Peragamon Press.

Hirisave, U., Oommen, A., and Kapur, M. (2002). *Psychological Assessment of Children in the Clinical Setting*, Bangalore: NIMHANS Publications.

Hoek, H.W., Brown, A.S. and Susser, E. (1998). The dutch famine and schizophrenia spectrum disorder. *Social Psychiatry and Psychiatric Epidemiology*, 33, 373-379.

Hollander, E., and Wong, C.M. (1995). Body dysmorphic disorder, Pathological gambling and Sexual compulsions. *Journal of Clinical Psychiatry*, 56 (Supl. 4), 7-12.

Hudson, J.I., and Pope, H.G. (1990). Affective spectrum disorder. Does anti-depressant response identify a family of disorder with a common Pathophysiology? *American Journal of Psychiatry*, 147, 552-564.

Karno, M., and Norquist, G.S. (1989). Schizophrenia: Epidemiology. In *Comprehensive Text Book of Psychiatry*, 5th edition, edited by Kaplan, H.I., Sadock, B.J., Baltimore, M.D., Williams and Wilkins, 699-705.

Kashani, J.H. and Orvaschel, H. (1988). Anxiety Disorders in mid adolescence-community sample. *American Journal of Psychiatry* 147, 313-318.

Kashani, J.H., Mc Gee R.O., Clarkson, S.E., et.al. (1983). Depression in a sample of 9-yr-old children : prevalence and associated characteristics. *Archives of General Psychiatry*, 40, 1217-1223.

Kaur, H. (2005). Parent training for child conduct problems. *Personality Study and Group Behaviour*, 25,131-139.

Kaur, H., Chavan, B.S., Lokraj (2005). Management of trichotillomania. *Indian Journal of Psychiatry*, 47, 235-237.

Kazdin, A.E. (2001) Behaviour Modification in Applied Settings (6th edition). New York: Thompson Learning Wadsworth.

Kelso, J. and Stewart, M.A. (1986). Factors which predict the persistence of aggressive conduct disorder. *Journal of Child Psychology and Psychiatry*, 27, 77-86.

Kemph, J.P., DE Vane, C.L., Lewin,G.M., et.al. (1993) Treatment of aggressive children with clonidine: results of an open pilot study. *Journal of American Academy of Child Adolescent Psychiatry*, 32, 577-581.

Lipowski, Z.J. (1988). Somatization: the concept and its clinical application. *American Journal of Psychiatry*, 145, 1358-1368.

Lorenz, J.M., Wooliever, D.E., Jetton, J.R., Nwaesei C.G., Young D.C., Byrne J.M. (1998). A qualitative review of mortality and developmental disability in extremely premature newborns. *Archives of Pediatrics and Adolescent Medicine*, 152, 425-535.

Machon, R.A., Mednick, S.A. and Huttunen, M.O. (1997). Adult major affective disorder after prenatal exposure to an influenza epidemic. *Archives of general Psychiatry*, 54, 322-328.

Malhotra, S. (2002). *Child Psychiatry in India*. New Delhi: Macmillan.

Martin, G. and Pear, J. (1996) *Behaviour Modification : What it is and how to do it.* (5th edition). New Jersey: Prentice Hall.

Mc Elrey, S.I., Phillips, K.A., and Keck, P.E. (1994). Obsessive compulsive spectrum disorders. *Journal of Clinical Psychiatry*, 55 (suppl.), 33-51.

Moustakas, C., (1959). *Psychotherapy with Children*, NewYork : Harper and Row.

Mussen, P.H., (1983). *Handbook of child psychology – socialization personality and social development*. New York : John Willy and Sons.

Offord, D.R., Boyle, M.H., Szatmari, P., Rae-Grant, N.I., Links, P.S., Cadman, D.T., byles, J.A., Crawford, J.W., Manroe, B.H., Byrne, C., Thomas, H., and Woodward, C.A., (1987). Ontario Child Health Study. II. six-month prevalance of disorder and rates of service utilization. *Archives of General Psychiatry*, 44, 833-836.

Otake, M., and Schull, W.J. (1984). In utero exposure to A-bomb radiation and mental retardation: A reassessment. *British Journal of Radiology*, 57, 409-414.

Peterson, A.L., Compise, R.L., and Azrin, N.H. (1994). Behavioural and pharmacological treatment for tic and habit disorders: A review. *Journal of Development, Behaviour and Pediatrics*, 15, 430-441.

Poznanski, E.O., Krahenbull,V., and Zrull, J. (1976). Childhood depression: a longitudinal perspective. *Journal of American Academy of Child Adolescent Psychiatry*, 15, 491-501.

Ramaa, S., (1992). *Handbook on learning disabilities*, Mysore: Regional College of Education (NCERT).

Rutter, M., and Herson, L., (1985). *Child and Adolescent psychiatry – Modern approaches*, NewYork: Blackwell Scientific Publications.

Rutter, M.,Taylor, E., and Herson, L., (1994). *Child and Adolescent psychiatry – Modern approaches*. Third Edition, NewYork: Blackwell Scientific Publications.

Saigal, S., et.al.(1991a). Learning disabilities and school problems in a regional cohort of extremely birth weight children and matched term controls. *Journal of Developmental Behavioural Paediatrics*, 12, 294-300.

Saigal, S., Szatmari, P., and Rosenbaum, P. (1990). Intellectual and functional status at school entry of children who weighed 1000 grams or less at birth: a regional perspective of birth in the 1980. *Journal of Pediatrics*, 116, 409-516.

Saigal, S., Szatmari, P., Rosenbaum, P., Campbell, D., King, S.(1991). Cognitive abilities and school performance of extremely low birth weight children and matched term controls at age 8 yrs: a regional study. *Journal of Pediatrics*, 118, 751-760.

Sandman, C.A., Wadhwa, P.D., Chicz-DeMet, A., Dunkel-Schetter, C., Porto, M. (1997). Maternal stress, HPA activity and fetal/infant outcome. *Annals of New York Academic Science*, 814, 266-275.

Schneider, M.L., Clarke, A.S., and Kraemer, G.W . (1998). Prenatal stress alters brain biogenic amine levels in Primates. *Developmental Psychopathology*, 10, 427-540.

Singer, L.T., Garber, R. and and Kliegman, R. (1991). Neurobehavioural sequelae of fetal Cocaine exposure. *Journal of Paediatrics*, 119, 667-672.

Slotkin,T.A. (1998). Fetal nicotine or cocaine exposure: which one is worse. *The Journal of Pharmacology and Experimental Therapeutics*, 285: 931-945.

Solomon, J.(1938). Active Play Therapy. *American Journal of Orthopsychiatry*, 8, 479-498.

Spiegler, M.D. and Guevremont D.C. (1998). *Contemporary behavior therapy* (3rd edition), Pasific Grove CA 93950: Brooks/Cote.

Szatmari, P., Offord, D.R and Boyle, M.H. (1990). Prevalence of Psychiatric disorder at five year of age among children born under 1000 grams of birth weight: a regional perspective. *Developmental Medicine and Child Neurology*, 32, 954-962.

Szatmari, P., Offord, D.R. and Boyle, M.H. (1994). Multiple risk and child psychiatry disorder. *International Journal of Mental Psychiatric Research*, 4, 231-240.

Tuthill, D.P., Stewart, J.H., Coles, E.C., Andrews, J., and Cartiledge, P.H., (1990). Maternal cigarette smoking and pregnancy outcome. *Paediatrics and Perinatal Epidemiology*, 13, 245-253.

Van Os, J. and Selten, J.P. (1998). Prenatal exposure to maternal stress and subsequent schizophrenia. *British Journal of Psychiatry*, 172, 324-326.

Weller, E.B., and Weller, R.A. (1986). Assessing Depression in prepubertal children. *Hillside Journal of Clinical Psychiatry*, 8, 193-201.

Weller, E.B., and Weller, R.A., (1984). *Current Perspective on Major Depressive Disorders*. Washington, DC: American Psychiatric Press.

Weller, E.B., Weller, R.A., Preskorn, S.H., and Glotzbach, R. (1982). Steady-state plasma imipramine levels in prepubertal depressed children. *American Journal of Psychiatry*, 139, 506-508.

Weller,E.B., and Weller, R.A.(1986a). Clinical aspects of childhood depression. *Pediatrics Annual*, 15, 843-847.

Werry, J.S., and Aman, M.G. (1975). Methylphenidate and haloperidol in children: effects on attention, memory and activity. *Archives of General Psychiatry*, 32, 790-795.

Wiener, J.M. (1999). *Textbook of Child and Adolescent Psychiatry*. Second Edition. Chennai : All India Publishers and Distributors.

World Health Organization (1992). *ICD-10 Classification of Mental and Behavioural Disorders*. Delhi: Oxford University Press.

16

EMDR : Therapeutic Prospects in Child Psychopathology

—Usha Verma & Tanusree Dutta

"The problem is not that there are problems. The problem is expecting otherwise and thinking that having problems is a problem"- Theodore Rubin.

Problems related to children include behavioral, emotional and motivational aspects which are a constant source of unrest not only for them but every significant other in their lives. These problems are nomenclated as disorders. Every child's mental health is important and families and communities should come together to solve these problems, as these problems can be painful and severe. According to an estimate of National Rehabilitation Association (2007) one in every five children and adolescent may have a mental health disorder that is identifiable and requires treatment. Problems of children include anxiety disorder, mood disorder, attention deficit hyperactive disorder, disorders pertaining to reading and writing (dyslexia), conduct disorder, eating disorder, autism, schizophrenia and a host of other disorders.

Many are of the opinion that young children are just too young to encounter problems relating to their everyday life and that they will ultimately outgrow it. But, available literature suggests that early detection and diagnosis of any disorder in children ultimately prevents the problem in magnifying and becoming a standard. It helps in early intervention also. Various therapeutic techniques such as cognitive behaviour therapy, systematic desensitization, play therapy, family therapy, and pharmacotherapy, have been tried to handle such problems specifically. EMDR (Eye movement desensitization and reprocessing) is one among such therapeutic techniques that has gained popularity over a period of time to solve specific problems of children.

EMDR is a complex method which combines elements of behavioral and client-centered approaches, in a manner which is hypothesized to stimulate and facilitate the innate psychological healing processes (Greenwald, 1995; Shapiro, 1995). All humans are understood to have a physiologically-based information processing system. This can be compared to other body systems, such as digestion in which the body extracts nutrients for health and survival. The information processing system processes the multiple elements of our experiences and stores memories in an accessible and useful form. Memories are linked in networks that contain related thoughts, images, emotions, and sensations. Learning occurs when new associations are formed with material already stored in memory. When a traumatic or very negative event occurs, information processing may be incomplete, perhaps because strong negative feelings or dissociation interfere with information processing. This prevents the forging of connections with more adaptive information that is held in other memory networks. When we receive sensory information it passes through an emotional filter (amygdala) in the right half of the brain. If there is nothing emotionally-charged, the information then passes through another structure (hippocampus) that processes the information for its time and space properties and allows it to pass to the left hemisphere. This experience is then stored normally in memory. However, when incoming sensory information is emotionally-charged (e.g. traumatic), it gets stuck in the Central Nervous System (CNS) in the right hemisphere of the brain. It does not get processed in time and space so, when reminders occur, the stuck memory is triggered and feels emotionally that it is happening in the present. This accounts for flashbacks, intrusive thoughts and nightmares.

EMDR therapists help clients reprocess their traumatic memories by using a process that involves repeated left-right (bilateral) stimulation of the brain while noticing different aspects of the traumatic memory. The bilateral stimulation is achieved through either rapid eye movements across the field of vision, auditory tones or clicks, or tactile stimulation of alternate sides of the body. It is believed that the bilateral stimulation of EMDR creates biochemical changes in the brain that aid processing of information. Negative and positive cognitions of the patient is asked and SUD scores (subjective unit of distress is noted). Shapiro (2001) further maintains that a negative sense of self, inappropriate emotional responses, and self-destructive behaviors are also manifestations of inadequately processed material, and that processing the etiological experiences underlying these current dysfunctions will transform them, allowing new self-perceptions, emotions, and behaviors to emerge.

It is not only major traumatic events, or "large-T Traumas" that can cause psychological disturbance. Sometimes a relatively minor event from childhood, such as being teased by one's peers or discouraged by one's parent, may not be adequately processed. Such "small-t traumas" can result in personality problems and become the basis of current dysfunctional reactions. EMDR has been successfully used to treat disorders namely PTSD, conduct disorder, mood disorder, phobic disorder and reactive attachment disorder of early childhood. A brief introduction of these behavioral problems and these treatment is as follows:

Post traumatic stress disorder or PTSD as it is commonly referred to was formally recognized as a psychiatric diagnosis in 1980 (Hamblen, 1998) and today it is a well established fact that children and adolescent are also susceptible to it apart from adults. Children who have survived natural (flood, epidemics, etc.) or man made calamities (rape, domestic violence, childhood sexual abuse or physical abuse, accident, etc.) are more vulnerable to PTSD. Symptoms of PTSD in children include sleep disturbances, separation anxiety, loss of acquired developed skill, visual flashbacks of the events, amnesia, trauma in play, and such other related behavioral problems. Mostly children avoid confronting traumatic memories and feelings because it makes them uncomfortable since they are not emotionally experienced or equipped enough to face them. This negative coping strategies of escape and avoidance of scary memories creates long term problems in children. In EMDR treatment procedure, a child is asked to think about that suppressed and frightening experience and it's a challenging task. Usually parents are also in state of denial of the impact of the trauma on child and do not recognize the behavioural symptoms of the child. Sometimes they also need counseling to participate effectively in the treatment and to meet the child's emotional need.

The following case reports demonstrate the effective treatment of children showing PTSD symptoms after a hurricane.

Illustrative Case Example

Paul was an eager, intelligent 11 year old boy who changed markedly following the hurricane, becoming apathetic, easily frustrated, pessimistic, and irritable. Although Paul's mother reported that the family was in counseling, she felt that Paul's changes were hurricane-related due to the timing of onset. Towards the end of the session Paul was asked to describe his most recent bad dream. It was two months prior to the session, and consisted of a radio announcement that a hurricane was coming. This seemed to indicate that Paul's mother's assessment was correct.

Although Paul expressed no motivation for treatment, and checked his watch frequently, he was co-operative. The treatment focus was the scariest hurricane memory, of huddling in a closet with the house falling apart around him. Paul found himself reexperiencing many associated upsetting memories, in a sequential manner. In addition to fear he expressed helplessness, saying "I can't do anything." However, he eventually expressed full confidence in the statements, "We're gonna make it better than before," and "I'm gonna get through this." His SUDS level went from 8 to 0, very gradually as he reexperienced different memory segments. The reexperiencing of a segment was often preceded by a physical sensation. For example, when asked what he noticed in his body, he would say "my ears are hurting," and then in the next set of eye movements he would reexperience the noise and the air pressure from the storm. He commented that "I get better and better at handling this as many times I go through it." Finally, he was able to imagine weathering another hurricane, but with less fear and more comfort and companionship.

At one week follow-up, Paul's mother reported a reduction in his symptoms, "just about back to normal." At four week follow-up, Paul's mother reported that a sadly anticipated family change had taken place: Paul's father took a job out of state, and was with his family only rarely. Despite this, the symptoms were down to nearly pre-hurricane baseline, a small additional improvement. His mother reported that he had caught up on his schoolwork and was doing well again, and that he had a "better attitude" in general. For example, he was more forgiving of himself, and didn't feel so badly after making a mistake. (Greenwald, 1994)

Conduct disorder also known as disruptive behavior disorder, is a very common childhood psychiatric problem. It has also been predicted that about 40% of the children suffering from conduct disorder will grow up to be adults with antisocial personality disorder. Children suffering from conduct disorder exhibit aggressive and or destructive behavior, lying, truancy and a host of other behavioral problems. Factors responsible for conduct disorder can be biological, environmental and mental factors. Environmental factors consist parental neglect, domestic violence, hostile home atmosphere etc, Greenwald (1994, 1995) proposed trauma as a key to understanding the development and persistence of conduct disorder in conjunction with other contributing factors. Trauma history is virtually universal in this population, and trauma effects can help to account for many features of the disorder including lack of empathy, impulsivity, anger, acting out, and resistance to treatment. The case illustrated below explains the EMDR treatment approach.

Illustrative case example

Rahul, a 15-year-old boy, was brought to the office by his mother. His mother explained that Rahul was suspended from school for assaulting a teacher and needed a "doctor's evaluation" before he could return to class. History revealed that this is Rahul's 10th school suspension during the past three years. He had previously been suspended for fighting, carrying a knife to school, smoking marijuana and stealing money from other students' bags. When asked about his behavior at home, Rahul reported that his mother frequently "gets on my nerves" and, at those times, Rahul left the house for several days. The family history indicated that Rahul's father was incarcerated for auto theft and assault. Rahul's mother frequently left Rahul and his eight-year-old brother unsupervised overnight.

Shapiro (1995, 2001) has proposed a 3 pronged approach of treatment plan. The past involving foundation memories and events underlying the psychopathology, present triggers as circumstances that triggers disturbance and future template i.e. the desired state with necessary skill/ attitude and behaviours to equip the child or adolescent to cope with his anger and also with his environment. First the traumatic memories are resolved with bilateral stimulation and then new coping strategies are taught using positive imagery again using bilateral stimulations and positive cognition is enhanced in 6 EMDR sessions.

After the treatment significant change in Rahul's impulsivity and anger outburst was reported and after a month's follow-up no incident of any stealing or fighting had been reported.

With respect to **mood disorder** one inherent problem with children is that they are not able to express their feelings due to which detection of mood disorder in children is the most under diagnosed category of illness. Essential features of mood disorder in children and adults are almost similar though their symptoms vary significantly (Brown, 1996). Mood disorders in children also put them at risk for other conditions (most often anxiety disorder, disruptive behavior, substance abuse disorders, and physical illnesses, including diabetes) that may persist long after the initial episodes of depression are resolved. Most likely, depression (and other mood disorders) is caused by a chemical imbalance in the brain. Life events (such as unwanted changes in life) may also contribute to a child's depressed mood.

Affective disorders aggregate in families and are considered to be multifactorially inherited. The factors are usually both genetic and environmental. Sometimes mood disorders are only secondary symptom of some other illness like medical condition of the child or of primary caregiver. Children may show symptoms like difficulty achieving at school, constant anger, rebellious behaviour, trouble with family, and difficulty with friends and peers.

Illustrative case example

Neera was a 16-year-old girl with severe mood lability, intense family conflict, psychiatric medication nonadherence, substance abuse, and imminent school failure. During initial interview her major complaint was that her 'family fights a lot'. She was reportedly exhibiting frequent emotional outbursts, elopement from home and school, alcohol and marijuana use, and self-injurious behavior (i.e., cutting) in her home. Her apparently low level of frustration tolerance was frequently manifested as anger and hostility towards family members as well as refusal to follow household rules and routines. In addition, she had thoughts of worthlessness, wishes to be dead, mood lability, anxiety, and distractibility. The reported, intense distress that she continually experienced was later conceptualized as moderated by the inaccurate, mood-altered perceptions of herself and her surroundings. At school, she was skipping classes, had poor grades, was noncompliant with teachers on a regular basis, and as a result was failing school and on her way to dropping out. Her mood lability and behavioral problems overwhelmed her family. They had exhausted all their resources, in addition, their work and other responsibilities were compromised. For example, when Neera became emotionally distraught, she would often contact her father over the telephone during work hours or visit her mother at her workplace for support. Family history was positive for several psychiatric conditions on both maternal and paternal sides, including depression, anxiety, panic, obsessions/ compulsions, suicidality, and substance and alcohol use.

EMDR sessions were started with preparation phase, involving safe place exercise and resource development and installation. She was also educated in skills of affect management.

Three pronged approach was applied for treatment. Negative cognitions were processed and positive cognitions were installed with future templates of desired behaviour, using imagery and better coping mechanisms to deal with anxiety and mood lability. Family intervention was also used, involving both parents. Significant changes occurred in her emotional outburst, and self injurious behaviour after 9 sessions of EMDR. She was motivated for treatment for alcohol and drug addiction. After one month and then 3 month follow up her grades at school become better and her symptoms of mood disorder were under control.

Reactive attachment disorder in children is reflected by severe physical, sexual, emotional abuse and neglect. Such problems develop in children due to abusive relationship received from significant others or caregivers to be more precise wherein the bonding or attachment is disrupted. The attachment relationship literally shapes the baby's coping mechanisms. If a baby is loved, cuddled, and has its physical and emotional needs well-met, its limbic system is set to interpret and remember things in a warm, friendly and loving way. Abandonment, abuse and neglect during this stage of life, however, mean that the limbic system is set to interpret the world as a hostile, frightening and bleak place. The attachment interaction between mother and infant in the first two years of human life literally shapes the circuits and biological structure of the brain and effects its maturation. The most deleterious trauma that occurs in childhood is relational. It comes from the social interpersonal environment and is cumulative. Prolonged and frequent episodes of intense, unregulated interactive stress in infants devastate development of stable and trusting atachment relationships and hinder the child's ability to regulate affect and to self-soothe or calm. Pathology is rooted in the individual's adaptive efforts to cope with the stress of overwhelming and frightening affects through the institution and use of defenses. Early experiences between the mother and infant are internalized, and this early attachment relationship either creates resilience against, or creates a high risk factor toward, the child developing psychopathology later on in life.

Joanne May, from The Family Attachment and Counseling Center of Minnesota, state that Attachment Disordered children have often experienced trauma in the first two years of life. The young child that is unable to use a fight or flight response will often "freeze" or disassociate. When parent cannot be relied on to provide protection and comfort, the adaptive survival response is vigilance. In order to remain vigilant, affect is disassociated (secondary or peritraumatic dissociation). This may account for the diminished affect (other than anger/rage) so often observed in Attachment Disordered children. Typical dysfunctional conclusions are: 1. The abuse I endured must mean I am bad or evil. 2. It is not safe to trust adoptive parents. 3. The only way I can survive is to be in control. 4. I am bad or evil and my behavior is who I am. 5. There is nothing I can do that is right. 6. I deserve to be hated. 7. Others deserve my hate.

When EMDR is used to revisit the original trauma, the child often gives a non-emotional, detailed observer account of past trauma and the spontaneously arrives at the conclusion that the abuse was not their fault and that the parents are not responsible.

Illustrative case example

Raghav was a 16 year old boy diagnosed with reactive attachment disorder. He had been studying in hostel since he was 7 years old. His mother was a gynecologist and father, a pathologist and both were very busy and shared a very strained relationship. He had one older and one younger brother, both in hostel. He was very intelligent but showed no interest in his studies. He wanted to live with his parents, but they wanted him to stay in hostel. His father once told him that he doesn't want him at home because of his misbehavior. He was a loner and had no friends because he could not trust them and also felt shy in introducing himself to anyone.

While going through the old memories, he told the therapist about an event when his mother had a fracture in her hand and she locked herself in a room and tried to cut her plaster while the boy, his father and a maid servant, outside the locked room were shouting and asking her not to do this. He was 5 years old then and can not remember the argument between his mom and dad. He was scared at that time but admitted that this memory does not disturb him anymore. The second event he told the therapist was, when he was 7 years old and his maternal grandfather took him home one day from hostel and returned him next day to hostel...He was crying and asking to stay over for one more day, but the warden told him to go and take his breakfast and then go with his grandfather, when he returned, his grandfather was not there. He was angry and sad. He thought that he was just a little obstinate but nothing was wrong with him and tried to justify that mom wanted him to stay in hostel so that he could study hard without any interference. He had been on antidepressant medicines for the last 2 years.

He had been in therapies (not EMDR) for last 2 years with different psychologists, and before coming for EMDR, had told his mom that he didn't want to listen to any more lectures on his behavior. First two sessions were devoted to safe place exercise, resource development and installation, and teaching affect tolerance techniques. Next sessions were used to process memories of abandonment. Mother was also involved in the sessions to reestablish the attachment, while doing the relaxation exercise together. After 5 sessions significant change in behaviour was reported and after one month the medicine had been stopped with the doctor's permission. After 2 months follow up showed further improvement in the relationship with parents and peers and a drop in impulsive and hostile behaviour.

Phobic disorder on the other hand involves an intense, unrealistic fear, which interferes with everyday living. This could be related to any object, event or situation. Phobias belong to a large group of mental problems known as anxiety disorders that includes obsessive-compulsive disorder (OCD), panic disorder, and posttraumatic stress disorder. The precise cause of most phobias is unknown. It has been found that children with one or more phobias consistently experience anxiety when exposed to the specific object or situation.

According to Shapiro, distressing events sometimes cause an imbalance of the human information processing system and remain unprocessed because the immediate biochemical responses to the incident have left it isolated in neurobiological stasis (Shapiro, 2001). She asserts that EMDR contains specific elements that stimulate the resolution of negative learning experiences. From an information- processing perspective, Shapiro's adaptive information processing (AIP) model posits that it is the combination of attention to a distracting stimulus and to a mental representation of a meaningful past experience and their associated states of mind that fosters the creation of new memory associations and the integration of previously isolated elements within the neural network maintaining the present pattern of dysfunction (Shapiro, 1995). To this end, the application of EMDR as a treatment of specific phobias can be conceptualized as the selection and the subsequent processing of a series of strategically important memories of earlier negative learning experiences concerning specific objects or situations. The following case example illustrates it clearly.

Illustrative case example

Roie was a 9-year-old boy who was terrified of terrorist attacks. His anxiety was intense and had generalized to many facets of his life. He did not want to go to school by himself or to visit friends. His fear often flung him into dissociative reactions. After establishing a safe place, his room at home, he began working on his fear that he might be blown up. He became so anxious that he used to stop and move around the room. He began to shoot darts. He was good at it, and his involvement in the game allowed him to move away from his fear. The therapist noticed his pride, joy, and excitement when he hit a high number, as well as his facial expression, his glad cry "yesh" (in Hebrew the equivalent of "great"!), and his open body position. She realized that she was looking at Roie's unique resources. These were the kind of resources that we all need in order to continue living in the face of uncertainty. This was certainly a frightened, quivering boy, but he also had within him the ability to feel competency and joy as he played.

Resource Connection: Identifying the Resource and Naming the Feelings, Sensations, and Thoughts

When he hit a high number and jumped up and down joyfully, the therapist called "Freeze" and asked him to stand still as a statue, "Where do you feel the "yesh" in your body?" Roie answered, "In my hands and my feet." The therapist asked, "What feelings do you have?" He said, "Happy." "What do you think of yourself now?" the therapist asked. He said, "I'm pretty good at this," "I can do stuff," and "This is fun."

Installation

During installation, the therapist said, "Think of all those feelings in your body and how you are pretty good at having fun and shooting darts, and look at my fingers," The therapist continued watching his game and calling "Freeze" when he succeeded. By the time he had hit the 100 mark on the target five times and had undergone five installations of his feelings of competency and pleasure, he was ready to continue processing to a positive and appropriate cognition. "*Eema* (mother) doesn't let me go to dangerous places. I' m safe. (Wizansky 2007).

The difference between EMDR outcomes and those of CBT may potentially be explained by new neurobiological theories with respect to differences between memory reconsolidation and extinction (Suzuki ,Josselyn, Frankland, Masushige, Silva and Kida, 2004). According to these theories, treatment that rely on extinction (such as exposure therapies) result in the formation of competing memories, rather than an alteration of the old ones. On the other hand EMDR's effects are based upon a different process known as *reconsolidation* that would involve the change and restorage of the altered targeted memory itself. It has been posited that longer exposures result in extinction, while shorter exposures result in reconsolidation.

REFERENCES

Brown, A. (1996). *Mood disorders in children and adolescents.* NARSAD Research Newsletter.

Greenwald, R. (1994). Applying eye movement desensitization and reprocessing (EMDR) to the treatment of traumatized children: Five case studies. *Anxiety Disorders Practice Journal, 1,* 83-97.

Greenwald, R. (1995).Eye movement desensitization and reprocessing (EMDR): A new kind of dreamwork? *Dreaming,* 5, 51-55.

Hamblen, J. (1998). PTSD in children and adolescents. *Journal of the American Academy of Child and Adolescent Psychiatry, 37,* 10.

Shapiro, F. (1995). *Eye movement desensitization and reprocessing:Basic principles, protocols and procedures.* New York: Guilford Press.

Shapiro, F. (2001). *Eye movement desensitization and reprocessing: Basic principles, protocols and procedures.* New York: Guilford Press.

Suzuki, A., Josselyn, S. A., Frankland, P. W., Masushige, S., Silva, A. J. and Kida, S. (2004). Memory reconsolidation and extinction have distinct temporal and biochemical signatures. *Journal of Neuroscience,* 24, 4787–4795.

Wizansky, B. (2007) Resource Connection in EMDR Work with Children *Journal of EMDR Practice and Research*, 1.

Index